# pentecostal grace

## by Laurence W. Wood

foreword by Robert E. Coleman

**FRANCIS ASBURY PRESS**
*of Zondervan Publishing House*
Grand Rapids, Michigan

TO MY FATHER AND MOTHER
THE REVEREND AND MRS. M. J. WOOD

PENTECOSTAL GRACE
Copyright © 1980 by Laurence W. Wood
All rights reserved.

FRANCIS ASBURY PRESS is an imprint of Zondervan
Publishing House, 1415 Lake Drive, S.E.,
Grand Rapids, Michigan 49506

**Library of Congress Cataloging in Publication Data**

Wood, Laurence W.        1941-
    Pentecostal grace.

    Includes bibliographical references and index.
    1. Experience (Religion)    2. Christian life —
Methodist authors.    3. Justification.    4. Sanctification.
5. Perfection.    I. Title.
BR110.W66        234        80-18192
ISBN 0-310-75041-5

*Printed in the United States of America*

84   85   86   87   88   89   90 / 10   9   8   7   6   5   4   3   2   1

# FOREWORD

Multitudes are seeking a deeper, more satisfying experience with Christ. Not that they have no present joy in following the Saviour, but that the dynamic of His Spirit — that abundant power so evident in the Book of Acts — is missing. Somehow life has no sparkle; there is no spring in the step, no glory in the walk.

For such disciples it is only natural to ask: Is this all that the ascended Lord has for His people? Must there be endless conflict in the pilgrimage of faith, and too often defeat? Or is there a dimension of Christian experience beyond regeneration, an effusion of Pentecostal grace which purifies the hidden motives of the heart and fills the longing soul with sweetness?

Dr. Laurence Wood answers this latter question in the affirmative. Reflecting the historic Wesleyan position on sanctification, he brings fresh insight to a subject much in the thinking of the church today. While drawing widely upon Methodist sources, he also ranges through other theological traditions, giving his thesis an unusual breadth of perspective. Impressive, too, is the author's biblical frame of reference. Not everyone will agree with his interpretation, of course. But one cannot help but appreciate his objective grasp of the subject, even when respectfully treating different points of view.

If one needs to earn the right to be heard, Dr. Wood deserves our attention. In addition to his baccalaureate, he holds three graduate degrees in theology, and has studied under leading theologians both in America and Europe. Presently he is serving with distinction as the Professor of Systematic Theology at Asbury Theological Seminary. He also serves as President of the Wesleyan Theological Society.

Scholar though he is, Dr. Wood does not write merely out of academic interest. His is the concern of a teaching evangelist — one who yearns that the truth of which he speaks will come alive in those who read. The Pentecostal reality, by whatever name it may be called, is a promise to be realized, not argued.

This is why perusing these pages can be more than a stimulating intellectual exercise. For the serious student of any theological discipline it brings hope along with challenge, and confidently points the way to that spiritual fulness which belongs to all the heirs of the Kingdom.

— Robert E. Coleman
Trinity Evangelical Divinity School
Deerfield, Illinois

# TABLE OF CONTENTS

# PREFACE

The charismatic movement which has swept across all sections of Christendom in recent years has served to some extent as a challenge to traditional theologies of all denominational bodies, especially in reference to the theology of the Holy Spirit. Books dealing with this subject have been numerous as a result of this phenomenon. What has come from this intensive concentration on the theology of the Holy Spirit has been a rethinking of the traditional understanding of what constitutes the Christian life.

Even prior to the outbreak of the charismatic revival, Roman Catholics and Angelicans in particular had been rethinking within the last thirty-five years their doctrine of confirmation. What impact the charismatic movement within the larger body of Christ might have had upon the need for this rethinking is not clear, though its presence surely accounts in some measure for it. At any rate, Roman Catholic and Anglican writers have addressed themselves in growing numbers to the validity of the idea of an experience of the Holy Spirit in confirmation which is subsequent to baptism. Some maintain that to stress a subsequent experience of the Spirit in confirmation takes away from the sacrament of baptism and should thus be dropped. Others maintain that the Scriptures and tradition teach that the Holy Spirit is not received until the subsequent rite of confirmation. For a discussion of this debate in Roman Catholic theology, see Austin P. Milner, *Theology of Confirmation* (Notre Dame: Fides Publishers, Inc., 1971); William J. O'Shea, *Sacraments of Initiation*

(Englewood Cliffs: Prentice-Hall, Inc., 1965); Karl Rahner, *A New Baptism in the Spirit: Confirmation Today* (Denville, New Jersey: Dimension Books, 1974).

For a full and enlightening discussion of the contemporary debate in Anglicanism, see G. W. H. Lampe, *The Seal of the Spirit* (2nd ed. rev.; London: SPCK, 1967), who argues against the idea of confirmation as being the second stage of initiation into the Church.

Scholars in the Reformed tradition have also addressed themselves to the question of the Pentecostal gift of the Spirit as a subsequent experience in the life of a Christian. To be sure, the Reformed tradition does not have anything like a concept of a twofold stage of becoming a Christian, yet the preponderance of books and movements in recent years on this concept has occasioned a number of critical studies from within the Reformed tradition on this theme. Frederick Dale Bruner, *A Theology of the Holy Spirit* (Grand Rapids: Wm. B. Eerdmans, 1970) attempts to show the inadmissibility of any idea of a second stage of the Christian life as advocated by the Wesleyan tradition and Pentecostalism (which he calls "primitive Methodism's extended incarnation," p. 37). James D. G. Dunn, *Baptism in the Holy Spirit* (SCM Press Ltd., 1970), argues against the Roman Catholic, Wesleyan, and neo-Pentecostal emphasis upon a second definitive stage of the Christian life. Karl Barth in the last part of the last volume of his *Church Dogmatics* (IV, Part 4) provides an invaluable exegetical-theological study concerning the relation between "baptism with the Holy Spirit" and "baptism with water." Barth's exposition of the "Baptism with the Holy Spirit" is one of the most fruitful and thought provoking works available on the subject, though he does not deal with the contemporary religious situation since his sole concern is exegetical-theological.

Not surprisingly, the Wesleyan tradition has been undergoing ferment in this area as well. While not much has been published to indicate this ferment, those who are in this tradition are aware of the "creative" tensions being felt everywhere. Two issues of *The Wesleyan Theological Journal*

(Volume 13, Spring, 1978; Volume 14, Spring, 1979) show a constructive attempt to deal with the exegetical, historical, and theological foundations for determining the relationship between the doctrine of Christian perfection and the Pentecostal gift of the Spirit.

The primary issue for the Wesleyan tradition is whether the doctrine of Christian perfection is to be equated with Pentecostal language. Other questions being asked are: Is Christian perfection only an aspiration or is it also a realizable experience in this life? In what sense is Christian perfection a second work of grace? Is circumcision of heart to be equated with Christian perfection? What does it mean to be cleansed from all sin? Is original sin to be conceptualized in substantialist or relational categories?

I have attempted to speak to each of these questions, but the primary concern is to show through an examination of Scripture, tradition, and contemporary scholarship that the Wesleyan concept of Christian perfection is to be directly linked with Pentecostal reality. More specifically, the thesis of this study is that the Wesleyan doctrine of Christian perfection can be best understood in the light of the Exodus-Conquest, Resurrection-Pentecost events of salvation history. That is, just as the Israelites under the Old Covenant experienced salvation through their personal re-living of the events of the Exodus from Egypt and the possession of the Promised Land in the cultic confessions, even so salvation under the New Covenant is realized through the believer's personal participation in Jesus' resurrected life (justification) and his personal indwelling of the Pentecostal Spirit (sanctification). In this respect, the Exodus and Conquest events prefigure Jesus' Resurrection from the dead and the sending of the Holy Spirit to dwell within believers. Hence this twofold sequence within salvation history is also normative for the believer's individual history of salvation.

This study is intended thus to be a constructive attempt in showing the biblical-theological foundation for the Wesleyan doctrine of Christian perfection; as such it is not intended to be a mere description of the thought of John Wesley. Nor is this intended to be a critical assessment of opposing points of view, though I have not hesitated to engage in dialogue with many different theological points of view. In this respect, I have not hesitated to draw from a number of sources whose exegetical conclusions could be used to support the thesis of this study even though I do not agree with their theological conclusions. Admittedly, exegesis and theology are not the same. It is one thing to collect exegetical findings; it is another thing to make inferences based on these findings. In this regard, all theologizing is a matter of making inferences. Hence I trust that my theological inferences are responsible and defensible as well as exegetically sound. At any rate, this is my understanding of the way that the doctrine of Christian perfection can be exegetically and theologically presented. I offer this work only in the hope that it will stimulate further study and help clarify some of the issues being discussed among Wesleyan scholars, as well as Anglican and Roman Catholic scholars.

One area which especially needs further examination is the relationship between Wesley's concept of perfection on the one hand, and the Roman Catholic and Anglican rites of confirmation on the other hand. Though I have included a chapter on this subject, it is largely exploratory and suggestive. What is needed is a full examination of this relationship which takes into consideration all the material dealing with the contemporary debate in the Catholic and Anglican traditions. Such a study could prove most profitable and enlightening for Wesleyan theology.

It should also be pointed out that I have not tried to speak to the issue of the gifts of the Spirit. This might appear to some to be puzzling since this work has to do with a study on the Pentecostal gift of the Holy Spirit. Yet this is by design, since the gift of the Spirit has to do primarily with the fruit of the Spirit, and the concern of this study is with the fruit of the Spirit (sanctification). However, a critical study dealing with the relationship between the fruit of the Spirit and the gifts of the Spirit is surely needed within the Wesleyan tradition.

Finally, a clarifying statement should be made about the meaning of Pentecost and the believer's reception of the Spirit. Since the focus of this study is upon the coming of the Holy Spirit on the day of Pentecost, the term, "Pentecostal Spirit," has been used to specify the unique relationship of the Holy Spirit to the world *after Pentecost*. To be sure, the Spirit is the same in his eternal essence, yet in an important sense the Spirit after Pentecost is not exactly the same as the Spirit before Pentecost. For the Spirit of Pentecost is the Spirit of the exalted Christ who has become incarnate in the Church (unlike the Spirit before Pentecost).

Just as there was a real difference between the pre-incarnate and incarnate Lord, even so there is a genuine distinction between the Spirit before Pentecost and the pouring out of the Spirit of the exalted Lord upon the Church at Pentecost. It is in this sense that the Church is the extension of the incarnate Lord, since the Spirit of Pentecost is the Spirit of Christ. More specifically, the Pentecostal Spirit is the agent through whom the saving work of Christ becomes efficacious in the world.

The language of the Spirit in the New Testament thus usually denotes the impartation of the fulness of Christ's righteousness. In this respect I have given considerable attention in Chapter II to Karl Barth's exposition of "the baptism with the Holy Spirit" in which he shows that the outpouring of the Spirit at Pentecost made available the fulness of righteousness. Although Barth thinks of this fulness largely in objectivistic and imputed terms, I believe that he is right to interpret Pentecost as bestowing sanctifying fulness.

This sanctifying fulness is what is implied in the phrase "to receive the Spirit." There are twelve places in the New Testament where "receiving the Spirit" is used as descriptive of Pentecostal fulness. This is a widely-understood interpretation in New Testament scholarship which will be dealt with throughout this study. However, it is most important to underscore the specific meaning of this phrase in order to avoid any possible misunderstanding. If one is to use this phrase in a biblical sense, then it should be used to imply a receiving of the *fulness* of the Spirit. Thus a believer has the presence of the Spirit in his life, though he may not have "received [the fulness of] the Spirit."

In order to see the meaning of this biblical phrase, it will be helpful to list each of the twelve passages in which it occurs.

Now this he said about the Spirit, which those who believed in him were to *receive*; for as yet the Spirit had not been given, because Jesus was not yet glorified" (John 7:39).

And I will pray the Father, and he will give you another Counselor, to be with you forever, even the Spirit of truth, whom the world cannot *receive*, because it neither sees him nor knows him; you know him, for he dwells with you, and will be in you (John 14:17).

And when he had said this, he breathed on them, and said to them, '*Receive* the Holy Spirit' (John 20:22).

You shall *receive* power when the Holy Spirit has come upon you (Acts 1:8).

And Peter said to them, "Repent, and be baptized every one of you in the name of Jesus Christ for the forgiveness of your sins; and you shall *receive* the gift of the Holy Spirit" (Acts 2:38).

Now when the apostles at Jerusalem heard that Samaria had received the word of God, they sent to them Peter and John, who came down and prayed for them that they might *receive* the Holy Spirit (Acts 8:14-15).

Then they laid their hands on them and they *received* the Holy Spirit (Acts 8:17).

Give me also this power, that any one on whom I lay my hands may *receive* the Holy Spirit (Acts 8:19).

Can anyone forbid water for baptizing these people who have *received* the Holy Spirit? (Acts 10:47).

Having believed, have you *received* the Holy Spirit? (Acts 19:2).

Did you *receive* the Spirit?  (Gal. 3:2).

That we might *receive* the promise of the Spirit through faith  (Gal. 3:14).

It is apparent that "receiving the Spirit" is linked to the Pentecostal event. It is also apparent that while the disciples possessed the presence of the Spirit before Pentecost, yet they did not "receive [the fulness of] the Spirit" until the day of Pentecost (John 14:17).

In Chapter VII it will especially be pointed out that the baptism with the Spirit (Acts 1:5), the Spirit "falling upon" (Acts 8:16), the Spirit "coming upon" (Acts 1:8), "filled with the Spirit" (Acts 2:4) are phrases which are more or less equivalent to "receiving the Spirit."

I have felt that in the preface it is most important to stress this understanding of the biblical phrase, "receiving the Spirit," as meaning a receiving of *the fulness* of the Spirit in order to avoid any possible confusion. I most certainly affirm that every believer in Christ has experienced the transforming power and presence of the Holy Spirit in his life, but not every believer has "received [the fulness of] the Spirit." This distinction can be popularly expressed this way: "Every believer has the Holy Spirit, but the Holy Spirit does not fully have every believer." Hence "to receive the Spirit" is the biblical phrase to describe the believer who has fully appropriated the fulness of Pentecostal grace.

# CHAPTER I.

# A THEOLOGY OF THE TWO STAGES
# OF THE CHRISTIAN LIFE – EASTER AND
# PENTECOST

The nature of the Christian life is impossible to understand unless one assumes a relationship between the Church and the congregation of Israel. However, it is not an easy task to unpack the complex issues involved in this relationship. At the very center of this relationship is the idea of grace. While the metaphors and ideas of the New Testament are largely presupposed in the Old Testament, yet the New moves beyond the Old in its concept of God incarnate. Hence the Christian experience of grace takes on a new dimension lacking, though anticipated, in the Old Testament.

It is not clear when the disciples of Jesus perceived the difference between Judaism and their proclamation. In fact, these earliest followers of Jesus were, from external appearances, only a Jewish sect like the Essenes. Further, it was not easy for the apostles to free themselves from those cultic practices of Judaism (Acts 15) which were not an essential part of their new charismatic reality.

Since these earliest Christians had deep roots in the traditions of the Jewish religion, it was only natural in the beginning that they should worship in the Temple in Jerusalem and in the various synagogues throughout the country. It is also understandable that they were concerned about Jewish rituals, food regulations, and especially the extremely bothersome problem of circumcision. Only through tense struggles did they free themselves from Judaism, thus allowing the Christian Church to be seen as a reality genuinely distinct from the Jewish congregation.

The question of the relationship between the Christian Church and the people of God in the Old Testament has been a thorny problem, not only for the earliest Christians, but continues to be discussed today.[1] Is the New Testament Church the continuation of the congregation of Israel? The answer seems to be a dialectical yes-and-no. The *ecclesia* (ἐκκλησία) of Jesus Christ embraces the congregation of Israel (*qehal Yahweh*), but also supersedes it. Whether or not this means that modern Israel is no longer participating in the Abrahamic covenant is a question that we shall leave aside. The focus here will be upon the relationship between ancient Israel and the Church, with special reference to the Exodus-Conquest theme and the Resurrection-Pentecost theme. The intent of this focus is to show that Jesus' *Resurrection* from the dead and *Pentecost* are the two determining events of the *Christian life*, even as the *Exodus* from Egypt and the *Conquest* of the Promised Land were the two determining events for the *national life* of Israel.

The clue to understanding the relationship between the Church and the congregation of Israel is in the idea of promise. This is particularly evident in the first thirteen chapters of the book of Acts which "compiles" (ἀνατάξασθαι, cf. Luke 1:1-4 with Acts 1:1-2) the very earliest preaching of the apostles. The content of this preaching is that the Church ultimately is the fulfillment of God's promise to Israel. This understanding of the Christ event as the final fulfillment of the Abrahamic covenant is the heart of the postresurrection teaching of Jesus *himself*. In fact, the primitive apostolic kerygma represents the gist of the postresurrection teaching of Jesus — a period of teaching lasting the forty days until his ascension.

The first postresurrection teaching of Jesus given to his disciples on the Emmaus road emphasized this connection between the history of Israel and its fulfillment in himself. The disciples "had hoped that he was the one to redeem

Israel" (Luke 24:21), but his crucifixion had dashed their hopes. Jesus then said to them: "'O foolish men, and slow of heart to believe all the prophets have spoken! Was it not necessary that the Christ should suffer these things and enter into his glory?' And *beginning with Moses* and all the prophets, he interpreted to them in all the scriptures the things concerning *himself*" (Luke 24:25-27).

This same theme connecting the history of Israel with the history of Jesus is immediately repeated as soon as the disciples had come together in Jerusalem where Jesus "opened their minds to understand" that he was the fulfillment of the promise of God to Israel (Luke 24:44-45). It is also significant that Luke says that his writings were intended to be a historical compilation of eyewitness reports and an orderly account (Luke 1:1-2) of what ". . . Jesus began to do [events] and teach [interpretation] " (Acts 1:2). Luke's intent was to show that the apostolic kerygma is none other than Jesus' interpretation of his own history.

In thus setting the stage for understanding Pentecost, Luke shows that the inseparable relationship between Israel and Jesus was the substance of his postresurrection teaching and that this teaching became the essence of the apostolic proclamation. In this respect, New Testament scholarship has pointed out that the first thirteen chapters in the book of Acts particularly reflect the earliest apostolic message which thus stands in close proximity to Jesus himself.[2] The primitiveness of Acts 1-13 is further indicated by its theological simplicity, with an emphasis on historical events in contrast to the more reasoned theological treatises of the epistles. In this respect, the sermons of Peter (Acts 2), Stephen (Acts 7), and Paul (Acts 13) are a recital of God's saving historical acts.

The theological simplicity of their sermons is in keeping with the simplicity which is characteristic of Israel's earliest cultic confessions which are a simple recital of God's mighty historical acts in behalf of his people. Typical of Israel's earliest cultic confessions is Deut. 26:5f.:

A wandering Aramean was my father; and he went down

into Egypt and sojourned there, few in number; and there he became a nation, great, mighty, and populous. And the Egyptians treated us harshly, and afflicted us, and laid upon us hard bondage. Then we cried to the Lord the God of our fathers, and the Lord heard our voice, and saw our affliction, our toil, and our oppression; and the Lord brought us out of Egypt with a mighty hand and an outstretched arm, with great terror, with signs and wonders; and he brought us into this place and gave us this land, a land flowing with milk and honey. And behold, now I bring the first of the fruit of the ground, which thou, O Lord, hast given me.

Of special significance in these cultic confessions is the use of the plural pronoun "we" which suggests the involvement of the worshiper in the two decisive saving acts of Yahweh — the Exodus and the Conquest. These two events are as salvific for the present experience of the worshiper as they were for those contemporary with Moses and Joshua. Likewise, the Resurrection of Jesus from the dead and the Pentecostal gift of his Spirit are salvific, not only because they happened at a dateable period of time in the history of the world, but because each person experiences (i.e., re-enacts) for himself Jesus' resurrected life and the indwelling of his Spirit.

The book of Acts thus reflects in the closest possible manner the connection between the history of Jesus and the history of Israel. This relationship is so closely linked that the apostles see nothing in their kerygma which is not already implicit in the ancient *credo*. Their worship, their ritual, their preaching assumes a direct relationship to the history of Israel. The essence of that relationship is that the *promise* to Abraham had its fulfillment in Jesus.

To be sure, Abraham comes before Jesus Christ in chronological time, but Jesus in a sense comes before Abraham (John 8:58). The concept of linear time (so widely discussed in contemporary theology) is misleading in articulating the biblical history of salvation if it suggests a literal sequence of "nows" in which the past is merely past and the future merely future. While the history of Jesus is a continuation of the history of Israel, there is an important sense in which it can be said that the history of Israel is legitimated only in the history of Jesus. In this respect, Jesus is not only the cornerstone of the church, but also in a qualified sense the same is true for the congregation of Israel. Any concept of a time-line used to describe the biblical history of salvation must be adjusted to allow for this flexibility and reversal of the time sequence. In this respect, the biblical idea of the *present* presupposes the priority of the *future*, for the present is meaningful only to the extent that it already participates in the future goal of history.

Hence the present is not simply the consequence of the past; rather the present, insofar as it is meaningful, is the partial arrival of the future. Israel's experience of grace was thus based upon the future of God incarnate in Jesus Christ. In Jesus the future goal of all history is already present, the kingdom of God is now come, and the Abrahamic promise is fulfilled. This realized eschatology (C. H. Dodd) is an important aspect of the apostolic proclamation. To be sure, Dodd's emphasis on a realized eschatology is misplaced because he failed to see the real future of God's coming kingdom, yet the present arrival of God's kingdom in Jesus is surely the focus of Acts 1-13.[3]

A fundamental implication of this relationship between Israel and Jesus is that the *historical pattern* of God's dealing with ancient Israel is embraced in the history of Jesus. It is this concept of a historical pattern linking the history of Israel and the history of Jesus that brings us to the very center of the apostolic preaching. The substance of this historical pattern can be stated in this thematic way : Jesus' Resurrection from the dead and Pentecost are theologically parallel events to Israel's Exodus from Egyptian captivity and the possession of the Promised Land. In this respect, the Exodus and Conquest events prefigure the Resurrection and Pentecostal events. It is this parallel which demonstrates that the idea of promise is the clue to understanding the relationship between the *ecclesia* and *qehal Yahweh*, for these historical events brought about the achievement of the Abrahamic promise.

Alan Richardson shows that "there can be no doubt that it

was upon the historical experiences of the *deliverance from Egypt* [italics mine] and the *establishment in Canaan* [italics mine] that the fundamental certainty of all biblical faith was based." He further points out: "But it is uniquely the genius of the Bible that the historical is transmuted by the eschato-logical, so that the action of God in the past becomes the type or foreshadowing of his action in the future."[4] Richardson then shows that these saving events are not just events of the past. Rather, "the salvation that was once-for-all wrought for the whole people is appropriated by each family or each individual as the family or the individual makes response in worship and thanksgiving (Exod. 12:26-27; Deut. 6:20-25; 26:1-11; John 6:53-58; I Cor. 10:16-17; 11:23-26)."[5] In reference to the Exodus event in particular, Richardson writes:

> The act of deliverance, so to speak, remains active and potent throughout the continuing history of the people for whom it was wrought; in the biblical view it is not a mere event of the past, but something that is ever and again made present and real in the lives of those who celebrate it in word and sacrament.[6]

Likewise Edmond Jacob has shown that there were two historical themes which formed the basis of Israel's *credo* — the Exodus and the Conquest. In addition to these two his-torical themes were two other memories which "were subordi-nate and whose links were of a sacred rather than an historical nature" — the Sinai and Temple themes. Later the Temple which occupied the center of the Promised Land was fused with the Conquest theme. In this respect, Jacob writes: "Thus the temple becomes very clearly the object of the Exodus, and by giving Jerusalem to the Israelites, David only continues the role of Moses, who promised a country to the people."[7]

Hence, the Promised Land and the Temple in Jerusalem symbolized the same reality — the Presence of God. This means that the Temple and the Conquest of the Promised Land are theologically equivalent — they are one and the same theme.

These two themes — the Exodus and the Conquest — became for all subsequent time in the history of Israel the normative pattern of God's dealing with his people. For example, the liturgy of Israel extolling the salvation of God (cf. Psalm 68; 77:11-20; 78; 114; 136:10-22) focuses upon these two decisive events. The *credo* of Deut. 26:5ff. is a reliving and personalizing of these two saving events. During their exile and captivity, the prophets envisaged Israel's salvation through a new Exodus and a new Conquest which would restore the Davidic kingdom in the Promised Land.[9]

In this respect, Edmond Jacob also shows that the Exodus and Conquest events were not merely the *formative* events of Israel's national beginnings, but rather they were the events upon which every Israelite experienced his own redemption. What happened to the nation of Israel as a whole was to be appropriated personally by every individual Israelite in all generations. Jacob writes:

> At the Passover feast, the departure from Egypt was enacted through the ritual, so clearly that it may be said that at least once a year the Exodus ceased to be a fact of the past and became a living reality, and that never, even after five centuries, did the Israelites consider themselves different from their ancestors who, under Moses' guidance, had experienced the deliverance (cf. Amos 3:2). . . . The *credo* of Deuteronomy 26 mentions the entry into Canaan as a second article; the deliverance of the Exodus was only made with a view to the possession of the country.[9]

While the Exodus-Conquest events were the *formative* events for the beginning of the national life of Israel, it can also be seen that they formed a *normative* pattern for the salvation of every Israelite in every new generation. The Passover feast was no mere memorial; rather, it was a personal appropriation of the Exodus event in the present.

This Exodus-Conquest pattern in achieving the Abrahamic promise is also decisive for the history of Jesus. In this respect, G. E. Wright says that these two events "are as important for the New Testament as for the Old. In Christ is the new exodus and the new inheritance."[10] The earliest apostolic kerygma presupposes this theme, as it shall be pointed out in the following expositions of Acts 1-13.

To be sure, this theological parallel is not systematically developed as such in the New Testament. It would be anachronistic to expect that it should be, since the genre of the New Testament is largely Hebraic, not Hellenic. In this respect, the New Testament writings do not give us a systematic theology, a biblical theology, or a theology of history. Their intent is to be hortatory, not a doctrinal textbook. Their categories are primarily functional, tacit, historical, and confessional; not ontological, explicit, theological, and systematic.

Not only is this characteristic of the Hebraic mind, but this is the way that it should be, since experience always precedes theory. Hence it is appropriate for the scriptures to be primarily kerygmatic rather than systematic. However, this observation about the biblical genre in no way relieves us of the responsibility to theologize, since there is an ontological structure implicit in the functional categories in Scripture. Without this implied ontology there could be no theologizing at all — no Christology, soteriology, ecclesiology, or eschatology.

In this respect, one may define theological reflection as making explicit the structure which is implied in the biblical experience of God. Without the possibility of making explicit this tacit dimension of religious experience, there could only be a Christian mythology instead of a Christian theology. A theological positivism which ignores the implied unity (and structure) of all biblical truth is just as superficial as a philosophical positivism which assumes that reality is merely a loose amalgamation of isolated data of sense experience. If one is not willing to sacrifice the depth of truth for alleged simplicity, then the functional and ontological categories must be held together. Otherwise theologizing will be at an end.

These remarks about the difference between the tacit and explicit dimensions of religious experience are especially apropos in regard to the difficult task of theologizing the history of Israel and the history of Jesus (from his birth to his death, resurrection, ascension, the Pentecostal outpouring of his Spirit, and his ongoing history in the Church). It is when this tacit dimension of the apostolic experience of the history of Jesus is theologically unpacked and made explicit that we enter the domain of doctrinal formulation — hence the doctrines of the Trinity, Christ, salvation, the Church. More specifically, in presupposing the Exodus-Promised Land, Resurrection-Pentecost motifs, the tacit dimensions of the earliest apostolic preaching in the book of Acts concerning the relation between the *ecclesia* and the *qehal Yahweh* is made explicit. The task of further developing the validity of this motif will now be undertaken.

It has already been pointed out that the data in the first thirteen chapters of the book of Acts represents the earliest apostolic proclamation and reflects the postresurrection teaching of Jesus himself. It was also pointed out that the key idea which demonstrates the validity of this motif is promise.

The concept of promise is a prominent theme of the Old Testament. To be sure, there is no Old Testament term which specifically denotes promise like the New Testament term ἐπαγγελία, yet the idea of promise is firmly rooted in the Old Testament belief that God's word is reliable. Hence the Septuagint often employs ἐπαγγελία when the idea of promise is indicated in the Old Testament.[11]

The whole purpose of God in entering into a covenant with Abraham and giving his descendants the land of Canaan was that they might have a hallowed land in which the Lord would be their God (Genesis 17:8). This means that the Promised Land was not only the intended place of settlement for the Israelite tribes, but "the land is the sanctuary of YHWH, his dwelling place on earth (Exod. 15:17)."[12] This idea of the sanctity of the land is first clearly expressed in the Song of Moses immediately after the Exodus. The Promised Land is "the place, O Lord, which thou hast made for thy abode, the sanctuary, O Lord, which thy hands have established" (Exod. 15:17). In their wanderings through the wilderness, worship had been limited to the altar before the tabernacle (the tent of meeting), but (as Yehezkel Kaufmann puts it) "when the people became rooted in the land, this restriction became obsolete; the sanctity of the land overshadowed that of the tent, and throughout the towns and settlements of Israel sanctuaries arose."[13]  In this respect, only Canaan was "the Lord's land," (Josh. 22:19) whereas "the other side of the Jordan is 'impure' land."[14]  That Canaan was the land of the Lord is thus the reason for the prohibition against idolatry. Idolatry might be tolerated beyond the Jordan (Josh. 22: 9-34), but not in Canaan land. The sanctity of Canaan land thus required a life of sanctity on the part of its inhabitants. The divine command to exterminate the idolatrous Canaanites must be understood in part on this basis.

God's purpose in thus delivering Israel from bondage in Egypt and bringing them into the Promised Land was that they might have a "holy land" (Zechariah 2:12) where they could worship their Lord with perfect love (Deuteronomy 10:12).   Living in Canaan Land, the sanctuary of the Lord, was conditioned upon an exclusive worship of God, i.e., a perfect love for God expressing itself in personal obedience and temple observance.   The locus of God's presence was in the Temple which came to be centralized in Jerusalem under David.  Hence it can be seen why the idea of the Temple and the possession of the Promised Land were merged into the same theme, since the intent of the Exodus was for God's people to be brought into the land of his abode and the place of his presence. This means that the Abrahamic promise was simply the idea of God's holy presence surrounding his people in the land of his abode.

In his sermon in Acts 13, Paul recounts the Exodus and the Conquest as the two decisive historical events which initially brought about the fulfillment of the Abrahamic promise (vs. 17-19). Yet he presents Jesus as the deliverer (Acts 13:23) who truly fulfilled the Abrahamic promise (Acts 13:32). Through his Resurrection from the dead (Acts 13:33), Jesus (like Moses) delivers his people from oppression. The superiority of the New Exodus, effected through Jesus' Resurrection from the dead, is indicated by Paul's reference to its spiritual significance as opposed to a political concept.

This New Exodus meant forgiveness of sins (Acts 13:38), not merely deliverance from political captivity. To be sure, the Old Testament did not interpret the Exodus simply in terms of political liberation. For example, the Psalmist links the redemption of Israel with forgiveness and deliverance from iniquity (Ps. 130:4,8). Yet the emphasis in the Old Testament understanding of the Exodus was upon political deliverance. Paul shows that by Jesus as the true deliverer "everyone that believes is freed from everything from which you could not be freed by the law of Moses" (Acts 13:39); hence the superiority of the New Exodus.

The theme of Stephen's sermon likewise was the Abrahamic promise (Acts 7:1-16) which was realized through the Exodus (Acts 7:17-43) and the Conquest (Acts 7:44-53). The purpose of the Exodus was deliverance from bondage; the purpose of the Conquest was to provide a place for exclusive worship (= perfect love) of God (Acts 7:45-50). Stephen portrays Moses' deliverance of Israel through the Red Sea as a prefiguration of Jesus' activity (Acts 7:36-37); he concludes his sermon with an emphasis on temple worship as the prefiguration of the Holy Spirit who indwells persons and not "houses made with hands" (Acts 7:48-49). Hence it is the Pentecostal Spirit whom his bearers with their uncircumcized hearts now reject, even as their idolatrous fathers did (7:51).

In a direct manner, Stephen shows that the history of Israel is thus fulfilled in the history of the risen Christ. Even as the purpose of entering the holy land (= the sanctuary of Yahweh) was to live holy and blamelessly before Yahweh (Deut. 18:9-13), even so, only through the reception of the Pentecostal Spirit can one truly love and worship God. Stephen further suggests this interpretation by associating "the coming of the Righteous One" with the Holy Spirit whom the Jews resisted (Acts 7:51-52). He further shows that true worship (= perfect love for God) does not occur "in houses made with hands" (Acts 7:48), but through the indwelling of the Holy Spirit.

In contrast to the Old Testament notion of a physical temple in which God dwelt, Stephen's sermon and life show that the true temple of God is one whose life is indwelt by the Pentecostal Spirit. In his dying moment, his being "full of the *Holy Spirit*" was a corollary to his being able to see "the glory of *God*, and *Jesus* standing at the right hand of God" (Acts 7:55). The Trinitarian significance of God, Jesus, and the Holy Spirit being brought together in such close identity at Stephen's death should not be overlooked. In this respect, Stephen's perfect love for God and his enemies was the result of his knowing the Father, Son, and Holy Spirit in the fullest and most personal manner. This deeper experience of the Trinity is what Wesley interpreted as the experience of those whom John called "fathers" (I John 2:14). That is, to be perfected in love is to "have known both the Father, and the Son, and the Spirit of Christ, in your inmost soul."[15] Stephen's martyrdom was ironically a concrete witness to the superiority of the New Covenant with its promise that perfect devotion and love for God can be realized through the Pentecostal Spirit (= the exalted Christ, cf. II Cor. 3:17).

The theme of Peter's sermon on the day of Pentecost (Acts 2) was that the Abrahamic promise had its fulfillment in the history of Jesus. The Pentecostal outpouring of the Spirit thus signified *the decisive historical moment* of the appropriation of that promise. Peter understood the fulfillment of this promise in accordance with the prevailing idea of every sincere Jew that the restoration of the Davidic kingdom would be accomplished through the long-awaited Christ who would be king. It is significant that just one week prior to his death Jesus was paraded through the streets of Jerusalem as *the king* of Israel. "Blessed is the King who comes in the name of the Lord! Peace in heaven and glory in the highest!" (Luke 19:38). These same people brought him to trial on the grounds that he was "perverting our nation, and forbidding us to give tribute to Caesar, and saying that he himself is . . . *king*" (Luke 23:2). Pilate was then intimidated into pronouncing the sentence of crucifixion upon him lest he should be considered disloyal to Caesar, but even so he was bold enough to have written over the cross: "This is the *King* of the Jews" (Luke 23:38).

It is against this background of the coming kingship of the

Christ who would restore the kingdom of David which serves as the setting for Peter's Pentecostal sermon (Acts 1:3,6; 2:16ff.). The establishment of the kingdom in the land of Canaan under David had completed the Conquest and thus marked the initial fulfillment of the Abrahamic promise. This promise of dwelling in the land of Yahweh came to be forfeited through disobedience, with the resulting captivity in Babylon; yet the prophets had written of a new Exodus and a new Conquest which would restore the Davidic kingdom in the Promised Land.

Peter links this new Exodus and new Conquest with Jesus' Resurrection and Pentecost. The Exodus event is recalled in Peter's words, "mighty works and wonders and signs" (Acts 2:22). These words served as a traditional formula to designate the Exodus event (Deut. 6:20-24; 26:5-10; Joshua 24:17; Deut. 4:34; 7:19; 11:3; 29:3; Jer. 32:20-21; Acts 7:36).[16] For Peter, this formula designates Jesus' Resurrection from the dead (Acts 2:22-24). Peter also equates Jesus' Resurrection with "having loosed the pangs of death" (Acts 2:24). This word "loosed" (λύσας) is related to the idea of Israel's being freed from Egyptian captivity. Λύω is the root word for λυτρόω (ransom), the word used in the Septuagint for Israel's deliverance from Egypt. Λύω is also used in Rev. 1:5-6 as an allusion to the Exodus which serves as the paradigm of Jesus' resurrection from the dead: "to him who loves us and has freed (λύσαντι) us from our sins by his blood [Exodus theme] and made us a kingdom [Conquest theme]; priests to his God and Father." Peter thus alludes to the Israelites being set free from the captivity of Egypt in describing the Resurrection of Jesus from the dead as the liberating event (the New Exodus) from the bondage of sin through his use of the language of the Exodus event — "mighty works and wonders and signs."

Peter also recalls the Conquest theme in alluding to the restoration of the kingdom (cf. Rev. 1:5), not in the political sense that David's kingdom would be literally restored in the Promised Land, but in the promised outpouring of the Holy Spirit of the exalted Christ (Acts 2:33) upon all believers.

Hence this Jesus who had been crucified because of his alleged intention to restore the kingdom of David was the message of Peter. Jesus' Resurrection from the dead which was accompanied by "mighty works and wonders and signs" and which "loosed the pangs of death" is the new Exodus (Acts 2:22-24). His being "exalted at the right hand of God" and our "having received from the Father the promise of the Holy Spirit" is the new Conquest (Acts 2:33). The Church in its collective singularity (κοινωνία Acts 2:42) is the temple of the Holy Spirit. Hence the exalted Christ reigns, not in a political, earthly kingdom, but in the hearts of believers.

In response to the announcement of the arrival of the kingdom, the people asked: "What shall we do?" (Acts 2:37). Peter exhorted them to have their own personal exodus and conquest: "Repent and be baptized (= the Exodus theme of deliverance), and you shall receive the gift of the Holy Spirit (the Conquest theme of Yahweh's reign over his people)" (Acts 2:38).

Peter also shows that the Abrahamic covenant with its promise of a universal blessing had its true fulfillment in the coming of the Spirit: "For the promise is to you and to your children and to all that are afar off" (vs. 39). God's promise to Abraham had been that all the nations would be blessed through his seed. Peter says that the promise is now extended to those who are "far off" by which he means the Gentiles.

Similarly Paul says that the Church is made up of those "who were far off" (Eph. 2:13) and those "who were near" (Eph. 2:17) and that "one new man in place of the two [Jew and Gentile]" has been created in Jesus Christ (Eph. 2:15).

Paul likewise shows here in this same context that the Abrahamic promise (Eph. 2:12) was realized through Jesus' Resurrection from the dead and the Pentecostal outpouring of the Spirit. Jesus' Resurrection from the dead means forgiveness of sins and peace with God: "But now in Christ Jesus you who once were far off have been brought near in the blood of Christ. For he is our peace" (Eph. 2:13-14). Those who have received this message of reconciliation through the death-resurrection of Jesus (Eph. 2:16) also have access to the (Pentecostal) Spirit (Eph. 2:18). Hence believers in Christ Jesus (= the Church) are "a holy temple in the Lord" (vs. 21) and "a dwelling place of God in the Spirit" (vs. 22).

To be truly *in Christ* (= the Church)* involves, thus, both forgiveness of sins (Resurrection theme) and the gift of the Spirit (Pentecost theme). It has been the intent of this chapter to show that the Exodus-Conquest and Resurrection-Pentecost themes are implicit in the whole of the apostolic proclamation. The initial fulfillment of the Abrahamic promise was accomplished through the Exodus and the Conquest; its ultimate fulfillment was accomplished through the Resurrection and Pentecost. It has also been the intention of this chapter to suggest that the Resurrection-Pentecost theme is the basis for understanding the two stages of the Christian life which Peter denotes in his exhortation: "Repent and be baptized, and you shall receive the gift of the Holy Spirit" (Acts 2:38). That these two stages are extended in time for each person, rather than being merely experienced in a single beginning moment of the Christian life, will receive further consideration in the following chapters. Yet even now it must be stressed that these two stages are not absolutely distinct as if they were only extrinsically related. Though they are distinct in time, they are also related through time. Rather than a break existing between them, they exist in a *continuum*. Hence sanctifying grace (Pentecost theme) is *really* begun in justification (Resurrection theme). This twofold emphasis upon these events being both related and distinct must be firmly kept in mind if the biblical stress upon a dynamic view of time is to be in proper focus. A static view of time, as if Easter and Pentecost were isolated facts, is thus altogether out of keeping with the understanding of the relationship between Easter (justification) and Pentecost (sanctification).

*Notice the frequent way the Church is denoted prepositionally especially in Ephesians 2:11-22: "In Christ Jesus . . . in himself . . . through him . . . in whom."

[1] Emil Brunner, *The Misunderstanding of the Church*, trans. Harold Knight (Philadelphia: Westminster Press, 1953); Oscar Cullman, *Salvation in History,* trans. Sidney G. Sawers (London: SCM Press Ltd., 1967), pp. 173ff., 236-247, 278ff.; Rudolf Bultmann, *Theology of the New Testament,* trans. Kendrick Grobel (New York: Charles Scribner's Sons, 1951), I, 53-62; Oscar Cullman, *The Early Church,* ed. A. J. B. Higgins (London: SCM Press Ltd., 1966), 105-137.

[2] Cf. R. J. Knowling, *The Expositor's Greek Testament,* ed. W. Robertson Nicoll (Grand Rapids: Wm. B. Eerdmans, 1961), pp. 18ff.; *The Acts of the Apostles, The Anchor Bible,* intro., trans., and notes by Johannes Munck, revised by W. F. Albright and C. S. Mann (Garden City: Doubleday, 1967), p. XLII.

[3] C. H. Dodd, *The Parables of the Kingdom* (New York: Charles Scribner, 1961), p. 35.

[4] Alan Richardson, "Salvation, Savior," *The Interpreter's Dictionary of the Bible*, ed. George A. Buttrick (Nashville: Abingdon Press, 1962), R-Z, p. 170.

[5] *Ibid.,* p. 172.

[6] *Ibid.*

[7] Edmond Jacob, *Theology of the Old Testament,* trans. Arthur W. Heathcote and Philip J. Allcock (New York: Harper and Brothers, 1958), p. 192.

[8] *Ibid.,* p. 192-193.

[9] *Ibid.,* p. 191.

[10] G. Ernest Wright, *God Who Acts* (London: SCM Press, 1962), p. 63.

[11] P. S. Minnear, "Promise," *The Interpreter's Dictionary of the Bible* , K - Q, p. 893.

[12] Yehezkel Kaufmann, *The Religion of Israel*, trans. and abridged by Moshe Greenberg (University of Chicago Press, 1960), p. 241.

[13] *Ibid.,* p. 258.

[14] *Ibid.*

[15]*The Standard Sermons of John Wesley*, ed. Edward H. Sugden (London: The Epworth Press, 1961), II, 157.

[16]*Kittel's Theological Dictionary of the New Testament*, VII (1971), 216, 241-243.

[17]*Kittel's Theological Dictionary of the New Testament*, IV (1967), 335-377.

# CHAPTER II.

# THE PROMISED LAND MOTIF AS A
# PREFIGURATION OF THE
# PROMISE OF THE FATHER

The history of Israel was a history of preoccupation with the idea of a political kingdom situated in the Promised Land of Canaan. The history of this concept of a kingdom began with the Abrahamic covenant in which Yahweh promised to Abraham's posterity a land which would be theirs forever (Genesis 17:8). In spite of its earthly-political meaning, this idea of a kingdom implied spiritual connotations which were to be made explicit and fulfilled ultimately through "the promise of the Father" (Luke 24:49; Acts 1:4). In this respect, the political idea of an earthly kingdom was "existentialized" in the outpouring of the Holy Spirit on the day of Pentecost.

Unlike Bultmann's existentialist exegesis which negates the historical aspect of the kingdom-idea,[1] the "existential" interpretation of the kingdom presupposed in the New Testament writings *includes* as well as *transforms* the older political connotations of the kingdom in ancient Israel. It *includes* the older conception since the kingdom of the exalted Christ means his rule will be coextensive with the whole of creation, but it also *transforms* this political connotation with its stress upon the spiritual and transcendent dimensions of the kingdom. Hence the kingdom begins in the inner being of believers in Christ through their reception of his Spirit, but its ultimate conquest will bring every person to his knees in submission before Jesus as Lord (Phil. 2:9-11; Rev. 11:15; 19:16). As Cullmann has put it, there is an "already" and a "not yet" aspect of the coming kingdom of God.[2] This kingdom "already" has arrived through the coming of Christ, but it is "not yet" consummated. Its final consummation will come only at the eschaton (glorification). The kingly reign of Christ was thus initially and formally begun through his death, resurrection, and ascension to the Father.

It can thus be said that the kingdom became an internal reality for believers through "the promise of the Father," i.e., the coming of the Holy Spirit as the exalted Christ.[3] In this respect, the kingdom of Israel situated in the Promised Land was a proleptic event of the reign of the exalted Christ. That is, "the promise of the Father" was the reality symbolized in the idea of the Promised Land. Yet the political idea of the Promised Land motif was no mere symbol. For it genuinely participated proleptically in the future reality of the exalted Christ. This means that the history of Israel was a redemptive history because it provisionally pre-actualized the coming of Jesus Christ, yet at the same time the history of Jesus Christ is redemptive because the God who was active in the history of Israel has acted decisively in the resurrection and exaltation of his Son. This interdependence between the history of Israel and the history of Jesus is a prerequisite for an adequate understanding of the Christian life.

The Promised Land had been the place where God dwelt with his people. Hence it was called the "holy land" (Zechariah 2:12). The "promise of the Father" was the promise of the Spirit dwelling within persons. Hence the Spirit is denoted as the *Holy* Spirit, since his dwelling in persons makes them holy even as Yahweh's dwelling in the Promised Land had made it holy. Saints in the New Testament are thus those who are made holy (οἱ ἄγιοι) by the indwelling Spirit.[4] This means that the true temple is a spiritual reality, whereas the Promised Land as Yahweh's sanctuary (Ex. 15:17) was largely a geographic concept.

The "promise of the Father" meant that God's presence

would no longer be confined to any one place or limited to any one group of persons. It meant the arrival of the kingdom on earth. The "promise of the Father" thus inaugurated Christ's reign on earth in the hearts of believers. This means that the Church is both the earthly setting of the body of Christ and the temple of the Holy Spirit. Hence the Church is the fellowship of believers *in Christ*, i.e., it is the corporate singularity of all those in whom the exalted Christ, through the "promise of the Father," dwells and reigns. In this respect, Bultmann defines the Church as "the vestibule" to the kingdom of God.[5] I, 37 Oscar Cullmann writes:

> The Church is the centre of this kingdom because it has been chosen to be the earthly setting of the body of Christ. It is now clear that the Church forms the centre, because it is the body of Christ as a human community which is the goal of the divine plan of salvation. The dominion which was prophesied for the Son of Man . . . in Daniel 7:27 is fulfilled in the Church as the body of Christ.[6]

The concept of the Promised Land as the earthly setting of Yahweh's kingdom carried with it enormous implications for the individual Israelite. No person could escape his responsibility to live holy before Yahweh. It was not enough for the land to be consecrated to Yahweh; rather, entire devotion (exclusive worship) to Yahweh was the obligation of every Israelite (Deut. 29:18-20). Likewise the Church is not merely a collective concept. What the Church is in its corporate wholeness *in Christ* must become appropriated personally by each believer. That is, the "promise of the Father" must be actualized in the life of every believer. This personal appropriation can be defined as the kingdom of God being established in the inner life of the believer in Christ. It is one thing to be a member of the kingdom of God through the believer's incorporation into the Church through justifying faith; it is another thing for the kingdom of God to be established within each believer in Christ through the sanctification of the Spirit.

It is this twofold differentiation which John Wesley presupposed when he defined Christian perfection (i.e., loving God with all the heart) as the kingdom of God being established within the believer.[7] For the reign of God presupposes perfect devotion on the part of those who are members of his kingdom. If one is taken into the church, then it is his obligation to let Christ reign in his heart. Bultmann's exposition of the grammatical use of the indicative and imperative moods is illustrative of this tension between being-in-Christ and Christ being formed in the believer. He shows that believers *are* holy by virtue of their *being in Christ*. Yet the believer *must* come to appropriate in his inner being the holiness of Christ.

> The Spirit is the 'Holy Spirit' $\pi \nu \epsilon \hat{\upsilon} \mu \alpha$ $\overset{\text{\'}}{\alpha} \gamma \iota o \nu$, and the use of the holiness-concept is likewise significant for the unity of the indicative and the imperative — i.e., of power and obligation. Believers are $\overset{\text{\'}}{\alpha} \gamma \iota o \iota$ $\overset{\text{\'}}{\eta} \gamma \iota \alpha \sigma \mu \acute{\epsilon} \nu o \iota$ ("holy," "made holy" — though English translations through the influence of the Vulgate conventionally render the first "saints" and the second "sanctified" or "consecrated" . . .) which means in the first place those who have been taken out of the world and transplanted into the eschatological existence by Christ's salvation-deed (I Cor. 1:2: as those "made holy in Christ Jesus") which in baptism was carried over to them (I Cor. 6:11: "but you were washed, you were made holy," etc.). Christ is to us "righteousness and consecration and redemption" (abstract expression for the concrete: "he who makes us righteous and holy and redeemed" (I Cor. 1:30). But from this very fact arises our obligation to the active "holiness" which God demands of us (I Thess. 4:3; Rom. 6:19,22); whoever disregards this demand disregards God who gave us His Holy Spirit (I Thess. 4:8). Our body is the Holy Spirit's temple, which must be kept clean (I Cor. 6:19). The congregation also is the holy temple of God, and God will destroy the destroyer of this temple (I Cor. 3:16f.). Similar are Paul's wishes that God, or the Lord, may establish believer's hearts "unblamable in holiness"

and utterly sanctify them (I Thess. 3:13; 5:23). The bestowal of holiness through baptism can be called "putting on Christ"; but in addition to the indicative, "you have put on Christ" (Gal. 3:27), we also find the imperative: "put on the Lord Jesus Christ" (Rom. 13:14).[8]

The believer's first step of being incorporated into Christ (with baptism as the sign and seal of this initiation) is participating in Jesus' resurrection from the dead (= justification by faith = Exodus theme of deliverance). On the other hand, the process of being made holy through the indwelling of the Spirit (Pentecost) is the second stage of initiation into Christ. This process is to be climaxed in total submissiveness to the reign of Christ. The Christian life is thus made up of two stages — the believer's being incorporated into the kingdom of Christ (justification) and the kingdom of Christ being established in the heart of the believer (sanctification).

This twofold initiation into Christ is suggested by Paul's use of the indicative and imperative moods in Romans 6. The indicative is used in Romans 6:1-11 where Paul describes the believer's incorporation into Christ through baptism into Jesus' death-resurrection. In vss. 12-23, Paul uses the imperative mood to indicate the obligation of the believer to make actual in his life what is his potentially by virtue of his being in Christ. Hence in Romans 6:4, Paul writes: "We were buried [indicative mood] therefore with him by baptism into death, so that as Christ was raised from the dead by the glory of the Father, we too might walk in newness of life." Yet in vs. 12, Paul's thought moves quickly to the imperative of Christ reigning supremely in the believer: "Let not [the principle of] sin reign . . . but yield yourself to God." For Christ to reign is to be "set free from [the principle of] sin and have become slaves of God, [and] the return you get is sanctification and its end, eternal life" (Romans 6:22). Here Paul relates Christ's reign to yieldedness = sanctification = slaves of God = freed from sin = the promise of eternal life.

The sanctification of the believer, of course, begins through

the Spirit's ministry of regeneration in the life of the repent-
ant sinner, yet the perfection of the believer's being (sanctification) is accomplished through the indwelling Pentecostal
Spirit. This means that it is the "promise of the Father"
who establishes the kingdom of God within the heart of the
believer so that it can then be said that the exalted Christ
reigns supremely. That Christ reigns supremely within the
believer implies perfect loyalty and perfect love for Christ.
Wesley's equation of the kingdom of God being established
within the believer and Christian perfection can thus be seen
to be appropriate.

Acts 1-2 substantiates the association of the "promise of
the Father" with this kingdom-idea. Luke shows that the
outpouring of the Spirit was identified with the expectation
of the restoration of the kingdom (Acts 1:3,6). In this respect, the "promise of the Father" was the fulfillment of the
prophetic vision of the New Covenant which was to restore the
ancient promise to Abraham and which was to be accomplished through a new Exodus and a new Conquest. In the previous chapter it was pointed out that the new Exodus corresponded to Jesus' Resurrection from the dead and that the
new Conquest corresponded to the Pentecostal gift of the
Spirit. It was also pointed out that these parallel events of the
Old and New Covenants are implicit in the sermons of Peter,
Stephen, and Paul in the first thirteen chapters of Acts. It
is now being pointed out that the concept of the "promise of
the Father" presupposes the Promised Land motif of the
Old Covenant.

The initial fulfillment of the Abrahamic promise meant that
Israel would be brought into the land of Canaan where the
demand of the Decalogue for exclusive worship of God was
to become a reality. Failure to love God perfectly resulted in
captivity. Hence the captivity of Israel had been a punishment
for Israel's sin of not obeying the first commandment, i.e.,
loving God perfectly, which was the focal point of the Ten
Commandments (Luke 10:27). [9] In this respect Moses had
made it clear from the beginning that the only basis for remaining in the Promised Land (Deut. 6:1-2) was a perfect love

and exclusive worship of Yahweh. "Hear, O Israel: The Lord your God is one Lord; and you shall love the Lord your God with all your heart, and with all your soul, and with all your might" (Deut. 6:4-5). Because they failed to love Yahweh perfectly they yielded to idolatry, and Yahweh "scattered them among the nations" (Ezek. 36:19). This punishment of exile from the Promised Land and the ensuing captivity was not the last word for Israel. Out of an act of sheer grace Yahweh freely chose to restore and renew the ancient promise which had been made with Abraham.

This hope of a New Covenant and a restored kingdom became the theme of the prophets of the exile. Edmond Jacob has shown that the language of this hope for a restored kingdom is the language of the Exodus and the Conquest.

> Ezekiel sees his own role in the light of that of Moses: as a sentinel with duty of warning the people, he will proclaim the coming of a new shepherd, a new David, who will take up on a vaster scale the work of Joshua. The people will be restored: just as in former times they had crossed the Red Sea and the Jordan, which in each case had been a passage through death — think of the lasting association of the sea with chaos — they will again pass from death to life (Ez. 36-37) and the Temple rebuilt in the centre of the country will be the guarantee of the dependability of this promise. So Ezekiel proclaims nothing which is not to be found already in the ancient *credo*, so convinced is he that the faithlessness of the people does not cancel the faithfulness of God.[10]

In reference to this restored kingdom which had its beginning at Pentecost with the initiation of the New Covenant (Acts 2), it is significant that Ezekiel equates the restoration of the Promised Land with the promised gift of the Spirit: "And I will put my Spirit within you, and you shall live, and I will place you in your own land" (Ezek. 37:14). What this restoration of the kingdom in the Promised Land further suggested was the sanctification of Israel and the perfecting of their love for Yahweh (Deut. 30:5,6,16; Ezek. 37:28).

Even before Israel had originally possessed the Promised Land, Moses had forseen that Israel would be removed because the people would fail to love God perfectly (Deut. 29:25ff.). He also saw that Israel would be regathered to the Promised Land where they would remain forever because "the Lord your God will circumcise your heart and the heart of your offspring, so that you will love the Lord your God with all your heart and with all your soul" (Deut. 30:6).

Likewise the prophets interpreted their captivity as a punishment for failure to love God perfectly, but they also perceived the inability of Israel to measure up to Yahweh's requirement within the context of the ancient Covenant. Yehezkel Kaufmann has shown in this regard that the prophets had come to see that "experience teaches that mankind as now constituted cannot keep God's covenant, hence a new mankind must be created whose heart God has refashioned."[11] Kaufmann has shown that the essence of this New Covenant is a perfect love for God[12] who "will purify them with pure waters, plant in them his spirit, and give them a 'heart of flesh' so that they will obey him forever."[13] This means that under the New Covenant there will be no tension or discrepancy between the moral law and Israel's intention to be obedient, for "this tension is resolved in the eschatological vision of the new heart that man is to get at the end of days which render him incapable of sinning (Jer. 31:31ff.; 32:39f.; Ezek. 22:19ff; 36:26f.)."[14] Edmond Jacob likewise shows that the New Covenant "will make fully real the ideal of a holy people."[15]

Luke's writings in particular show that the Pentecostal event fulfills this eschatological hope of the kingdom restored in the Promised Land. However, he shows that Jesus' understanding of the restored kingdom was radically different from the popular notion. The true kingdom brought about by the Pentecostal event means that the exalted Christ reigns in the life of believers through the indwelling Spirit. In this respect, it is of symbolic significance that "the promise of the Father" which brought about the inauguration of this spiritual kingdom occurred in Jerusalem, the capital city of the Promised Land! (Acts 1:3-4).

As background to the Pentecostal event, Luke shows in his Gospel that the earthly Jesus had been hailed as the Messiah-king who would restore the Davidic kingdom. In his triumphal entry to the city, Jesus was paraded in the streets of Jerusalem as the Messiah-king on a donkey — a symbol of royalty. The people greeted him as a king: "Blessed is the King who comes in the name of the Lord!" (Luke 19:38). During his triumphant ride through the streets Jesus wept over the impending doom which would sweep away their mistaken dreams of a restored kingdom (Luke 19:41ff.).

Immediately following his arrival in Jerusalem the focus of his activity, significantly enough, was in the Temple and the cluster of events during the last days of his life centered on the concept of the restored Davidic kingdom. Parenthetically, it should be kept in mind that the kingdom and the Temple motifs had come to denote the same theme since the days of David's reign.[16]

His trial consisted largely of trumped-up charges of sedition that he would establish a political kingdom and overthrow Caesar. That Pilate was not disposed to take these charges seriously does not lessen the fact that Jesus' apparent understanding of himself as the Messiah did in fact come dangerously close to sedition. At any rate, Jesus did re-interpret the kingdom-temple theme of the Old Covenant as symbolic of his reality. The true temple is not the one that was to be torn down in three days, but the one what was to be raised in three days (John 2:19). The true kingdom was not the literal restoration of the Davidic kingdom in the city of Jerusalem, but was a spiritual kingdom whose capital was the glory of heaven from which Christ would rule with his Father (Luke 24:26; John 18:36).

It is significant that Jesus expected his kingdom to conquer the world, not through swords, but by word of mouth. As the reigning and risen Lord his commission to the disciples was that they were to bear witness to his Resurrection from the dead. This proclamation of the Resurrection was to be God's offer of forgiveness of sins to those who repented (Luke 24:44-48). Hence participation in Jesus' Resurrection from the dead was the meaning of the prophetic hope of the new

Exodus from captivity. Anyone from all nations could participate in this new Exodus and become a member of the true
kingdom.

Jesus' commission to his followers had stipulated that their
proclamation should begin at Jerusalem (the capital of the
Promised Land) and then extend to the ends of the earth
(Luke 24:47). The power with which they were to conquer
the world for the sake of God's kingdom was the power derived from the "promise of the Father" (Luke 24:49; Acts
1:8). This is why the disciples were to wait in Jerusalem until
the Pentecostal gift of the Holy Spirit had come to dwell
within them. Only then could they be strengthened with the
power of the Spirit to conquer the world for Christ's kingdom.
Only then, too, could it be truly said that the kingdom had
come and the Temple fully restored to its former glory. For
the Church as the body of Christ is the temple of the Holy
Spirit and the earthly center for the kingdom of Christ.

Hence the "promise of the Father" had two implications.
First, it meant for the disciples, and all the believers, the personal appropriation and sanctifying grace through the infilling
of the Holy Spirit (Luke 3:16; Acts 15:8-9). This means they
were thus empowered to conquer the world because the
kingdom had been established in their hearts. Second, the
"promise of the Father" meant the rise of the Church which
was the "vestibule" to the coming kingdom of God.

Bultmann has shown in this regard that "the dominant
concept of Jesus' message is the *Reign of God*."[17] He further
shows that this eschatological concept is fulfilled in Jesus
himself as the exalted Christ (who is functionally identical
to the Pentecostal Spirit). His kingdom is none other than
"his presence."[18] Wolfhart Pannenberg has written: "This
resounding motif of Jesus' message — the imminent Kingdom
of God — must be recovered as a key to the whole of Christian
theology."[19]

That the idea of the kingdom is "the dominant concept"
and "the resounding motif of Jesus' message" is surely sufficient to justify the claim that it is "a key to the whole of
Christian theology." Yet what has often not received suffi-

cient attention is that the "promise of the Father" as the indwelling Holy Spirit is the full *presence* of the exalted Christ enthroned in the heart of believers. Consequently, the Christian life has been interpreted largely in terms of participation in Christ's resurrected life ( = justification by faith) without a corresponding emphasis upon the kingdom becoming confirmed and established within the believer through the indwelling Spirit ( = sanctification). Like those who were delivered from Egypt through the Exodus event, believers are allowed to wander in the wilderness without crossing Jordan into the Land of Promise. They have the promise of the Kingdom through their participation in the Exodus event, but they have not become permanently established in the Land of Promise where they can enjoy "the fruit of the land" (Joshua 5:12 = the symbol of "fruit of the Spirit").

Wesley's equation of the imagery of the promised rest of Canaan land with perfect love is highly relevant and appropriate. His hymns often allude to the imagery of Canaan land as descriptive of Christian perfection. The following two verses cited in his *Plain Account of Christian Perfection* link Pentecostal language, perfect love, and the Promised Land:

> Choose from the world, if now I stand,
>   Adorn'd with righteousness divine;
> If, brought into the promised land,
>   I justly call the Saviour mine;
> Thy sanctifying Spirit pour,
>   To quench my thirst, and wash me clean;
> Now Saviour, let the gracious shower
>   Descend, and make me pure from sin.
>
> Oh that I now, from sin released,
>   Thy word might to the utmost prove,
> Enter into Thy promised rest,
>   The Canaan of Thy perfect love.[20]

Wesley on occasions equates the "rest which remaineth for the people of God" (Hebrews 4:9) as descriptive of Christian perfection.[21] An exposition of Hebrews 3:7-4:11 provides warrant for this equation of the symbol of the promised rest with perfect love. Those who were released from captivity through the Exodus event failed to enter the promised rest in the land of Canaan even though that was God's design for them (3:18-19). Unbelief and an incomplete devotion to God accounted for their failure to enter the promised rest (3:7-11). Surely the Hebrew writer did not intend to suggest that those who failed to enter this promised rest missed eternal life; otherwise Moses would have to be counted among them!

That this symbol of the promised rest is not to be identified with heaven can be seen in the way that the writer intends it to be achieved in this life. (1) Repeatedly he affirms that this promised rest is to be achieved "today" (3:7,15; 4:7). (2) He uses the present tense in speaking of the appropriation of this rest (4:1,3,6,9,10). (3) The writer also uses the aorist tense in exhorting the appropriation of this rest, "Let us therefore hasten ($\sigma\pi o\upsilon\delta\acute{a}\sigma\omega\mu\epsilon\nu$) to enter ($\epsilon\acute{\iota}\sigma\epsilon\lambda\theta\epsilon\hat{\iota}\nu$) that rest" (Heb. 4:11). The use of the aorist tense suggests the idea of completed action, and the word $\sigma\pi o\upsilon\delta\acute{a}\sigma\omega\mu\epsilon\nu$ denotes haste and eagerness. Hence the writer could hardly intend this rest to be identical with the heavenly rest. (4) This promised rest is to be achieved by faith in the present moment (4:3). (5) This rest in the Promised Land, which was secured initially by Joshua, is only a foretaste of the spiritual rest of faith which the exalted Christ gives (4:8). (6) Finally, this rest of which the writer speaks is for those who are already the people of God and who have presumably already experienced their exodus from captivity. Hence this rest is not offered to those who are still unbelievers (4:9).

Inasmuch as the Promised Land symbolized the abode of Yahweh where his people served him with perfect love and where idolatry was totally excluded, the idea of the promised rest naturally lends itself to the symbol of the perfect Christian life of exclusive worship and love for God. Wesley's hymn which he quotes in the *Plain Account of Christian Perfection* catches the significance of this symbol of rest:

> Lord, I believe a rest remains
> To all Thy people known;

A rest where pure enjoyment reigns,
   And Thou art loved alone.

A rest where all our soul's desire
   Is fixed on things above;
Where doubt, and pain, and fear expire,
   Cast out by perfect love.

From every evil motion freed
   (The Son hath made us free),
On all the powers of hell we tread,
   In glorious liberty.

Safe in the way of life, above
   Death, earth, and hell we rise;
We find, when perfected in love,
   Our long-sought paradise.

O that I now the rest might know,
   Believe, and enter in!
Now, Saviour, now the power bestow,
   And let me cease from sin!

Remove this hardness from my heart,
   This unbelief remove;
To me the rest of faith impart,
   The Sabbath of Thy love.

Come, O my Saviour, come away!
   Into my soul descend;
No longer from thy creature stay,
   My Author and my End.

The bliss Thou hast for me prepared
   No longer be delay'd;
Come, my exceeding great reward,
   For whom I first was made.

Come, Father, Son, and Holy Ghost,
   And seal me Thine abode!
Let all I am in Thee be lost;
   Let all be lost in God.[22]

That the promised rest of Canaan Land symbolizes the perfection of the Christian life which is effected through the "promise of the Father" is also in accord with Karl Barth's interpretation of Pentecost. His exposition occurs in a highly significant chapter in *Church Dogmatics* entitled, "The Baptism with the Holy Spirit."[23] A summary of some of his thoughts will be helpful in understanding the significance of the "promise of the Father."

That the Resurrection and Pentecost are the two events which are the sole bases of the Christian life is a well established consensus in the history of theology and in New Testament studies. Karl Barth writes: "The New Testament witnesses, too, counted upon the Christian life only on the basis of these factors [of the Resurrection and Pentecost]."[24] This distinction between Easter and Pentecost has also figured prominently in the sacramental theology of Roman Catholicism. Easter is the sacrament of baptism in which one begins the Christian life, and Pentecost is the basis of the sacrament of confirmation in which the believer is strengthened to live the Christian life through the reception of the Spirit.[25] John Fletcher, the first systematic theologian of Methodism and John Wesley's chosen successor of the Methodist movement, likewise grounded Wesley's distinction between conversion and Christian perfection on the basis of these two distinct events.[26]

That the Exodus event prefigures the Resurrection event is generally recognized.[27] What has not received adequate consideration is that the Promised Land motif prefigures the "promise of the Father" ( = baptism with the Spirit). Karl Barth specifically calls attention to this idea, though he does not fully develop it. He describes the believer as "constantly marching" toward the Promised Land with "a never-resting striding."[28] While the baptism with the Spirit denotes the completeness of the Christian life which the Promised Land symbolizes, [29] it is impossible for the believer to appropriate now "the perfect life."[30] Nor is "the rest which is available for him" in the formal sense actually appropriated except "provisionally."[31] Rather, "he is constantly chasing this

perfection which awaits him."[32] In other words, Barth understands sanctification exclusively in terms of progression with
no allowance for Christian perfection in this life. For Barth,
the promised rest of Canaan Land symbolizes the perfection
of the Christian life, yet the believer never crosses the Jordan
into the land of perfect love this side of eternity.

Barth's exegesis of the baptism with the Holy Spirit is,
on the whole, highly illuminating. He shows that the Pentecostal outpouring of the Holy Spirit marked the realization of
the New Covenant anticipated by the exilic prophets. In particular, he equates the baptism with the Spirit, circumcision of
heart, and loving God with all the heart.[33]

Barth brings together these equations in his exegesis of
Romans 2, in which Paul shows that the real Jew is one whose
circumcision "is that of the heart by the Spirit and not the
letter."[34] Barth writes:

Paul is here describing the strange fulfillment of the
radiant Old Testament promise of the future establishment of a completely renewed Israel which is awakened
to obedience to God and empowered and ready to keep
his commandments. Thus we read in Jer. 31:33ff.:
"But this shall be the covenant that I shall make with
the house of Israel after those days (the days of the
breaking of the covenant and the ensuing rejection),
saith Yahweh: "I will put my law in their inward parts,
and write it in their hearts; and will be their God, and
they shall be my people. And they shall teach no more
every man his neighbour, and every man his brother,
saying, Know the Lord: for they shall all know me,
from the least of them unto the greatest of them, saith
Yahweh." In the decisive matter Jer. 32:39f. is even
stronger: "I will give them another heart and another
way, that they may fear me for ever." Stronger still is
Ezek. 11:19f. (cf. 36:26f.); "I will . . . put a new spirit
within you; and I will take the stony heart out of their
flesh, and will give them an heart of flesh, that they
may walk in my statutes, and keep mine ordinances,
and do them." Also, Deut. 30:6 (cf. Jer. 4:4): "Yahweh,
thy God, will circumcize thine heart, and the heart of

thy seed, to love Yahweh, thy God, with all thine heart, and with all thy soul, that thou mayest live."[35]

Barth shows that the implication of all this is: "If God's Law is written on his heart, if his heart is circumcized, if he acquires a new and different heart, this means that he himself, in so far as this has a decisive bearing *on his whole being and act* [italics mine], becomes another man."[36] He further shows that the baptism with the Holy Spirit "cleanses, renews, and changes man *truly and totally* [italics mine] ."[37] This "divine change, at the baptism of the Spirit . . . is the totality of salvation, the full justification, sanctification, and vocation of man brought about in Jesus Christ."[38] Further, he shows that "man's baptism with the Holy Spirit, is not half-grace, or half-adequate grace; it is whole grace and wholly adequate grace." [39]

Barth's understanding of this "baptism with the Holy Spirit" is theologically disappointing, though his exegetical considerations are otherwise impressive. The theological interpretation that he gives to his exegesis leads him to an extreme imputation theory.[40] The baptism with the Holy Spirit is exclusively "a divine event" which happens position-ally and formally *in Christ*. This baptism with the Spirit is perfect freedom, but "the reality and perfection of his liber-ation and empowering for it, the direct validity of the com-mand given him therewith, cannot be negated or even dimin-ished by the brokenness of his disobedience, however severe. Once and for all, perfectly and with full adequacy, he is empowered and liberated."[41] This totality of the Christian life is the objective, "*divine decision*" which is imputed to the believer in contrast to the subjective, "*human decision*" and experience of the grace of God.[42]

For Barth, baptism with water is the sacrament which represents the subjective appropriation of God's grace.[43] It represents the beginning and incomplete experience of grace,[44] whereas the baptism with the Spirit represents the totality of the Christian life.[45] It is impossible for the Chris-tian actually to appropriate now "the perfect life,[46] which the baptism with the Spirit denotes in a formal sense.[47]

Baptism with water parallels the Exodus event;[48] it denotes repentance in man;[49] it denotes regeneration;[50] it signifies conversion.[51] "Baptism is for those who newly join the community the first concrete step of faith, love, hope, and service."[52] Deliverance, conversion, forgiveness of sins are thus the things signified in Christian baptism and are grounded in the Resurrection.[53]

Baptism with the Holy Spirit (Pentecost) signifies the totality of sanctifying grace;[54] it signifies the establishment of the kingdom of God;[55] it signifies purifying fire. The imagery of fire which John the Baptist associated with baptism with the Spirit means a "judgment on the sin that is plainly robbed of any possible basis . . . ; hence there can be no Pentecost, no baptism with the Holy Ghost, unless one receives Him ὡσεὶ πυρός (Acts 2:3)."[56]

Baptism with water has as its goal the baptism with the Holy Spirit.[57] Baptism with water denotes the beginning of the Christian life.[58] On the other hand, the baptism with the Spirit denotes the "confirmation of the Easter event."[59] In this sense, baptism with the Spirit is the goal of (Christian) baptism with water.[60] Hence the baptism with water, though distinct from baptism with the Spirit, is related to it. The beginning of the Christian life, symbolized in water baptism, will be perfected at "the last definitive and universal revelation of Jesus Christ."[61] In this respect, the reality denoted by the baptism with the Spirit will not be achieved until the eschaton. For Barth, this perfection is already present in the Church (i.e., *in Christ*) from the day of Pentecost onward, but its actualization will take place for believers only in the eschaton.

Barth thus does not equate conversion with Pentecostal language. Rather he shows that "Christian baptism, as it is the form of the petition for the coming of the kingdom, is far from being itself in any sense the baptism of the Spirit."[62] Rather, Christian baptism is "the petition for this — that the outpouring of the Spirit might take place again, and especially on these newcomers to faith."[63] Hence Barth shows that baptism only grants the right to pray for and expect the baptism in the Spirit. He refers to the Samaritan's baptism as illustrative of this distinction between Christian baptism and the baptism in the Spirit.[64] To be sure, Barth understands the Spirit to be given in Christian baptism, but the Spirit's *"fulness* [italics mine] promised to Christians in and with this beginning" in Christian baptism is progressively realized in further outpourings of the Spirit.[65]

Barth is thus explicit in his distinction between one becoming a Christian and his further experiences of the Spirit's outpourings and baptisms. Water baptism puts one "in a position to ask for Him [the Holy Spirit]." He further shows in his exegesis of Pentecostal passages (Acts 8:15f.; 10:45f.; 18:25f.; 19:2f.) that water "baptism, which obviously does not guarantee reception of the Holy Spirit but can only be a prayer for Him, cannot be in any sense dispensible for those who have received Him, since they have to receive Him again, and hence to pray for Him."[66]

Barth thus stresses that the baptism in the Spirit denotes the fulness of the Christian life and is to be equated with the coming kingdom of God since "Βασιλεία and the πνεῦμα ἅγιον . . . denote one and the same divine human reality which is present and yet also future."[67] For Barth, this fulness of the Holy Spirit is to be achieved only in the eschaton when the kingdom of God has fully come, though through repeated outpourings of the Spirit one is always progressively realizing this fulness.[68]

In contrast to Barth, Wesley believed that the Kingdom of God could be established in full power within the heart of each believer who is enabled thus to serve Christ with perfect devotion (exclusive worship), yet he allows that in the more objective sense the kingdom of God will not embrace the scope of God's creation until the end time.

Barth's exegesis of the baptism with the Spirit is , on the whole, compatible with Wesley's emphasis that Pentecost signifies the fulness of the Christian life. The point of theological difference from Barth is that Wesley believes that the perfect Christian life can be realized in this life, not merely in the eschaton. To be sure, only in glorification at the eschaton will the believer actually be able to lead a life of perfect obedience, but through the perfection of love experienced in this life Wesley believed that one could at least *intend* perfect obedience, even though he does not actually succeed altogether in *performing* perfect obedience. In this respect, Barth is certainly right to speak of the future fulfillment of the reality which the baptism with the Spirit denotes. Yet Wesley insisted upon the possibility of a perfect heart in this life because of the present possibilities of Pentecostal grace. Perhaps Wesley went too far in minimizing the possibilities of grace prior to Pentecost, yet his theology is distinctly clear in affirming the possibility of perfect love for those living in the Pentecostal era. Wesley writes:

> But elsewhere Solomon says, "There is no man that sinneth not." Doubtless thus it was in the days of Solomon; yea, and from Solomon to Christ there was then no man that sinned not. But whatever was the case of those under the law, we may safely affirm, with St. John, that since the Gospel was given, "he that is born of God sinneth not."
>
> The privileges of Christians are in no wise to be measured by what the Old Testament records concerning those who were under the Jewish dispensation; seeing the fulness of time is now come; the Holy Ghost is now given; the great salvation [a term consistently used by Wesley to denote Christian perfection] of God is now brought to men by the revelation of Jesus Christ. The kingdom of heaven is now set up on earth, concerning which the Spirit of God declared of old time (so far is David from being the pattern or standard of Christian perfection), "He that is feeble among them at that day shall be as David; and the house of David shall be as the angel of the Lord before them" (Zech. xii.8).[69]

It is not the intent of this writer to deal with the practical implications of Wesley's conception of perfect love, but it should be pointed out that Wesley believed that perfect love was compatible with living in a fallen world, even though the believer inevitably succumbs to innumerable mistakes and infirmities. Only in the eschaton, when the believer's body will be glorified, will these consequences of sin be removed. Wesley's concept of perfection thus implies only a perfect intention, not perfect behavior.[70]

It will be helpful to conclude this chapter with the following summary statements:

1.    Baptism with water recalls the Exodus through the Red Sea (I Cor. 10:2) and specifically denotes Jesus' Resurrection from the dead (Romans 6:3-5; Col. 2:12; I Peter 3:21).

2.    Baptism with water as the sacrament of the Resurrection event means forgiveness of sins, justification, regeneration (Rom. 6:8; I Cor. 15:17; Eph. 2:1-2, 5-6; Acts 5:30-31; 13:37-38; Gal. 2:20-21).

3.    Baptism with the Holy Spirit ( = "promise of the Father") recalls the Promised Land motif ( = kingdom-temple theme, Acts 1:3-4) and specifically denotes Pentecost.

4.    Baptism with the Holy Spirit as the ongoing event of Pentecost effects perfect love (Rom. 5:6; I John 4:13-21; Deut. 30:6) and full sanctification (Acts 15:8-9; Ezek. 36:25-27).

5.    Baptism with water denotes the first step of the Christian life. Its cleansing is a relative renewal.

6.    The baptism with the Spirit, as Barth puts it, "cleanses, renews, and changes man truly and totally."[71]

7.    Even as the crossing of the Jordan River into the Promised Land symbolized the ultimate goal of the Exodus (Exod. 3:8) and the complete removal of the reproach of Egypt from the people of Israel (Josh. 5:9), even so the baptism with the Spirit completes the sanctifying grace begun in the symbol of Christian baptism with water.

8.    Just as Pentecost was the "confirmation of the Easter event" (Barth),[72] even so baptism with the Spirit is the confirmation, or establishing, of the grace begun in conversion.

These summary statements are intended to show that the Promised Land motif is a prefiguring of the "promise of the Father." In this respect, Pentecostal reality is the ultimate fulfillment of the grace symbolized in the Conquest of Canaan.

[1] Rudolf Bultmann, *History and Eschatology* Edinburg: The University Press, 1957) pp. 36, 121; Bultmann, "Prophecy and Fulfillment," *Essays on Old Testament Interpretation,* ed. Claus Westermann, Trans. James Luther Mays (London: SCM Ltd. 1963, pp. 63, 71-74.

[2] Oscar Cullmann, *Salvation in History*, trans. Sidney G. Sowers (London: SCM Press Led., 1967), pp. 172ff.

[3] *Ibid.*, p. 245; Bultmann, *Theology of the New Testament*, I, 27; Cullmann, *The Early Church*, ed. A. J. B. Higgins (London: SCM Press Ltd., 1966), pp. 116f.; Georgia Harkness, *The Fellowship of the Holy Spirit* (Nashville: Abingdon Press, 1966), pp. 68-71; George S. Hendry, *The Holy Spirit in Christian Theology* (Philadelphia: Westminster Press, 1956), pp. 21-25, 30, 36, 39; Hendrik Berkhof, *The Doctrine of the Trinity* (Richmond, VA.: John Knox Press, 1964), p. 94.

[4] Bultmann, *Theology of the New Testament*, I, 338.

[5] *Ibid*, I, 37.

[6] *The Early Church*, p. 131.

[7] Fletcher, *Checks to Antinomianism* (New York: Hunt and Eaton, 1889), II, 622, 657. Cited hereafter as *Checks*. Cf. Fletcher, *Checks*, I, 593 and *The Standard Sermons of John Wesley*, I, 154; II, 163.

[8] Bultmann, *Theology of the New Testament*, I, 338-339.

[9] Kaufmann, *The Religion of Israel*, p. 233.

[10] Jacob, *Theology of the Old Testament*, p. 193.

[11] Kaufmann, p. 426.

[12] *Ibid.*, p. 425.

[13] *Ibid.*, p. 442.

[14] *Ibid.*, p. 75.

[15] Jacob, p. 216.

[16] *Ibid.*, p. 192.

[17] *Theology of the New Testament*, 1, 4.

[18]*Ibid.*, p. 7.

[19]Wolfhart Pannenburg, *Theology and the Kingdom of God* (Philadelphia: The Westminster Press, 1969), p. 53.

[20]*A Plain Account of Christian Perfection* (London: The Epworth Press, 1970), pp. 31-32.

[21]*Ibid.*, p. 26.

[22]*Ibid.*, pp. 26-27.

[23]*Church Dogmatics*, trans. G. W. Bromiley (Edinburgh: T. & T. Clark, 1969), IV., Part IV.

[24]*Ibid.*, IV., Part IV, 30.

[25]See below, Chapter VI.

[26]Fletcher, I, 526.

[27]William J. O'Shea, *Sacraments of Initiation* (Englewood Cliffs: Prentice-Hall, 1966), pp. 24, 30; F. X. Durrwell, *The Resurrection*, trans. Rosemary Sheed (New York: Sheed and Ward, 1961), pp. 17-18, 187.

[28]*Church Dogmatics*, IV, Part 4, 39.

[29]*Ibid.*, p. 34.

[30]*Ibid.*, p. 40.

[31]*Ibid.*

[32]*Ibid.*

[33]*Ibid.*, pp. 7-8.

[34]*Ibid.*, p. 7.

[35]*Ibid.*, p. 8.

[36]*Ibid.*

[37]*Ibid.*, p. 34.

[38]*Ibid.*, p. 34.

[39]*Ibid.*

[40]*Ibid.*, 38, 40, 41, 42.

[41]*Ibid.*, pp. 34-35.

[42]*Ibid.*, p. 41.

[43]*Ibid.*, pp. 41ff.

[44]*Ibid.*, pp. 38, 46.

[45]*Ibid.*, p. 34.

[46]*Ibid.*, p. 40.

[47]*Ibid.*, pp. 34-35.

[48]*Ibid.*, p. 45.

[49]*Ibid.*, p. 46.

[50]*Ibid.*, p. 120.

[51]*Ibid.*, pp. 90, 136.

[52]*Ibid.*, pp. 72, 116.

[53]*Ibid.*, p. 84.

[54]*Ibid.*, p. 34.

[55]*Ibid.*, pp. 76, 78.

[56]*Ibid.*, p. 80.

[57]*Ibid.*, pp. 71, 86.

[58]*Ibid.*, pp. 52, 132.

[59]*Ibid.*, p. 89.

[60]*Ibid.*, p. 86.

[61]*Ibid.*, p. 89.

[62]*Ibid.*, p. 70.

[63]*Ibid.*

[64]*Ibid.*

[65]*Ibid.*

[66]*Ibid.*, p. 78.

[67]*Ibid.*

[68]*Ibid.*, p. 76.

[69]*A Plain Account of Christian Perfection*, p. 17; cf. *The Standard Sermons of John Wesley*, II, 159ff.

[70]*A Plain Account of Christian Perfection*, pp. 42-43.

[71]*Church Dogmatics*, IV, Part IV, 34.

[72]*Ibid.*, p. 89.

# CHAPTER III.

## PENTECOSTAL LANGUAGE AS CANAAN LAND LANGUAGE

The language of Pentecost is the language of Canaan Land. This should not be surprising since all that Canaan Land symbolized had come to be fulfilled in the reality of Pentecost. The New Covenant language assumes and enriches the language of the Abrahamic covenant and promise which initially had been brought to pass under Moses (Heb. 3:3) and Joshua (Heb. 4:8) who prefigure Christ.

In the previous chapter the concept of the restored kingdom was shown to be presupposition for understanding Luke's account of Pentecost. The intent of this present chapter — to show that the language of Canaan Land, along with the language of the prophetic hope of a New Conquest — is appropriated in the proclamation of the New Covenant. To be sure the New Testament writers did not attempt to theologize.in an explicit and precise manner, but this was not necessary for them since their minds were so thoroughly saturated with the language and thought of the Old Testament. Hence it was sufficient for them to imply these theological truths through allusions to the Old Testament imagery, events, and language. But for us, we are not so steeped in the imagery and thought of the Old Testament, and the distance in time between first century Palestine and our modern world easily obscures the tacit meanings of these Old Testament allusions shared by the New Testament writers. Our task now is to make explicit these tacit theological truths presupposed in the New Testament.

In this respect, it should be observed that the language of Jesus' Resurrection from the dead is the language of the Exodus — redemption (Ex. 6:6; Eph. 1:7); deliverance (Ex. 3:8; Gal. 1:4; Col. 1:13); ransom (I Peter 1:18-19; I Tim. 2:6); release (Ex. 6:6; Acts 2:24; Rev. 1:5). Just as the Exodus from bondage symbolized forgiveness of sins (Psalm 130:4,8),[1] even so, Jesus' Resurrection from the dead is the basis of forgiveness of sins (Titus 2:14).*

On the other hand the language of Canaan Land includes the following words: promise, blessing, rest, dwelling, kingdom, gift, established, fruit, abundance, riches, inheritance, sanctification, purity, obedience, temple, peace, joy. Each of these words can be used interchangeably to describe the one and same reality of dwelling in the Promised Land. The sameness of these words is indicated in the description of the initial Conquest, as well as in the subsequent hope of the exilic prophets for a New Conquest.

An exposition of two passages in the book of Deuteronomy (12:5-12; 28:7-12) will illustrate the similarity between the language of Canaan Land and the language of the New Covenant.

1. Canaan Land as the *habitation* of God (Deut. 12:5,11) prefigures the Church as the habitation of God through the Spirit (Eph. 2:22).

2. The promised *rest* of Canaan Land (Deut. 12:9,10) prefigures the promised rest of faith given to God's people (Heb. 4:9).

---

*Titus 2:14 illustrates the twofold stages of the Christian life; "Jesus Christ . . . gave himself for us to redeem us from all iniquity [Exodus-Resurrection theme] and to purify for himself a people of his own who are zealous for good deeds [Conquest–Pentecost theme]." Even as possession of Canaan Land is a concomitant of Israel's sanctification (Ezek. 37:28; cf. Is. 4:3-4) and obedience (Ezek. 36:27); so under New Covenant possession of the pentecostal Spirit is a concomitant of sanctification (II Thess. 2:13; Heb. 10:29) and obedience (Heb. 10:16).

3. The *peace* of the Promised Land (Deut. 12:10; Lev. 26:6,7) prefigures the peace of the exalted Christ (Phil. 4:7), which is bestowed through the Pentecostal Spirit (John 14: 26-27).

4. The idea of a settled and *established place* where God *dwells* with his people (Deut. 12:11; 28:9) prefigures the idea of being "rooted and built up in him and established in the faith" (Col. 2:7). It also prefigures the idea of God having "blessed us in Christ with every *spiritual* blessing ($\pi\nu\epsilon\nu\mu\alpha\tau\iota\kappa\hat{\eta}$ = Pentecostal Spirit)* in the *heavenly places*" (Eph. 1:3).

5. The idea of the Promised Land as a *gift* of God (Deut. 12:10) prefigures the Pentecostal *gift* of the Spirit to believers (Acts 2:38).

6. The *fruit* of the land (Deut. 28:11) prefigures the *fruit* of the Spirit (Gal. 5:22).

7. The idea of *blessing* (Deut. 28:8) prefigures the blessing of Christ which is identical to "the promise of the Spirit through faith" (Gal. 3:14).

8. The idea of *abundance* (Deut. 28:11) prefigures the abundance and riches of Christ's kingdom (Eph. 2:7; 3:8).

9. The idea of being *established* in the land as a corollary to the *holiness* of Israel (Deut. 28:9) prefigures the New Covenant idea of the believer's heart being *established* unblamable in *holiness* (I Thess. 3:13).

10. Even as *obedience* was the condition for dwelling in the land (Deut. 28:9), so in the New Covenant the believer must "lead a life worthy of God, who calls you into his own kingdom and glory" (I Thess. 2:12).

11. Even as the Promised Land was Israel's *inheritance* (Deut. 12:9), so in the New Covenant the sanctification of God's people (Acts 20:32) and the possession of the promised Spirit are their *inheritance* (Eph. 1:13-14).

12. The command to rejoice before the Lord in the Promised Land for the riches of his blessing (Deut. 12:7) prefigures the New Covenant command to "rejoice in the

---

*The word, "spiritual," is unique to the New Testament and always denotes the Holy Spirit.

Lord" (Phil. 4:4). The presupposition in the New Covenant for worshiping the Lord "with all your heart" and "*always* and for everything giving thanks" is being "filled with the Spirit" (Eph. 5:18-20).

An exposition of Ezekiel 37:12-28 will also show the similarity between the language of the subsequent hope of the exilic prophets for the restored kingdom in Canaan Land and the language of the New Covenant.

1. That the New Covenant is to be accomplished through a new Exodus and a new Conquest is recalled in Ezek. 37:12; "Behold, I will open your graves, and raise you from your graves, O my people [which recalls the Exodus theme of deliverance from captivity and prefigures the believer's deliverance from sins' captivity through Jesus' Resurrection from the dead, Eph. 2:1, 5-6]; and I will bring you home into the land of Israel [which recalls the Conquest theme of Joshua's bringing the Israelites into Canaan Land (Deut. 6:23) and prefigures the Pentecostal theme of the inauguration of the reign of Christ, Acts 2:30-36]."

2. The New Conquest through which the Kingdom of God will be restored to the land of Canaan will be accomplished through the indwelling Spirit (37:14). This prefigures the Pentecostal outpouring of the Spirit who brought the Church (as the earthly focal point of the coming kingdom of God) into being.

3. This restored kingdom will have as its king "my servant David" (37:24). The kingship of David prefigures the exalted Christ who became the true Messiah-king who sits upon the throne of God's kingdom (Acts 2:30-32).

4. The indwelling Spirit will enable God's people to live holy (37:14) through cleansing them (37:23). Their sanctification will be effected through the Spirit's presence in their midst: "Then the nations will know that I the Lord sanctify Israel, when my sanctuary is in the midst of them for evermore" (37:28). Likewise, Pentecostal reality effected the sanctification of God's people when they become the sanctuary of the Holy Spirit (Acts 15:8-9; II Thess. 2:13; I Peter 1:2; Heb. 10:29).

5. To dwell in the land permanently when the kingdom had been restored (37:25) prefigures, especially, the Johannine concept of the exalted and reigning Christ dwelling in the believer. Cullman has shown in this regard that John's Gospel is in a sense "the real Gospel of the Church."[2] Its presentation of the life of Jesus already presupposes the kingdom of the exalted Christ. It stresses even more so than the Synoptics[3] the idea of salvation history in which the reign of the exalted Christ occurs in the hearts of believers through the indwelling Spirit.[4]

The promise of the earthly Jesus that he and his Father would come to make their dwelling in the heart of his disciples through the Pentecostal Spirit (John 14:15-20) is prefigured in the prophetic vision of God dwelling with his people in the land (37:27). The twofold hope of the exilic prophets that "they shall dwell in the land" (37:25) and that "my dwelling place shall be with them" (37:27) anticipates the reality of Pentecost, when the Church as the earthly setting for the coming Kingdom of God became the "dwelling place" (temple) of the Holy Spirit. According to the prophetic vision, the indwelling Spirit of the New Covenant would guarantee their unfailing devotion and perfect worship of Yahweh (37:14,23,27,28). In this respect the following concepts are closely related: the indwelling Spirit; dwelling in the land; perfect worship of Yahweh; God's dwelling place being with them; the sanctification of Israel; the land as the sanctuary of Yahweh. Dwelling in the land, with all its implications, prefigures the idea of dwelling in Christ.

Of special significance in this regard are those passages in John 14, 15, 16 where dwelling (abiding) in Christ equals unbroken fellowship with God. Dwelling in Christ suggests the idea of having a spiritual home in Christ as a permanent residence, comparable to Ezekiel's hope of his people being brought "home into the land of Israel" (Ezek. 37:12), which was to be their permanent and established settlement (37:22,25).

In defining the meaning of Christian perfection, John Wesley shows that this idea of dwelling in Canaan Land corresponds to the idea of abiding in Christ. He writes:

> God is mindful of the desire of them that fear Him, and gives them a single eye and a pure heart; He stamps upon them His own image and superscription; He createth them anew in Christ Jesus; He cometh unto them with His Son and blessed Spirit; and, fixing His abode in their souls, bringeth them into the "rest which remaineth for the people of God."[5]

Paul speaks the language of Canaan Land where he tells the Colossians to "let . . . Christ dwell in you richly" (3:16).

1.  For Christ to dwell within the believer means that he will render to God proper worship (vs. 16), and corresponds to the theme of temple worship in Canaan Land.

2.  A coordinate idea to Christ dwelling within the believer is letting "the peace of God rule in your hearts" (vs. 15). This idea of the peace of God recalls the Canaan Land idea of the peace of the land (Lev. 26:6) in which there will no longer be any division and in which the people will dwell with safety and rest (Lev. 26:5; Deut. 12:10).

3.  For Christ to dwell within the believer also recalls the kingdom idea of Canaan Land. Paul indicated that the believer is one who has been raised with Christ (Exodus-Resurrection theme) and who seeks to be submissive to the reigning Christ who is "seated at the right hand of God" (Pentecost theme, 3:1). This submissiveness is seen in the believer's whole-hearted devotion to Christ (3:2) and his being obedient in all things (3:17). This kingdom-idea is also recalled in Paul's affirmation that the rule of the exalted Christ is universal and sovereign (3:11).

The First Letter of John especially draws upon this idea of God dwelling in the believer's heart through the indwelling Spirit of Christ.

1.  Even as perfect love ( = exclusive worship of Yahweh, Ezek. 37:23) was the concomitant of dwelling in the land, even so perfect love is the test of dwelling in Christ: "If we love one another, God dwells in us and his love is perfected

in us. By this we know that we dwell in him and he in us, because he has given us of his own Spirit" (I John 4:12-13). "Whoever keeps his word, in him truly love for God is perfected. By this we may be sure that we are in him: he who says he dwells in him ought to walk in the same way in which he walked" (I John 2:5-6).

2. Even as the restoration of Israel to the land of Canaan was to be a permanent establishment for God's people and continuous victory over their enemies; so Christ dwelling in believers means power and strength to overcome the enemies of God (I John 2:14). Wesley interprets the Johannine concept of "fathers" in contrast to "babes" to mean that they *"are strong* in the Lord" and are " 'perfect men,' being grown up to 'the measure of the stature of the fulness of Christ.' "[6]

3. Even as the indwelling Spirit enabled Israel to live holy (Ezek. 37:14, 28), so the believer is enabled to live obediently through Christ dwelling within him by the Holy Spirit: "All who keep his commandments dwell in him, and he in them. And by this we know that he dwells in us, by the Spirit which he has given us" (I John 3:24).

It will not be possible to explore in depth the entire language of Canaan Land as it relates to the New Covenant. Primary attention will be given to the concepts of inheritance and blessing as they prefigure Pentecostal reality. An exposition of these concepts will also focus upon the two stages of the Christian life.

*Canaan Land and Pentecostal reality are described as an inheritance.* Closely related to this concept of inheritance are *lot, part, portion,* and *place.* These words suggest the idea that "Israel did not conquer the land by its own achievements or indeed plan its conquest, but that God's free disposition gave Israel the land as its share, and that it has thus been conquered and possessed by Israel as a legitimate portion."[7] Figuratively, the idea behind these words is the Old Testament "awareness of a God who exercises concrete control of history, leading the people into the land of Canaan."[8] The language of inheritance and its cognates — lot, part, portion, and place – are appropriated in the New Covenant to designate admission into the kingdom of Christ.  These words suggest a gift of God, not something achieved through human effort.[9]  An analysis of the use of these words will indicate the relation between the Promised Land motif and Pentecostal reality.

After Joshua had led the Israelites through the Jordan River into the Promised Land, each tribe was assigned his own particular *lot* (LXX, κλῆρος) which constituted his *inheritance* (LXX, κληρονομία, Num. 26:55; 33:54). They were to "inherit the land by lot" (Josh. 13:6).  The word *lot* was first used as the method for dividing the land among the twelve tribes (Numbers 26:55; Joshua 14:2).  It denoted an *inheritance* of property (Josh. 17:14; Psalm 16:5-6), and was also used interchangeably with "portion" (Josh. 17:14)[10]

Casting lots (ἔδωκαν κλήρους, cf. Acts 1:26) was the method for apportioning the land of Canaan to each of the twelve tribes (Josh. 18:8-10). Metaphorically, lot, place, part, portion, came to mean inheritance – a man's lot (κλῆρος) was his inheritance (κληρονομία).

It can be seen that in Acts 1:26, casting lots for a successor to Judas was not intended to be a magical practice, since this practice extends back to the method which Joshua had used to divide up the Promised Land among the twelve tribes. In this respect the idea of casting lots was not to make room for chance, but to eliminate human decision in favor of the divine decision.  In apportioning the Promised Land among the 12 tribes, "Joshua cast lots for them in Shiloh *before the Lord*; and there Joshua apportioned the land to the people of Israel, to each his portion" (Josh. 18:10).  There is here no practice of witchcraft – which was forbidden – for it was the Lord who does the deciding, not chance or magic.[11] Likewise, the practice of the apostles in casting lots for a successor to Judas, who had originally obtained a lot (κλῆρος, Acts 1:17) among the twelve followers of Jesus, was only repeating the same method that Joshua had used to divide up the Promised Land among the twelve tribes. The apostles in casting lots were not themselves deciding, but they – like

Joshua – were casting lots before the Lord (Acts 1:24) who alone chose Matthias, even as he had chosen the previous eleven apostles. The significance of casting lots was that this practice typified the apportioning of Canaan Land among the twelve tribes of ancient Israel. Now that Pentecost was about to usher in the New Kingdom, it only seemed appropriate that lots should be cast to decide who would constitute the twelve apostles as the New Israel (cf. Rev. 21:14).

Another instance of "lot" (κλῆρος) in the book of Acts which recalls the apportioning of the tribes in the land of Canaan occurs in association with the word "part" (μερίς) – "You have neither *part* nor *lot* in this matter" (Acts 8:21). Arndt and Gingrich specifically point out the parallel between Acts 8:21 and Deuteronomy 12:12 (LXX, οὐκ ἔστιν αὐτῷ μερίς᾿ οὐδὲ κλῆρος μεθ᾿ ὑμῶν),[12] and Cremer has shown that "part" (μερίς) and "lot" (κλῆρος) are used together as a technical designation of Israel's possession of Canaan Land (Deut. 10:9; 12:12; 14:27,29; 18:1; Isa. 57:6).[13] It is highly significant that these words are used in this context, since undoubtedly Peter was presupposing that the kingdom established in Canaan Land prefigured the kingdom of Christ which was established on earth through the gift of the Holy Spirit. An analysis of Acts 8:4-25 will indicate this.

Simon Magus had attempted to obtain the gift of God, i.e., the Pentecostal gift of the Spirit, with money (8:18-19). Peter informed him that he was not prepared to receive this gift, for repentance (Resurrection theme) is the prerequisite for receiving this gift (Pentecost theme, vss. 22-23). It is also significant that as a result of Philip's preaching the Samaritans had been converted through "receiving the Word of God" and being baptized (Resurrection theme). Three days later Peter came to Samaria so that they might receive the Spirit (Pentecost theme). With the exception of Simon Magus, the Samaritans were prepared to receive the Pentecostal Spirit, since they had already experienced their exodus from sin's captivity by believing and receiving the word of Christ (8:12,14). On the other hand, Simon Magus did not have a proper relationship to Christ which was the prerequisite for receiving the Pentecostal Spirit: "You have neither *part* nor *lot* in this matter, for your heart is not right with God. Repent therefore of this wickedness of yours, and pray to the Lord that, if possible, the intent of your heart may be forgiven you" (Acts 8:21-22). Peter's identification of Canaan Land with the Pentecostal event is suggested by his appropriation of the technical phrase, "part and lot." This technical designation of Canaan Land as Israel's inheritance is used by Peter to denote the believer's experience of the indwelling Spirit.

That Peter is assuming that life in Canaan Land prefigures life in the Spirit is also suggested by his use of the phrase "gall of bitterness" (cf. Heb. 12:15), which recalls Deut. 29:18 (LXX reads ρίζα ἄνω φύουσα ἐν χολῇ καὶ πικρίᾳ)[14] In Deut. 29:19, Moses specifically warns against anyone saying after his arrival in the Promised Land: "I shall be safe, though I walk in the stubbornness of my heart." If one thinks he can enjoy the blessing of the covenant while harboring anything contrary to God's love in his heart (Deut. 29:19) then "the anger of the Lord and his jealousy would smoke against that man, and the curses written in this book would settle upon him, and the Lord would blot out his name from under heaven. And the Lord would single him out from all the tribes of Israel for calamity, in accordance with all the curses of the covenant written in this book of the law" (Deut. 29:-20-21). That Peter recalls this specific passage is further supported by the "curses" and "calamity" which Peter pronounced upon Simon Magus (Acts 8:23-24).

Peter's further description of Simon Magus in this same verse as still being in the "bond of iniquity" recalls Isa. 58:6, where the Exodus theme of deliverance from oppression is alluded to.[15]

Peter is saying to Simon Magus that since he has not experienced an exodus from spiritual captivity, he is not prepared to receive the inheritance. After all, the inheritance is promised only to those who have made their exodus from captivity. That is, there can be no Conquest until first there has been an Exodus. This means there can be no Pentecost for Simon Magus until he has experienced Jesus' resurrected life which is signified in Christian baptism. He has "neither part nor lot in this matter" of entering into the promised rest, because he is still living in the captivity of wickedness and unrepentance.

That Simon Magus was still in "the gall of bitterness" and "the bond of iniquity" even though he had been baptized does not mean that the other Samaritans were also unconverted until they had received the Pentecostal Spirit. Such an interpretation has been suggested.[16] However, it should be seen that Simon Magus' baptism was insincere, since he still lived in "the gall of bitterness." His insincerity was like the individual Israelite whom "the Lord would single . . . out from all the tribes of Israel for calamity" (Deut. 29:21), because he had only pretended to be sincere while enjoying the blessing of the covenant. That an individual Israelite should, from outward appearances, participate in the blessing when he in reality is in "the gall of bitterness" (Deut. 29:18) does not negate the authenticity of the experience of the rest of the people. Likewise, Peter's remarks to Simon Magus, which presuppose this passage in Deut. 29:18, are not intended to negate the experience of faith which the other Samaritans had professed in baptism.

Another instance of "part" and "lot" being used together is in Col. 1:12, where Paul says that God qualifies believers to possess the "part and lot" ($\epsilon\grave{\iota}\varsigma$ $\tau\grave{\eta}\nu$ $\mu\epsilon\rho\acute{\iota}\delta\alpha$ $\tauο\grave{\upsilon}$ $\kappa\lambda\acute{\eta}\rho\upsilonυ$) of the saints of light.[17] The language in this verse, along with its context, is the kingdom-idea of Canaan Land. Paul is describing the Spirit-bestowed reality of the New Covenant. The next verse (Col. 1:13) in particular illustrates this: "He has delivered us from the dominion of darkness (Exodus-Resurrection theme) and transferred us to the kingdom of his beloved Son (Canaan Land-Pentecost theme)."[18]

Another instance of Canaan Land language being used in reference to Pentecostal reality is in Acts 20:32; "The word of his grace, which is able to build you up and to give you an inheritance among all them which are sanctified" (cf. Eph. 1:18).

1.   "To build you up" recalls the Canaan Land concept of settlement.

2.   "To give you" recalls the idea of the Promised Land as

a gift rather than a human achievement.

3. The decisive thing about Canaan Land was its sanctity and its sanctifying influence on the people (Ezek. 37:28). Pentecostal reality denotes the sanctity (οἱ ἅγιοι) of God's people, affected through the Word of his sanctifying grace (cf. John 17:17; Heb. 10:29).

4. The concept of inheritance recalls the idea of the Holy Land as a gift to Israel. The exalted Christ, whose sanctifying presence rules within believers through the sending of his Spirit (Pentecost), is the inheritance of the new Israel.

In Acts 26:16-18, Paul also suggests a parallel between the Exodus-Conquest theme and the Resurrection-Pentecost theme. In his testimony before Agrippa he recalls Christ's commission to him: "I have appeared to you for this purpose, to appoint you to serve and bear witness to the things in which you have seen me and those in which I will appear to you, delivering you from the people and from the Gentiles — to whom I send you to open their eyes, that they may turn from darkness to light and from the power of Satan to God, that they may receive forgiveness of sins [Exodus-Resurrection theme] and a place [κλῆρος, Canaan Land language] among those who are sanctified [Pentecost theme] by faith in me."

The following comparisons between Moses and Paul in this passage will show the relationship between the New Covenant and the Old Covenant.

1. Like Moses, Paul had met God personally and audibly (Moses at the burning bush, and Paul on the Damascus Road).

2. Even as God said to Moses: "I will send you to Pharaoh" (Ex. 3:10); so Paul was sent by Christ to the Gentiles to be a witness of God's saving power.

3. As Moses had been delivered from Pharaoh; so Paul had been delivered "from the people and from the Gentiles."

4. As Moses had delivered his people from captivity through the Exodus event; so Paul was called of Christ to lead the people out of the bondage of sin through participation in Jesus' resurrected life ( = forgiveness of sins).

5. As Moses was called to lead his people to occupy their

place in Canaan Land; so Paul was appointed to lead God's people to their place *in Christ* (vs. 18, "in me"). To occupy *this place* is to be sanctified (Pentecost theme of the Holy Spirit whose ministry is to sanctify, II Thess. 2:13).

6.  As God told Moses that the possession of Canaan Land was a gift (Deut. 4:1); so Christ told Paul that the sanctification of the believer's heart, as the dwelling place of God, is by a gift of faith.

Paul specifically linked the concept of inheritance with the kingdom of God (Eph. 5:5). In this respect, it should be noted that the concept of inheritance as the kingdom of God has a present and an eschatological meaning. On the one hand, the believer's inheritance is already realized through being "sealed with the promised Holy Spirit." Yet this inheritance, though already obtained through the Spirit, is still in the future "until we acquire possession of it" (Eph. 1:14).

In Col. 1:12-13, Paul speaks of the believer already sharing in the inheritance and having already been translated into the *kingdom of God* ( = inheritance, cf. Eph. 5:5). Yet he exhorts believers to be faithful since "you will receive [future tense] the inheritance as your reward" (Col. 3:24). Hence, the inheritance-kingdom is already arrived; it it is also to come.

Peter speaks of being "born anew to a living hope through the resurrection of Jesus Christ from the dead [Easter theme], and to an inheritance [Pentecost theme] which is imperishable, undefiled, and unfading [unlike the Davidic kingdom in Canaan Land, which was destroyed], kept in heaven for you" (I Peter 1:3). Here Peter implies a present and eschatological meaning of the inheritance-kingdom.

This tension between the "already" and "not-yet" aspects of the coming kingdom of God has received much attention in contemporary theological scholarship. Oscar Cullmann in particular has called attention to this twofold significance of the coming kingdom of God in his discussions with Bultmann-ian theology which rejects any concrete objective significance to the coming kingdom of God. Cullmann has used the imagery of "D-Day" and "V-Day" to illustrate that through Christ's resurrection the decisive battle has been won and

Christ's kingdom has "already" come. Yet "V-Day" will be the final battle when Christ's kingdom shall be fully triumphant in the eschaton.[19] The Church is not coextensive with the kingdom of God, but it will be in the eschaton.

What has often not received sufficient attention is that the *present* aspect of the coming kingdom of God has a corporate and personal significance. This can be seen in Ephesians and Colossians, where Paul specifically discusses the nature of the Church. On the one hand, he speaks of being "in Christ" which is a technical phrase to designate the meaning of being a member of the Church as the body of Christ. It is characteristic of Paul to designate the Church prepositionally as being "in Christ," "in whom," "in him," etc. (cf. Eph. 1:2-10).[20]

While the kingdom of Christ is a present reality for all believers *in Christ* ( = the Church), the kingdom must also be firmly established within the believer through his own personal experience of the fulness of the Pentecostal Spirit. Paul exhorts believers to be "filled with the Spirit," so that they can worship — i.e., perfectly love and serve — "the Lord with all your heart" (Eph. 5:18-19).

The kingdom thus has both an objective signification — what is imputed to the believer — and a subjective significance — what is imparted inwardly to the believer. This means that all believers are members of the kingdom in a formal and corporate sense. Yet when the believer's heart is infused with perfect love, then it can be said that Christ truly *reigns* within the believer.

The subjective appropriation of the kingdom being established within the believer who is already corporately *in Christ* (Eph. 1:1) is set forth in Ephesians 3:14-19:

> I bow my knees before the Father, from whom every family in heaven and on earth is named [the kingdom of God is inclusive of all reality], that according to the riches of his glory he may grant you to be strengthened with might [$\delta\acute{v}\nu\alpha\mu\iota\varsigma$] through his Spirit [cf. Acts 1:8] in the inner man, and that Christ [the Messianic title of Christ above all denotes kingship] may dwell [$\kappa\alpha\tau o\iota\kappa\tilde{\eta}\sigma\alpha\iota$

= κατά / οἰκέω, which suggests domination and habitation] in your hearts through faith; that you, being rooted and grounded in love, may have power [ἐξισ-χύσητε = to be fully able] to comprehend [καταλαμ-βάνω suggests the idea of taking possession of an inheritance and making it one's own] with all the saints what is the breadth and length and height and depth, and to know the love of Christ which surpasses knowledge, that you may be filled with all the fulness of God [ = Pentecostal fulness of the Spirit].

Wesley particularly understood this Pauline prayer to designate the meaning of "entire sanctification." He cites it as one of the strongest Scriptural references for supporting the doctrine of Christian perfection, since it is both a prayer and a command.[21]

Likewise, with the Colossians who are *in Christ* (1:2), Paul exhorts them to make actual the righteousness which is already theirs: "Put on love, which is the bond of perfection [σύνδεσμος τῆς τελειότητος]. And let the peace of Christ *rule* [ = perfect love, which denotes total surrender to the reign of Christ] in your hearts, to which indeed you were called in the one body [i.e., now that you are formally in the kingdom of God, it is incumbent to make actual the righteousness which is yours by virtue of being in the body of Christ, since that is what you have been called to]. And be thankful. Let the word of Christ dwell [ἐνοικείτω = ἐν/οἰκέω, which literally means *indwell* in the strong sense of being a permanent place of domination and residence] in you richly" (Col. 3:14-16).

This distinction between *being in Christ* and *Christ dwelling within* the believer corresponds to the distinction between the indicative (justification) and the imperative (sanctification) of the Christian life. The kingdom has both a formal and personal signification. In participating in Jesus' resurrected life, one is delivered from the captivity of evil; and through his standing in Christ (imputed righteousness) he is incorporated into the kingdom of God (justification). Yet through his subsequent personal appropriation of the perfect love of Christ (imparted righteousness), the believer's heart becomes fully submissive to the *reign* of Christ (sanctification).

To be sure, in justification one becomes a new person through the regenerating and sanctifying power of the Spirit. Yet the focus of conversion is upon the fact of being justified in Christ. This justification denotes, in a formal sense, the believer's complete restoration to God. John Calvin is surely right to stress that while the believer really experiences the beginning of a transformed life in the new birth, the important thing is that *in Christ* the believer is *now* fit for heaven.[22] Justification by faith denotes both the forgiveness of sins and, in a formal sense, release from the very presence of sin. However, in sanctification (i.e., the kingdom of God being established within the believer) this righteousness is made actual.

Calvin believed imparted righteousness was only an incomplete process this side of eternity.[23] Wesley taught that it was both a realizable experience, and yet an ever-increasing experience within the process of time. In this respect, Wesley and his counterpart, John Fletcher, defined the experience of imparted righteousness as the kingdom of Christ being established with the believer.

One of Wesley's favorite expressions for the kingdom of God is Rom. 14:17: "The kingdom of God is not meat and drink; but righteousness, and peace, and joy in the Holy Ghost."[24] Wesley defined the kingdom of God as denoting primarily the fruit of the Spirit (sanctification). Wesley writes: "And what is 'righteousness,' but the life of God in the soul; the mind which was in Christ Jesus; the image of God stamped upon the heart, now renewed after the likeness of Him that created it? What is it but the love of God, because He first loved us, and the love of all mankind for His sake?"[25] Each of these definitions of righteousness corresponds to Wesley's usual descriptive phrases of Christian perfection.[26] In his sermon, "The Way to the Kingdom," Wesley further defines the righteousness of the kingdom to mean perfect love. He shows that loving God with all the heart is "the first and great branch of Christian righteousness."[27] This means that "having given Him thy heart, thy inmost soul, to reign there without a rival, thou mayest well cry out, in the fullness of thy heart, 'I will love Thee, O Lord, my strength."[28]

Yet Wesley makes it clear that the kingdom is also inclusive of those believers who are not entirely sanctified: "This inward kingdom implies . . . the righteousness of Christ *imputed* [italics mine] to us."[29]  In this respect, John Deschner has rightly pointed out that Wesley understood the concept of the kingdom to denote both the sanctification of the believer and his incorporation into the body of Christ. Deschner writes: "The kingdom of grace is an inward, spiritual kingdom, with two primary references: the sanctification of the individual and the gathering of the church."[30]  The gathering of the church denotes "the whole body of true believers, whether on earth or in paradise."[31]  Deschner further shows that for Wesley the kingdom of God has already arrived through the outpouring of the Spirit on the day of Pentecost.[32]  It can be seen that for Wesley the kingdom of God has both corporate and personal implications. On the one hand, it denotes sanctification of the believer; on the other hand, it denotes the body of Christ.

John Fletcher also speaks of the personal implication of the kingdom of God. He writes: "Perfection is nothing but the unshaken Kingdom of God, peace, righteousness, and joy in the Holy Ghost, or by the baptism of the Holy Ghost."[33]  He further says: "Christian perfection is nothing but the full kingdom in the Holy Ghost."[34]

A weakness of Fletcher's position is that he fails to stress the corporate aspect of the Church. It should be emphasized that the kingdom of God, which is the believer's *inheritance*, is first of all by virtue of his *faith in Christ* ( = incorporation into the Church); and yet this kingdom which is righteousness, peace, and joy (the fruit of the Spirit) must become his through an inward appropriation (sanctification). The concept of *inheritance* usually denotes in a specific way the idea of inherent righteousness. The believer's inheritance is already given to him through his being "sealed with the promised Holy Spirit" (Eph. 1:13-14), though its final appropriation will come in the eschaton.

*The "Blessing" of the Abrahamic Covenant Prefigures the
"Blessing" of the New Covenant.* We have already examined
in some detail the relationship of the Pentecostal event to the
idea of promise. Closely related to this idea of promise is
*blessing* (Deut. 1:11; Heb. 6:13-15). Originally the word
*blessing* was linked to the possession of the Promised Land
(Deut. 11:26,29; Genesis 12:2-3). The word blessing is used
on many different occasions in Scripture, which usually implies something that God graciously gives to his people; or
else it implies worship (adoration) which God's people offer to
him.[35] Yet there is an identity between the concepts of promise and blessing as they relate to the inheritance of the
Promised Land (Deut. 1:11).

The writer to the Hebrews, in particular, interprets the
promised blessing to Abraham as being fulfilled in the exalted Christ (Heb. 6:13-20), who has entered into the sanctuary of heaven (Heb. 6:20; 9:24). The significance of His
exaltation to God's throne is that "he is the mediator of a
new covenant" (9:15) who "has perfected for all time those
who are sanctified" (10:14); in contrast to the Old Covenant,
"which cannot perfect the conscience of the worshiper"
(9:9). The Holy Spirit is the inner witness to the sanctifying
work of the exalted Christ (Heb. 10:14-15). In this respect,
the exalted Christ is functionally identical to the Pentecostal
Spirit ("the Son of God" = "the Spirit of Grace," 10:29).
The promised blessing to Abraham that his posterity would
inherit Canaan Land had its true fulfillment through a participation in the person of the exalted Christ "who through the
eternal Spirit offered himself without blemish to God," so
that He might "purify your conscience from dead works to
serve the living God" (Heb. 9:14). The Old Covenant had
failed to bring about the requirement of a perfect heart and
obedience for dwelling in Canaan Land. The New Covenant is
written on the heart by the indwelling Spirit of the exalted
Christ; so that one can truly worship the living God (Heb.
10:1-18,29).

Paul also shows that the *blessing* promised to Abraham had
its ultimate fulfillment not in the Promised Land, but in the

exalted Christ ( = the Holy Spirit). This blessing was accomplished, not through the Exodus and Conquest, but through Jesus' resurrection from the dead and the Pentecostal gift of his Spirit: "Christ redeemed us from the curse of the law, having become a curse for us — for it is written, 'Cursed be every one who hangs on a tree' [Easter theme]* — that in Christ Jesus the blessing of Abraham might come upon the Gentiles, that we might receive the promise of the Spirit through faith (Pentecost theme)" (Gal. 3:13-14).

This passage is especially significant because it shows that Easter and Pentecost are the two decisive historical events for the maintenance of the Christian life. This means that the promised blessing to Abraham had its true fulfillment, not through the Exodus and Conquest, but through Jesus Resurrection from the dead and through the Pentecostal outpouring of the Spirit of the exalted Christ.

Paul's emphasis is upon justification and sanctification, grounded in Jesus' Resurrection from the dead, and the Pentecostal bestowal of the Spirit. "Christ has redeemed us from the curse of the law . . . that [$\ddot{\iota}\nu\alpha$ = purpose clause] in *Christ Jesus* the *blessing* of Abraham might come upon the Gentiles" (Gal. 3:13-14). Ernest De Witt Burton has shown that the curse of the law meant that judgment was pronounced "on those who do not perfectly obey its statutes."[36] Perfect obedience had been the condition for the "blessing of Abraham" being initially fulfilled in the possession of the Promised Land. Disobedience was the occasion of Israel's exile and captivity. Now the "curse of the law" has been abrogated through the believer's justification in Christ. Through His redemption we are justified (Gal. 3:6,11,13-14).[37]

There is an additional purpose clause here which is a co-ordinate of the previous purpose clause: "that we might receive the promise of the Spirit through faith" (vs. 14). Not

---

*John Calvin points out that "whenever mention is made of his death alone we are to understand at the same time what belongs to his resurrection" (*Institutes of the Christian Religion*, ed. John T. Neil, trans. F. L. Battles [Philadelphia: Westminster Press, 1960], I, 521.

only is the blessing of Abraham realized through our redemption in Christ Jesus, but the blessing of Abraham also is defined in reference to the gift of the Holy Spirit. Burton writes:

> It is possible that the second final clause is to be taken as . . . epexegetic of the first [final clause] that the Holy Spirit is a definition of the blessing of Abraham. In that case the apostle refers to the promise to Abraham and has learned to interpret this as having reference to the gift of the Spirit. This possibility is in a measure favoured by the use of ἐπαγγελία in vv. 16, 17.[38]

Here the blessing of Abraham refers to the believer's justification by faith in Christ, but also, "this blessing is identified with the Spirit's coming *through faith* (as in vss. 1-5)."[39] Ridderbos shows in this verse that "the gift of the Spirit is now designated as the content of the promise to Abraham. It is the guarantee or pledge of the perfected redemption which Abraham was promised."[40]

That the gift of the Spirit denotes something distinct from the believer's justification is suggested by Paul's equation of the gift of the Spirit with the fruit of the Spirit (Gal. 5:22). To "walk by the Spirit" (sanctification) is just the opposite of yielding to the "desires of the flesh" (5:16). This means that those believers who are Spirit-endowed (πνευματικοι) evidence the fruit of the Spirit (6:1). In this respect, the Spirit-endowed believer is one of whom it can be said that "Christ is formed in you" (4:19).[41]

This distinction between the believer's redemption in Christ (justification) and reception of the *Holy* Spirit (sanctification) is further expressed in Gal. 4:4-7: "But when the time had fully come, God sent forth his Son, born of woman, born under the law, to redeem those who were under the law, so that we might receive adoption as sons. And because you are sons, God has sent the Spirit of his Son into our hearts, crying, 'Abba! Father!' So through God you are no longer a slave but a son, and if a son then an heir."

Paul here distinguishes between "sending his Son" and "sending the Spirit." The sending of the Son (ἐξαπέστειλεν, historical aorist), once and for all time, effected redemption; sending the Spirit (ἐξαπέστειλεν, historical aorist), once and for all times effected the confirmation of our being adopted sons of God, whereby we are the true *heirs* (Canaan Land language) of Abraham's blessing (Gal. 4:7).

Not only is there a historical distinction between the sending of the Son and the sending of the Spirit, but it can also be implied that there is in the life of the believer an experiential distinction between receiving the Son and receiving the Pentecostal Spirit. Jesus' disciples were genuinely converted (Luke 10:20) before their subsequent experience with the Pentecostal Spirit. To be sure, the Spirit was with them before Pentecost, but he did not dwell *in* them (John 14:17). Hence in their case their experience of the Son and the Spirit were historically distinct. It is also significant that Jesus said that only those who were already believers could receive the Spirit (John 14:17). Yet there is a sense in which one could be "born of the Spirit" even before Pentecost (John 3:5), though after Pentecost one could receive the gift of the indwelling Spirit in his fulness (John 14:15-20; cf. Acts 2:4).

If one accepts at face value the accounts in Acts 8:14-17 and Acts 19:1-7, the Samaritans and the Ephesians were believers prior to their reception of the Spirit. The Samaritans were baptized and received the word of God three days before their reception of the Pentecostal Spirit (Acts 8:14-17), and the Ephesians already believed in Jesus through the witness of John's disciples. The faith of the Ephesians was acknowledged through their being called "disciples" (Acts 19:1). After their being baptized in the name of Christ, Paul laid hands on them in order that they might receive the Pentecostal Spirit. It can be thought that the two kinds of physical symbols – baptism and the laying on of hands – signified the two different aspects of the Christian life. Baptism represents justifying faith in Christ; laying on of hands represents the sanctifying anointing of the *Holy*Spirit. These same two symbols were also used respectively to distinguish the Samaritans reception of the Word of Christ and three days later their reception of the Spirit (Acts 8:12,17).

There is no hesitation at all in Paul's question to the Ephesians concerning their reception of the Spirit which might suggest that he thinks they were not really believers. Like Apollos (Acts 18:25), they were believers in Jesus, even though their understanding of Christ had been mediated through the followers of John the Baptist. If there had been any doubt about their conversion to Christ, Luke would not have unequivocally called them disciples. F. F. Bruce specifically points this out by showing that when Luke calls someone a disciple he always means a Christian disciple.[42] Nor would Paul have acknowledged them to be believers if, in fact, they were not.

It should also be noted that Paul's question can be translated, "Have you received the Holy Spirit since you believed?" (KJV), or "Did you receive the Holy Spirit when you believed?" (RSV). The context of the question favors the former translation. Quite literally, Εἰ Πνεῦμα Ἅγιον ἐλάβετε πιστεύσαντες can be translated: "Have you received the Holy Spirit, having believed?" Since εἰ is only an interrogative particle, with the leading verb and the participle in the aorist tense, the sentence does not specify the time sequence of the action of the verbs.[43] If Paul had intended to suggest the equation, believing = receiving the Spirit, then his question would seem to have been meaningless. The context seems to require the time sequence: "Have you received the Holy Spirit *since* you believed?" However, this is an instance where theological orientation may dictate what the translation will be. It may well be that the KJV translates the verse, "Have you received the Holy Ghost since ye believed?" since the Church of England had already used this verse as a text for confirmation, which was the ordinance for receiving the Pentecostal Spirit subsequent to baptism. Nonetheless, the context seems to justify this particular translation.

It is puzzling that Paul re-baptized these believers, since they had already some knowledge of Jesus and were disciples of John the Baptist whose baptism pointed to Jesus. F. F.

Bruce has suggested that possibly John's baptism was no longer thought to be valid since the day of Pentecost and perhaps they came to be believers in Christ through some of John's disciples after Pentecost; hence the re-baptism.[44] Even if Paul did not really consider them true believers until he baptized them — which is not likely — it cannot be thought that baptism = receiving the Spirit. For the Spirit was not given until the "laying on of hands;" which denotes some-thing in addition to Christian baptism. Otherwise, why would there be two physical symbols to denote one and the same experience (cf. Heb. 6:1-2). It is not at all clear just what "laying on of hands" denoted.[45] It seems questionable for Roman Catholic theology to see this as a *sacrament* of confirmation; but it does seem highly probable that this physical symbol denoted a definitive experience of the Pente-costal Spirit subsequent to their becoming believers.

To argue that the Ephesian believers were not truly be-lievers because they had not received the Holy Spirit and were unconverted and unregenerate is not warranted. To be sure, the Ephesian believers were incomplete Christians because they had not received the Pentecostal Spirit; but so is every baptized believer an incomplete Christian until he receives the Spirit. That is why Catholic theology speaks of two initiary events in the process of becoming truly Christian; and that is why Wesleyan theology speaks of two works of grace — justi-fication and sanctification — as necessary for the perfecting of the Christian life.

Though Roman Catholic theology interprets the Christian life too onesidedly in sacramentalist terms, its exegetical considerations for interpreting the two stages of the Christian life as receiving the Son and receiving the Pentecostal Spirit seem to be sound. Father Durrwell, a New Testament scholar, specifically points out the exegetical bases of the two stages directly in reference to Gal. 4:6: "The sending of the personal Spirit indeed presupposes that we have first been integrated into the Son — at least if the most natural rendering of Gal. iv.6 is also the right one: 'Because you are sons, God hath sent the Spirit of his Son into your hearts.'"[46]

Father Durrwell, in further pointing out the exegetical bases for distinguishing between the two stages of the Christian life, writes:

> According to the Acts, baptism incorporates us *into* the Church, the expression in the world of that Kingdom of God that was set up when Christ was glorified. (ii.41.) Administered in the name of Jesus (ii.38; viii.16; x. 48), it sets the seal of the Lord's possession upon those who believe; it confers remission of sins (ii.38), and the right to receive the Holy Ghost (ii.38), which are graces that belong to the risen Christ (v.31-2). But it seems as though only the *right* to receive the Spirit is given.[47]

In reference to the statement in Gal. 4:6 (ὅτι δέ ἐστε υἱοί, ἐξαπέστειλεν Θεὸς τὸ πνεῦμα τοῦ Υἱοῦ αὐτοῦ εἰς τὰς καρδίας ἡμῶν, "And because you are sons, God has sent the Spirit of his Son into our hearts.") Burton has shown that "the clause ὅτι . . . υἱοί is naturally interpreted as causal, giving the reason in the divine mind for the act ἐξαπέστειλεν . . . ἡμῶν. . . . Nor is there any sufficient reason for departing from this obvious interpretation."[48] He shows that sonship is "here spoken of being antecedent to and the ground of the bestowal of the Spirit."[49] This accords with Jesus' statement to his disciples that only those who are already believers can receive the Holy Spirit (John 14:17). Burton further interrets Gal. 4:6: "The direct affirmation of the sentence is that the sonship is the cause of the experience of the Spirit."[50] Likewise, Marvin Vincent interprets verse 6 to mean: "The Spirit would not be given if ye were not sons."[51] He points out that the reception of the Spirit "is not a *proof* of the fact of sonship that the apostle is giving, but a *consequence* of it."[52] Likewise, Bultmann has shown that faith is not the gift of the Spirit, but the gift of the Spirit is given to the one who already has faith.[53]

It might be argued that Paul is assuming only a logical difference, without any time sequence between conversion to

Christ and receiving the Spirit. But a more natural understanding would be that he is assuming a real temporal distinction, since the context speaks of the two historical events of
"the sending of the Son" and "the sending of the Spirit."
That is, just as the coming of the Son and the coming of the
Spirit were extended in time, so for the individual the two
salvific events of conversion to Christ and the reception of
the Spirit are extended in time.

This twofold differentiation might appear to contradict
what Paul says in Rom. 8:9: "But you are not in the flesh,
you are in the Spirit, if in fact the Spirit of God *dwells* in
you. Any one who does not *have* the Spirit of Christ does
not belong to him." However, for Paul to say that every
believer *has* ($\check{\epsilon}\chi\epsilon\iota$) the Spirit, is not identical to the statement
that the Spirit of God really *dwells* ($o\iota\kappa\epsilon\hat{\iota}$) in you. The idea of
"having" ($\check{\epsilon}\chi\epsilon\iota$) is not the same as "dwelling" ($o\iota\kappa\epsilon\hat{\iota}$). All
Christians have ($\check{\epsilon}\chi\epsilon\iota$) the Spirit in the same sense in which
Jesus spoke of the Spirit being with the disciples, but who as
yet did not dwell in them (John 14:17 — $\pi\alpha\rho'$ $\dot{\upsilon}\mu\hat{\iota}\nu$ $\mu\acute{\epsilon}\nu\epsilon\iota$
$\kappa\alpha\grave{\iota}$ $\dot{\epsilon}\nu$ $\dot{\upsilon}\mu\hat{\iota}\nu$ $\check{\epsilon}o\tau\alpha\iota$). As Bultmann has shown, Paul distinguished
between "babes in Christ" who were not Spirit-endowed and
those "perfect" ($\tau\acute{\epsilon}\lambda\epsilon\iota o\iota$) believers who were Spirit-endowed
(I Cor. 2:6; 3:1).[54] Here in Rom. 8:9, Paul also suggests a
difference between a Christian who in some degree has the
Spirit and the Christian in whom the Spirit really dwells.

As Sanday and Headlam, in *A Critical and Exegetical Commentary on the Epistle to the Romans*, point out, Paul means
in saying that all Christians have ($\check{\epsilon}\chi\epsilon\iota$) the Spirit nothing
more than "that all Christians 'have the Spirit' in greater or
lesser degree."[55] However, when Paul says, "But you are
not in the flesh, you are in the Spirit, if in fact the Spirit of
God dwells ($o\iota\kappa\epsilon\hat{\iota}$) in you," he means that the believer's heart
has become a dwelling-place ($o\iota\kappa\acute{\iota}\alpha$) of the Pentecostal Spirit,
even as he assumes that the Spirit-endowed believers at
Corinth were those who were no longer "men of the flesh, as
babes in Christ" (I Cor. 3:1). In this respect, it is one thing to
have ($\check{\epsilon}\chi\epsilon\iota$) the Spirit; it is another thing for the Spirit fully
to have us ($o\iota\kappa\epsilon\hat{\iota}$ $\dot{\epsilon}\nu$ $\dot{\upsilon}\mu\hat{\iota}\nu$, Rom. 8:9).

This distinction between the two stages of the Christian life has a parallel in other Pauline metaphors. For example, it is one thing to be *in Christ* ( = the Church, Eph. 1:1; Gal. 1:2); it is another thing for Christ to be formed in the believer (Gal. 4:19). It is one thing to live by the Spirit; it is another thing to walk by the Spirit (Gal. 5:25). It is one thing to have "peace with God" ( = justification, Rom. 6:1); it is another to "let the peace of Christ rule in your hearts" (sanctification, Col. 3:15).

In distinguishing the two stages of Christian life, John Fletcher understands Romans 8 as a description of the "glorious liberty,"* which God's children enjoy in their souls, under the perfection of the Christian dispensation.[56] He understood Romans 7:7-23, as descriptive of a struggling Jew groaning under the curse of the law.[57] In Romans 7:24-25, Paul describes the transition state between an awakened Jew and his participation in the fulness of the Christian life.[58] Fletcher interpreted Romans 8 as a description of the fulness of the Christian life.[59] Assuming the validity of this interpretation of Romans 8, it seems appropriate for Skevington Wood to refer to Romans 8, as "Paul's Pentecost" by which is meant a personal appropriation of the Spirit subsequent to justifying faith.[60]

Burton indirectly supports this idea of the believer's appropriation of the Spirit subsequent to his justification. He has pointed out that Paul's reference to the believer's participation in the Holy Spirit denotes "the full possession of the relationship of sons to God."[61] He shows that the language of Romans 8:14-15 is "open to interpretation as an argument from effect to cause, in which case there also adoption [like Galatians 4:6] precedes possession of the Spirit."[62]

Burton also shows that to be an "heir of God" ($κληρονόμος$ $διὰ Θεοῦ$, Gal. 4:7; Rom. 8:17) means, to be "recipients of the blessing promised to Abraham's seed" and that this bless-

---

*"Glorious liberty" was a term that Wesley and Fletcher used interchangeably with Christian perfection (Fletcher, *Checks*, I, 14.)

ing is "defined as justification, acceptance with God, possession of the Spirit."[63] According to Oriental custom, one was
automatically the heir to the Father's inheritance if he were a
son. Sonship preceded the actual receiving of the blessing of
the inheritance.[64] Likewise, the blessing of the Holy Spirit
as the believer's inheritance comes to those who are already
sons (Gal. 4:6-7).

Inasmuch as Paul differentiates in Gal. 4:4-7 between the
two ephochal events — Jesus' resurrection from the dead and
the Pentecostal gift of the Spirit — and then shows that these
two decisive events brought about the fulfillment of God's
promised *blessing* to Abraham; it is not without warrant that
Wesley spoke of the experience of perfect love as a "second
blessing."[65] Such terminology is also suggested by Paul's
speaking of the fulness of the blessing of Christ (Romans
15:29: "I know that when I come to you I shall come in
the fulness of the blessing of Christ." The blessing of Christ
is the spiritual reality prefigured in the blessing of Canaan
Land which was promised to Abraham. Paul indicates this in
Gal. 3:14, where he equates the "blessing of Abraham" with
being "in Christ Jesus" and having received "the promise of
the Spirit."

This identity of *blessing* and the *Spirit* is made in Eph.
1:3-4: "Blessed be the God and Father of our Lord Jesus
Christ, who has blessed us with every *spiritual blessing* in the
heavenly places in Christ, even as he chose us in him before
the foundation of the world, that we should be holy and
blameless before him." This concept of God having *blessed
us* recalls the Abrahamic blessing: "I will bless you" (Gen.
12:2ff.). Abraham's blessing was to be fulfilled in the land of
Canaan, in contrast to the Christian believer whose blessing is
fulfilled in the exalted Christ ( = $\dot{\epsilon}\nu\,\tau o\hat{\iota}\varsigma\,\dot{\epsilon}\pi o\upsilon\rho\alpha\nu\acute{\iota}o\iota\varsigma\,\dot{\epsilon}\nu\,\chi\rho\iota\sigma\tau\hat{\omega}$,
Eph. 1:3). Possession of the blessing of Canaan Land was
achieved through the crossing of the Jordan River, whereas,
possession of the blessing of the exalted Christ (which is
identical to possession of the Spirit) was achieved on the Day
of Pentecost. In this respect, "*spiritual* blessing" ($\epsilon\upsilon\lambda o\gamma\acute{\iota}\alpha$
$\pi\nu\epsilon\upsilon\mu\alpha\tau\iota\kappa\hat{\eta}$) is the blessing of the Spirit — blessing = the Spirit

= the exalted Christ (ἐν πάσῃ εὐλογίᾳ πνευματικῇ ἐν τοῖς ἐπουρανίοις ἐν χριστῷ).

Even as Abraham and his posterity had been called of God to serve him in a chosen place (Gen. 17:8) with a perfect heart (Gen. 17:1; Deut. 6:1-8), even so, God "chose us in him before the foundation of the world, that we should be holy and blameless before him" (Eph. 1:4). The intent of the "spiritual blessing" is that the believer be "holy" and "blameless."

It can thus be seen that the idea of "spiritual blessing" denotes particularly sanctifying grace. T. K. Abbott, in *A Critical and Exegetical Commentary on the Epistle to the Ephesians and to the Colossians*, shows that "spiritual blessing" in Eph. 1:3 does not mean "the blessing of the Spirit" in the sense that gifts of the Spirit are intended. The "spiritual blessing" refers to "the nature of the blessings, not their source." He further writes: "these blessings are not to be limited to the extraordinary gifts of the Spirit." Rather, it is "more generally what St. Paul enumerates as the fruit of the Spirit in Gal. v. 22, love, joy, peace, and all Christian virtues."[66]

Alford has defined "spiritual blessing" as the "blessing of the Spirit."[67] What he seems to imply is not the gifts of the Spirit, but the sanctifying graces (fruit) of the Spirit. This difference between the fruit of the Spirit (Gal. 5:22) and gifts of the Spirit (I Cor. 12) is of fundamental importance. The *gift* of the Spirit (Acts 2:38) and the *gifts* of the Spirit also should be clearly distinguished. Likewise the blessing of the Spirit ( = "spiritual blessing") does not denote the gifts of the Spirit. Rather, the fruit of the Spirit = the gift of the Spirit = the blessing of the Spirit. Each of these terms denotes the actual grace and inner reality of the Spirit, not manifestations and gifts of the Spirit. S. D. F. Salmond, in the *Expositor's Greek Testament*, puts it this way: "It is best, therefore, to take πνευματικῇ to define the blessings in question as *spiritual* in the sense that they are the blessings of grace. . . . It is true that these come from God through the Spirit. But the point in view is what they are, not how they reach us."[68]

The word "spiritual" is unique to the New Testament and always means "Holy Spirit." It never means spiritual in our modern sense of that which is the opposite of material.[69] Paul indicates that this "spiritual blessing" ( = sanctifying grace of the Holy Spirit) is to be *fully* appropriated. He speaks of "*every* spiritual blessing" (ἐν πάσῃ εὐλογία πνευματικῇ). Alford shows that by πάσῃ (all, or every) Paul means "all richness and fulness of blessing."[70] Paul means by "all spiritual blessing" that one possesses the fulness of the blessing of the grace of the Holy Spirit.

In the light of Paul's identification of the "blessing of Christ" with the reality of the Holy Spirit in Gal. 3:14 and Eph. 1:3-4, for him to say that he possesses "the fulness of the blessing of Christ" (Rom. 15:29) suggests that he has personally appropriated the full presence of the Holy Spirit in his life. Though all believers in a formal sense (imputed righteousness) are heirs to the promise, through their participation in Jesus' resurrected life (even as the Israelites who had made their Exodus from Egyptian captivity were heirs to the promise of Canaan Land), not all believers have appropriated their inheritance of the promised Holy Spirit in his sanctifying fulness.

This identity between the Pentecostal Spirit and the Abrahamic blessing is anticipated in the prophetic vision of a new covenant: "For I will pour my Spirit upon your descendants, and my *blessing* on your offspring" (Isa. 44:3). Durrwell has exegetically-theologically shown the sanctifying significance of this Pentecostal fulness:

> Israel had already known the Spirit. But the Prophets had foretold that in the last age the outpouring of the Spirit would exceed anything known before; that the Spirit would do greater things than ever, establishing a more sublime creation than the one he had produced when the world began. "In that day," he was to sanctify the messianic community and cleanse it of all defilement (Isa. iv. 4.)"[71]

For Durrwell this pentecostal fulness is to be received subsequently to Christian baptism.[72]

These exegetical-theological considerations concerning the differentiation between the Son and the Spirit are supposed in Roman Catholic theology, which teaches that the true Christian life has two initiatory events — the new birth and the reception of the Pentecostal Spirit. Ives Congar, a Roman Catholic scholar, in pointing out the two stages of the Christian life, speaks of "an unquestionable duality" of Easter and Pentecost, as they are personally experienced; but he also insists upon "the necessity of unity" of the two stages.[73] He further writes:

> We cannot deny a certain duality or push it out of sight. . . . There is a duality because there are two missions, that of Christ and that of the Holy Spirit; but we know these two missions are for one and the same work. To deny one or other of these two terms [of Easter and Pentecost] is not the answer; the answer is to hold fast to both in their unity and to make their harmony with one another real to ourselves, for that is the nature of God's work.[74]

Congar further shows that "Christ is one divine person, the Holy Spirit is another, a person in himself (cf. Jn. 14:16f.); but he is the Spirit *of Christ*."[75] He succinctly shows the distinct yet inseparable relation between the saving work of Christ and the sanctifying work of the Holy Spirit:

> Thus the Holy Spirit has a "mission," a "coming," of his own; just as the Father sent the Son into this world and the Son came in Jesus Christ, so the Father sends the Holy Spirit to dwell in those who follow Christ. But the work of the Holy Spirit's mission is not *his* work, something independent and self-contained; it is the work *of Christ*, who has already done the Father's work, given the Father's message. . . . The Spirit consecrates and sanctifies *Christ's* apostles; he gives them understanding of what *Christ* taught them.[76]

In contrast to this distinction between baptism and reception of the Spirit, Bultmann thinks that for the earliest

Christians it was generally. presupposed that at baptism the Holy Spirit is given.[77]  However, the references which he cites (Acts 2:38) can also be interpreted to mean that at baptism *only the right to receive the Holy Spirit* is granted, as Durrwell has shown.[78]  However, Bultmann interprets Acts (representing "Jewish Christianity") as identifying baptism and reception of the Spirit.*  He writes:  "The passages, Acts 8:14-17;  10:44-48, in which the receipt of the Spirit and baptism are not contemporaneous, are only an apparent exception.  In reality, the intent of both passages is to teach precisely the inseparability of baptism and the receipt of the Spirit."[79]  There can be no doubt that baptism (signifying the new birth) and the receipt of the Spirit are "inseparable," but such inseparability does not necessarily mean the two events are "contemporaneous."  In the case of the Samaritans (Acts 8:14-17), they were baptized and "received the word of God" three days before their receipt of the Spirit.  For Cornelius (Acts 10:44-48), he was already a God-fearer, worshipping in Jewish synagogues; and his godly life did not go unnoticed by the God of the Jews.  During Peter's message, he received the Pentecostal Spirit, and only afterwards did he receive baptism.  This could indicate that while the sacrament of baptism is necessary to fulfill our Lord's command, it is not necessarily identifiable with the experience of saving grace.  That he received the Holy Spirit immediately during Peter's sermon, even though there is no mention of his repentance prior to his reception of the Spirit, may be because he already had a saving relation with God.  After all, his devotion to God is stressed (Acts 10:2-3,22).  As one who already sustained a trusting relationship to God, his heart was prepared to receive the Pentecostal Spirit.

---

*Barth shows, in contrast to Bultmann's exegesis, that in Acts the baptism in the Spirit is not the same as Christian baptism; and that the outpouring of the Spirit is not necessarily identifiable with the new birth.  Rather, entrance into the Christian life through Christian baptism gives one the right to receive the Holy Spirit.  And this outpouring of the Spirit is, for Barth, to be repeated often as one grows in grace (see Chapter II).

That the new birth and the receipt of the Pentecostal Spirit are not necessarily "contemporaneous" is further attested by Bultmann's exegesis of Paul's thoughts:

> Paul (I Cor. 2:13-3:3) distinguishes between people in the Church who are Spirit-endowed (πνευματικοί) and those who are "unspiritual" (ψυχικοί; KJ: "natural") or "men of flesh" (σαρκικοί; KJ: "carnal") — contrary to the proposition that all the baptized have received the Spirit. He similarly distinguishes between the Spirit-endowed in the Church and those whom some trespass has overtaken and who therefore cannot be regarded as Spirit-endowed (Gal. 6:1). It means the same thing when he makes a distinction between "the mature" (τέλειοι, Phil. 3:15) and others; for according to I Cor. 2:6 (compared with 2:13ff.) "the mature" are identical with the "Spirit-endowed."[80]

Bultmann significantly shows that at least for Paul there is a difference between an "unspiritual" Christian and the Spirit-endowed Christian. Bultmann shows that the Spirit-endowed Christians (πνευματικοί) are identified with the perfect Christians (τέλειοι) ; whereas the "babe in Christ" is identified with the "unspiritual" (ψυχικοί) .

Bultmann thinks that Paul's distinction between the two kinds of Christians is in blatant contradiction to the rest of the New Testament, where it is assumed that all Christians are Spirit-endowed. For Paul to assume that some Christians are carnal and some are Spirit-endowed, "perfect Christians," is to go against the earliest proclamation of Jewish Christianity.[81] "In the inconsistency — in fact, the contradictoriness — of these conceptions, a significant fact in regard to the Spirit is reflected."[82] However, Bultmann thinks this ambiguous and contradictory interpretation of the Christian life "is appropriate to the nature of the Spirit."[83] Apparently Bultmann means to say that it is of the nature of Spirit not to be mechanically programmed to function in a prescribed manner. If so, this could be an important insight for understanding the dynamics of the Christian life — what appears to be contradictory is only an indication that life cannot be stereotyped. In this respect, to *require* either the idea of one decisive beginning moment of the Christian life or to prescribe in a static sense two decisive moments would be claiming more for a theological position than can be exegetically defended.

Bultmann has, however, suggested an interpretation which shows that the apparent contradiction is not a real contradiction. He writes:

> The view that all Christians receive the Spirit in baptism does not rest upon the idea that the individuals baptized have special 'spiritual' or emotional experience during the act of baptism, however much that may occasionally have been the case. Rather, it rests basically upon the fact *that the Spirit is given to the Church*, into which the individual is received by baptism.[84]

Here Bultmann shows that "there now arises the question how participation in the Spirit becomes a reality in all individuals [who are already members of the Church]."[85]

In other words, every believer initiated into the Church through baptism had the right to receive the Holy Spirit, since the Church is the fellowship of the Spirit, but not every believer in Christ has necessarily appropriated the Spirit. In this way, it is not necessary to think of this distinction as a real contradiction. Yet Bultmann says that it is a "contradiction that on the one hand the Spirit is the origin of a new attitude and capacity in the Christian, and on the other hand that his attitude qualifies him for ever-new endowment with the Spirit."[86]

It is difficult to know why Bultmann thinks this twofold experience of the Spirit is a real contradiction, unless it grows out of his understanding that Paul represents Hellenistic Christianity as opposed to Jewish Christianity. Bultmann thinks that Hellenistic Christianity posited a time difference between baptism and the reception of the Spirit; whereas the earliest Christian community (i.e., Jewish Christianity) assumed that baptism and reception of the Spirit were contemporaneous.[87]   Otherwise, Bultmann's exposition of Paul's thought significantly shows that there is a difference between being baptized into Christ and a subsequent receiving of the Pentecostal Spirit. To be sure, Bultmann's theological understanding does not assume "two works of grace" as such; but his exegetical consideration indirectly lends support to the thesis being maintained here.

That there is a distinction between the Son and the Spirit within the one reality of God corresponds historically to God's revelation of Himself in the Incarnation and Pentecost. It has frequently been noted among biblical scholars that "*Holy* Spirit" occurs only twice in the Old Testament, and in neither case is the concept of the Spirit as a distinct personality of his own indicated.[88]   That the Spirit is a distinct reality within the triunity of God did not become evident until Pentecost, even as the distinct personality of the Son did not become truly evident until His resurrection from the dead. Even as the Son after his incarnation and Resurrection from the dead was not altogether identical to the pre-existent Christ, even so, the Spirit after Pentecost was not altogether identical with the Spirit before Pentecost.

This genuine difference between the Spirit before Pentecost and after Pentecost is often not taken seriously enough. The Spirit before Pentecost is not altogether the same as the Spirit after Pentecost, because the Spirit before Pentecost was not the Spirit incarnate, as Karl Rahner points out.[89]   The Spirit after Pentecost is the Spirit of the exalted Christ. Rahner, with precision and clarity, writes: "This Spirit was not there before Christ, and since Pentecost it has been revealed that *this* Spirit is the Spirit of *Christ*, that in its outpouring and its work in the world it shares in the finality of Christ himself."[90] The Pentecostal Spirit is "not merely the Spirit who moves intermittently and mysteriously here and there, who takes a prophet and uses him as his 'instrument' so long as he wills to do so, but who never remains lastingly among men, and who provides no lasting sign of his presence and power, but the Spirit of the Son who has become man."[91]   In this respect, Bultmann has also shown exegetically that there is no difference in meaning between "being in Christ" and "being in the Spirit," for the exalted Christ is functionally identical to the Holy Spirit.[92]

Rahner further shows that the meaning of Pentecost was that the Holy Spirit possesses "within itself all the fulness of perfection, and has already imparted this fulness to the world."[93] This implies that the fulness of the Spirit is the perfection of the Christian life.

Wesley also implies this sanctifying fulness of the Pentecostal reality when he writes:

> Thy sanctifying Spirit pour,
> To quench my thirst, and wash me clean;
> Now, Saviour, let the gracious shower
> Descend, and make me pure from sin.[94]

---

[1]R. C. Dentan, "Redeem, Redeemer, Redemption," *The Interpreter's Dictionary of the Bible*, R-Z, p. 22.

[2]Oscar Cullman, *Salvation in History*, p. 278.

[3]*Ibid.*, pp. 268ff.

[4]*Ibid.*, pp. 271-274, 283.

[5]John Wesley, *A Plain Account of Christian Perfection*, pp. 25-26.

[6]*The Standard Sermons of John Wesley*, II, 157, 169; Fletcher points out that "a being strengthened, stablished, and settled" and "being rooted and grounded in love" are favorite terms of Wesley's to describe Christian perfection (cf. Fletcher, I, 14).

[7]*Kittel's Theological Dictionary of the New Testament*, III (1965), 760.

[8]*Ibid.*, p. 761.

[9]*Ibid.*, 762-763; cf. Hermann Cremer, *Biblico-Theological Lexicon of New Testament Greek*, trans. William Urwick (4th ed. rev.; Edinburgh: T. and T. Clark, 1962), I, 357.

[10]*Kittel's Theological Dictionary of the New Testament*, III, 763; Cremer, I, 357.

[11]F. D. Gealy, "Lots," *The Interpreter's Dictionary of the Bible*, K-Q, p. 164.

[12]*A Greek-English Lexicon of the New Testament* (University of Chicago Press, 1957), p. 506.

[13]Cremer, p. 357.

[14]A. C. Hervey, *Acts of the Apostles, The Pulpit Commentary,* ed. H. D. M. Spence and Joseph S. Exell (Chicago: Wilcox and Fallet Co., n.d.), I, 252.

[15]*Ibid.*, I, 253.

[16]James D. G. Dunn, *Baptism in the Holy Spirit* (London: SCM Press, 1970), pp. 64-65.

[17]*Kittel's Theological Dictionary of the New Testament*, III, 763.

[18]Wright, *God Who Acts*, p. 63.

[19]Cullmann, *Christ and Time*, trans. Floyd V. Filson (London: SCM Press Ltd., 1951), p. 39.

[20]Richard Longenecker, *The Ministry and Message of Paul* (Grand Rapids: Zondervan Publishing House, 1973), p. 99; P.S. Minear, "Church, Idea of," *The Interpreter's Dictionary of the Bible, A-D*, p. 616.

[21]Wesley, *A Plain Account of Christian Perfection*, p. 36.

[22]*Institutes of the Christian Religion,* ed. John T. McNeill, trans. Ford Lewis Battles (Philadelphia: The Westminster Press, 1960), I, Book II, Chapter XVII.

[23]*Ibid.*, I, 602ff.

[24]John Deschner, *Wesley's Christology, An Interpretation* (Dallas: Southern Methodist University Press, 1960), p. 130; *The Standard Sermons of John Wesley*, I, 148.

[25]*The Standard Sermons of John Wesley*, I, 327.

[26]*Harald Lindstrom, Wesley and Sanctification* (Nashville: Abingdon Press, 1946), pp. 131-132; Wesley, "On Perfection," *Sermons on Several Occasions* (New York: T. Mason and G. Lane, 1839), 169ff.

[27]*The Standard Sermons of John Wesley*, I, 151.

[28]*Ibid.*, I, 150.

[29]*Ibid.*, I, 327.

[30]Deschner, p. 126.

[31]Wesley's comment on Heb. 12:23 in his *Explanatory Notes on the New Testament*; Deschner, p. 131.

[32]Deschner, p. 13.

[33]Unpublished letter (January 16, 1773) in manuscript, researched by Dr. Timothy Smith in the John Rylands Library, Manchester.

[34]Unpublished letter (July, 1774) in manuscript, researched by Dr. Timothy Smith in the John Rylands Library, Manchester.

[35]Cremer, I, 770.

[36]Ernest DeWitt Burton, *A Critical and Exegetical Commentary on the Epistle to the Galatians, The International Critical Commentary* Edinburgh: T. and T. Clark, 1964), p. 168.

[37]*Ibid.*, pp. 168f.

[38]*Ibid.*, p. 177.

[39]Victor Paul Furnish, "The Letter of Paul to the Galatians," *The Interpreter's One-Volume Commentary on the Bible*," ed. Charles M. Layman (Nashville: Abingdon Press, 1971), p. 829; Donald Guthrie, *Galatians, The Century Bible* (Camden, N.J.: Thomas Nelson and Sons, 1969), p. 104.

[40]Hermann W. Ridderbos, *The Epistle of Paul to the Churches of Galatia, The New International Commentary on the New Testament*, ed. F. F. Bruce (Grand Rapids: Wm. B. Eerdmans, 1953), p. 128.

[41]Cf. Bultmann, I, 329-340.

[42]F. F. Bruce, "The Holy Spirit in the Acts of the Apostles," *Interpretation*, 27:2 (April, 1973), 176.

[43]Arndt-Gingrich, *A Greek-English Lexicon of the New Testament* p. 218.

[44]Bruce, *Interpretation*, p. 176.

[45]M. H. Shepherd, Jr., "Hands, Laying on of," *The Interpreter's Dictionary of the Bible*, E-J, 521-522.

[46]F. X. Durrwell, *The Resurrection*, trans. Rosemary Sheed (New York: Sheed and Ward, 1961), p. 219.

[47]*Ibid.*, p. 315.

[48]Burton, p. 221.

[49]*Ibid.*

[50]*Ibid.*

[51]*Word Studies in the New Testament* (Grand Rapids: Wm. B. Eerdmans, 1946), IV, 136.

[52]*Ibid.*, IV, 136-137.

[53]Bultmann, *Theology of the New Testament*, I, 330; cf. Wolfhart Pannenberg, *Revelation as History* (New York: Macmillan Co., 1968), p. 136.

[54]*Ibid.*, I, 158.

[55]William Sanday and Arthur C. Headlam, *A Critical and Exegetical Commentary on the Epistle to the Romans, The International Critical Commentary* (Edinburgh: T. and T. Clark, 1967), p. 197.

[56]John Fletcher, *Checks*, II, 539.

[57]*Ibid.*, II, 538, 540, 549.

[58]*Ibid.*, II, 543.

[59]*Ibid.*, II, 538f.

[60]A. Skevington Wood, *Paul's Pentecost* (Exeter Devon: The Paternoster Press, 1963), pp. 22f.

[61]Burton, p. 222.

[62]*Ibid.*

[63]*Ibid.*, p. 225.

[64]*Kittel's Theological Dictionary of the New Testament*, III, 769.

[65]*The Letters of John Wesley*, IV, 133, V, 333.

[66]T. K. Abbott, *A Critical and Exegetical Commentary on the Epistles to the Ephesians and to the Colossians, International Critical Commentary* (Edinburgh: T. and T. Clark, 1964), pp. 4-5.

[67]Henry Alford, *The New Testament for English Readers* (Chicago: Moody Press, n.d.), p. 1203.

[68]S. D. F. Salmond, *The Epistle to the Ephesians, The Expositor's Greek Testament*, ed., W. Robertson Nicoll (Grand Rapids: Wm. B. Eerdmans, 1956), III, 246.

[69]Alford, p. 1203; Bengel, *Gnomon of the New Testament*, II, 385.

[70]Alford, p. 1203.

[71]Durrwell, p. 255.

[72]*Ibid.*, p. 56.

[73]*Yves M. J. Congar, OP, Theologians Today*, ed. Martin Redfern (New York: Sheed and Ward, 1972), pp. 31-32.

[74]*Ibid.*, p. 32.

[75]*Ibid.*, p. 28.

[76]*Ibid.*,

[77]*Theology of the New Testament*, I, 138-139.

[78]*Ibid.*

[79]*Ibid.*, I, 139.

[80]*Ibid.*, I, 158.

[81]*Ibid.*, I, 160.

[82]*Ibid.*

[83]*Ibid.*

[84]*Ibid.*

[85]*Ibid.*, I, 160-161.

[86]*Ibid.*, I, 163.

[87]*Ibid.*, I, 160, 161, 189.

[88]Georgia Harkness, *The Fellowship of the Holy Spirit* (Nashville: Abingdon Press, 1966), p. 26.

[89]Karl Rahner, *Theological Investigations*, trans. David Bourke (New York: Herder and Herder, 1971), VII, 189.

[90]*Ibid.*, VII, 197.

[91]*Ibid.*, VII, 189.

[92]*Theology of the New Testament*, I, 335.

[93]*Theological Investigations*, VII, 197.

[94]Wesley, *A Plain Account of Christian Perfection,* p. 114.

# CHAPTER IV.

## SPACE – TIME AND A TRINITARIAN CONCEPT OF GRACE

The concept of time presupposed in Scripture is of fundamental importance in understanding the nature of grace. Each of these concepts has received a great deal of attention in the history of recent thought, though there is still a wide difference of opinion regarding their significance. Generally speaking, however, grace can be defined as unmerited favor, whereas time is the moving points and ongoing series of events within space. Samuel Alexander in *Space, Time and Deity* has pointed out that "time and space in their pure reality remain as the framework of history."[1] Hence, space-time (creation) is the objective framework in which grace is experienced through God's self-revelation.[2]

It will not be the intent of this chapter to provide a philosophical or scientific analysis of the different concepts of time. Nor will any attempt be made to reproduce a biblical word study on time, such as Oscar Cullmann's *Christ and Time* or James Barr's *Biblical Words for Time*. And no attempt will be made to argue for an "evangelical" as opposed to a "sacramentalist" concept of grace. Rather, the intent of this chapter is to indicate that God's grace has had a real history in the sequence of time and that this salvation history *(Heilsgeschichte)* is simultaneously the self-revealing history of the triune God, who is the transcendent unity of all time. It will be pointed out in this regard that the history of grace has had decisive turning points in time corresponding to those events in which God revealed himself as Creator (Father), Redeemer (Son), and Sanctifier (Holy Spirit). It will also be pointed out that the decisive points within the saving-revealing history of God are the normative pattern for understanding the sequence of grace as experienced in the life of the Christian.

### 1. The Freedom of God and the Reality of Time

Karl Barth has given considerable attention to the theological exposition of time in relation to God's eternity. He speaks of "time before the fall," "fallen time," and "revelation time." The revelation of Jesus Christ is the time of the Lord of time who redeems "fallen time."[3]  His time for us is the time of grace. The significance of Barth's exposition is that he seeks to show that time is an objective reality, not a human creation or merely a subjective concept (Kant).  Rather, time is a "reality, as accessible to God as is human existence."[4] Without this presupposition of time as an objective reality instead of a mere human creation there could be no concept of a self-revelation of a triune God, because there could be no history in which this revelation could take place.[5]  This means that there could be no theological basis for an experience of grace.  The creation of space-time is the essential framework for understanding the nature of the covenant.

Barth's stress upon the objectivity of time has been a helpful corrective to the existentialist narrowing down of time to a mere timeless moment of grace without any continuity to the past or future.  Such a subjective notion of time, along with its idea of a non-historical faith, has become quite pervasive in contemporary theological thought, primarily through the influence of Bultmann's existentialist exegesis.  Yet its consequences for the Christian life are enormous, since it precludes any possibility of a real participation in the events of Easter and Pentecost through the sacramental and evangelical means of grace.  What has become an essential task of theology today is to rediscover the biblical emphasis upon creation as the point of departure for understanding the trinitarian concept of grace. Otherwise, the historical bases of the Christian life are undermined, along with the organism-concept of the Church as the real body of Christ.

The first thing to be seen in this respect is that the creation of space-time itself (Genesis 1) is an act of sheer grace. This is the meaning of the classical theological term *creatio ex nihilo*. God spoke space-time into existence from nothing (Rom. 4:17; Heb. 11:3). There was no pre-existent stuff out of which God made the world. Nor did God create the world out of the substance of his own being. Such a concept would be pantheism. Nor did God create the world out of a need for his own well-being; otherwise, God would not be self-existent and infinite in his being (Acts 17:24-25). Rather, he *willed* (i.e., freely chose) the world into existence out of pure love from sheer nothing. Without this concept of creation *ex nihilo*, grace is no longer grace and God's freedom is no longer pure freedom.[6]

To be sure, to affirm that the sole reason for God's creating the world was that he freely willed it to be so seems like circular reasoning. But such reasoning about God's being is necessarily limited and "circular," though not "a vicious circle." This limitation of finite logic is a witness to God's mystery. Without this concept of mystery, whereby God is acknowledged to be beyond all human definitions, God would no longer be God. At least, the God of Jesus who is transcendent and sovereign would be denied. Hence, grace is the corollary to God's mystery. The possibility of knowing that God is and that he is pure love is by grace through faith alone. This knowledge of God is not a human discovery, but a divine gift (Eph. 2:8); which is to say that knowledge of God comes through revelation, not through human reasoning.[7]

Though there is this essential difference between God and the world, space-time is, nonetheless, the finite manifestation of God's infinite being (Rom. 1:20). God does not need the world of space-time for his own personal existence. Søren Kierkegaard points out that God "is not moved by some need, as if he could not endure the strain of silence, but had to break out in speech. But if he moves himself, and is not moved by need, what else can move him but love?"[8]

Love in the highest sense means freely giving. It is this kind of love which motivated God to will for there to be life other than himself. On the other hand, there is a sense in which it can be said, as Kierkegaard does, that "God needs no man. It would otherwise be a highly embarrassing thing to be a creator, if the result was the creator came to depend upon the creatures."[9] The concept of *agape* love as unmerited love is understandable only in the light of the concept of *creatio ex nihilo*.

This *ex nihilo concept* is not to suggest a dualistic notion in which God and the world are wholly different categorical realities but, as Karl Rahner puts it, "the difference between God and the world is of such a nature that God establishes and is the difference of the world from himself, and for this reason he establishes the closest unity precisely in the differentiation."[10]

On the other hand, the world of space-time could not survive apart from the sustaining grace of God. More fundamentally, history as the ongoing events within space-time are meaningful only to the extent that events are grounded in the self-revealing God who freely redeems the fallenness of space-time. He redeems it *as freely* as he originally created it. In this respect, the Bible sets the stage for the history of salvation with the account of creation (Gen. 1-3). God's covenant with Abraham presupposes space-time as God's creation.

Just as the creation of space-time *ex nihilo* was an act of sheer grace, even so God's covenant with Abraham, which brought into being "God's own people" who once were "no people" (Gen. 12:2; Deut. 10:14; Hos. 1:9f.), was based solely on God's grace. Just as creation was based on God's free choice; so God's covenant with Israel was the result of free choice. Yehezkel Kaufmann has shown the significance of this absolute freedom of God which stands in sharp contrast to naturalistic religions, such as polytheism, pantheism, as well as the modern concept of panentheism:

Israel did not descend from gods; YHWH is not Israel's kinsman; Palestine is not his natural habitat; Israel's cult is not the source of his vitality. The relation between Israel and YHWH is a covenant relation. . . . YHWH's relation to Israel could be conceived of only in terms of election and free choice.[11]

## 2. The Triune History of God and Two Works of Grace

The story of creation (space-time) is the setting for Israel's history; it is the framework for understanding the history of the Abrahamic covenant which had its final fulfillment in Jesus Christ.[12] Biblical history may be generally defined as the record of unique events through which God's grace is mediated. This means that space is the time in which grace is offered to humanity.

A purely scientific concept of sequential time is inadequate for understanding the time of grace. Time is not simply linear. The biblical concept of time rather presupposes a transcendent unity which serves as the basis for continuity among the past, present, and future. Only through this concept of a transcendent dimension of time can the experience of grace as a present reality be based on something which happened in the past or which is anticipated in the future. God as Creator *ex nihilo* transcends all finite time, and his saving acts in space-time are embraced in his eternal reality through which these saving events of the past (or future) are extended into the present time of the believer.

More specifically, the temporal events of Easter and Pentecost have saving significance today through faith in Jesus Christ, since those events are not simply past and done with. Rather, Jesus Christ is the transcendent unity of all time and he mediates grace into the present through allowing us to participate in his resurrected life and his Spirit of power. This participation in the temporal events of Easter and Pentecost is not figurative but profoundly real; since present time in a dialectic sense includes past time and future time, because Jesus Christ is the transcendent unity of all time. Without his transcendent unity of all time, the idea of the saving events of the past having any significance for the present experience of grace would be unintelligible.

Alan Richardson has shown that "biblical theology is essentially recital — the recitation of the great things which God has done in history for his people; the biblical doctrine of salvation is an assertion of something which actually happened."[13] Salvation comes through personal participation in these past events which become contemporary through Word and sacrament. Richardson especially points out the saving significance of the Exodus and Jesus' Resurrection from the dead. The Exodus-Resurrection theme of deliverance

> remains active and potent throughout the continuing history of the people for whom it was wrought; in the biblical view it is not a mere event of the past, but something that is ever and again made present and real in the lives of those who celebrate it in word and sacrament; the salvation that was once-for-all wrought for the whole people is appropriated by each family or each individual as the family or the individual makes response in worship and thanksgiving (Exod. 12:26-27; Deut. 6:20-25; 26:1-11; John 6:53-58; I Cor. 10: 16-17; 11:23-26).[14]

He further shows that "there is no divorce or contradiction between the historical and eschatological; because the former, by becoming active in the present and no mere past-and-gone event, is the matrix and type of the latter"[15]

Oscar Cullmann[16] has noted that the writer to the Hebrews presupposed this dialectic understanding of time when he defined faith as a present participation in the saving events of the past and future: "Faith is the assurance of things hoped for (future saving events), the evidence of things not seen (past saving events)" (Heb. 11:1). In this respect, faith is both historical and eschatological. It was in the experience of faith's relationship to God that he was seen to be the Creator *ex nihilo* (Heb. 11:3). It was through the concrete events within the history of God's creation that grace was mediated to the Israelites. It is significant that the phrase "by faith" always had reference to some particular event (Heb. 11:4-39). Yet the concrete events of history which served as the framework of Israel's faith were salvific only because they already, in a provisional manner, participated in the future event of Jesus Christ (Heb. 11:39; 12:2). The writer of the letter to the Hebrews shows that faith is based in the two decisive saving events of Jesus' Resurrection from the dead and his exaltation ( = Pentecostal outpouring of the Holy Spirit; (Heb. 12:2; cf. Acts 2:33; John 16:4-7). This means that faith is always faith in the saving history of Jesus Christ who is "the pioneer and perfector of our faith, who for the joy that was set before him endured the cross despising the shame (Easter event), and is seated at the right hand of the throne of God (Pentecostal event)."

Whether the idea of *salvation* history (Cullmann) or *revelation* history (Pannenberg) is the more comprehensive theological term is not a question of importance in this context. Rather, both concepts are inseparably related in understanding the nature of the Christian life.[17] It is God's self-revelation which was historically based in Easter and Pentecost which constitute the foundation of the Christian life. God's trinitarian self-revelation in history is simultaneously the history of salvation. This can be seen in Jesus' teaching concerning the coming of the Pentecostal Spirit, which suggests the idea that the knowledge of the Father, Son, and Holy Spirit are related yet distinguishable. Jesus talked about those who "have not known the Father, nor me" (John 16:3). In this same context, Jesus spoke of the disciples' future experience of the Spirit (John 16:13). Yet, Jesus showed that knowledge of the Father also implies a relationship to the Son and to the Holy Spirit who proceeds from the Father and Son (John 15:26). However, the quality of one's relationship to God is dependent upon the depth of his relationship to the three persons of the Trinity (John 14:15-17). All who really know the Father will come to accept the Son, and all who come into a relationship with the Son will come to be filled with the Holy Spirit.

This trinitarian concept of grace presupposes in the first place that God is Creator and Father of all things (Isa. 45:7-13; 64:8). God the Father can be seen to be the Creator of Israel because he is Creator of heaven and earth (Isa. 43:1, 7, 15, 21; 44:2, 21, 24). This revelation that God the Father is Creator was first made explicit in the Exodus event. B. W. Anderson puts it this way:

> Just as the Creation points forward to the Exodus and the making of the covenant, so the covenant faith reaches backward and includes the Creation. The theological movement of Israel's thought is not from the confession 'God is the Creator' to 'Yahweh, the God of Israel, is the Redeemer,' but in just the opposite direction.[18]

In this respect, the Exodus event had "decisive significance" for the interpretation of the whole sweep of history from its very beginning with creation.[19]

Likewise in the New Testament the whole sweep of history, beginning with creation, is given a Christological interpretation in the light of Jesus' Resurrection from the dead (Eph. 1:7-10; Col. 1:15-20).[20] That Jesus is "the first-born from the dead" (Col. 1:18) is proof that God is creator of all things. As Barth has shown, the Christian concept of God as Creator is based on his "knowledge of God as the Lord over life and death, as the God of Good Friday and Easter."[21] This creator God who is, in a unique sense, the Father of our Lord Jesus Christ also becomes uniquely the Father of all those who participate in the sonship of Jesus (Gal. 4:4-7; I John 3:1-2).

The strength of Paul's argument in Rom. 4:13-25 concerning the universal availability of salvation presupposes the idea of God as Creator *ex nihilo*.[22]

1. God created the world *ex nihilo*: "calls into existence the things that do not exist" (4:17).

2. God created a new people *ex nihilo* by his promise to Abraham: "I have made you the Father of many nations"

(4:17). Abraham and his descendents were redeemed solely by grace, through faith in this creator God (4:16). Hence Abraham and his descendents have no grounds for self righteousness.

3. God created anew within time-space in an absolutely unique sense, through his raising of Jesus from the dead (4:24).

4. Everyone can now be justified through faith in Jesus, whom *God* raised from the dead (4:24). Faith is a *real* participation in Jesus' Resurrection.

The Old Testament concept of God as Creator who provides for the needs of his people naturally suggests the idea of God as a Father (cf. Psalm 89). Yet as C.F.D. Moule has shown, Jesus "gave a new depth to the conception of God as Father." He shows that Jesus' teaching revealed "a new attitude of sonship."[23]  Moule further points out that for the New Testament concept of God, "most important of all, he is designated as Father. This conception, although not itself new, was evidently enormously deepened and enriched by the life and words of Jesus, and the idea of the fatherhood of God has ever since dominated Christian thinking."[24]

Moule shows that the New Testament unquestionably affirms Christ's divine sonship. The idea of Christ's sonship is meant to imply his oneness with God's essence (cf. John 5:18; 19:7). That Jesus differentiated between "your Father" and "my Father" suggests a qualitative difference in Jesus' sonship from the disciples' sonship (John 20:17). In this respect, "the disciples are to receive from the unique Son a derived sonship."[25]  Moule further writes: "The mission of Jesus seems to have been so to reveal and import his sonship that — although in a most important sense unique — it might nevertheless be entered into and shared" (cf. Matt. 11:27; Luke 10:22; Rom. 8:29; Heb. 2:11).[26]  This sharing in Jesus' sonship is the significance of Peter's interpretation of Jesus' Resurrection from the dead: "Blessed be the God and Father of our Lord Jesus Christ! By his great mercy we have been *born anew* to a living hope through the Resurrection of Jesus Christ from the dead (Easter), and to an *inheritance* (Pentecost) . . . kept in heaven" (I Peter 1:3). Believers are "born anew" and granted the inheritance ( = kingdom of God) which are the bases for their "living hope" of an ultimate destiny in heaven.

One of the insights of form criticism has been to point out that the earthly life of Jesus is interpreted from the perspective of his Resurrection. Unlike some form critics, Oscar Cullmann believes that it is possible to get back to the real Jesus of history. However, he shows that it is possible to do so only by taking into account the Resurrection kerygma.[27] The Resurrection is the basis for understanding who Jesus was. The Resurrection is the confirmation of his claim to unique sonship (Rom. 1:4-6).[28]

The idea of revelation-salvation history stands or falls with the reality of the Resurrection event. Not only can there be no hope for salvation if Christ be not raised, but the trinitarian concept of God is seriously compromised (I Cor. 15:14-15).[29] Barth has shown that the Resurrection of Jesus Christ is the foundation of the trinitarian revelation of God.[30] It will not do to speak of the "Easter faith" without the "Easter Message" (Harnack). As Barth points out, the whole of Christian faith with its belief in Jesus Christ as the Son of God is based on "the Easter story, Christ truly, corporally risen."[31] It is this "event which is the proper object of all other narratives and teachings in the New Testament."[32] Without the concreteness of this event, there could have been no exaltation of the Son to the Father and, hence, no Pentecost. A rejection of the historicity of Jesus' Resurrection from the dead and the Pentecostal outpouring of the Spirit of Christ is a rejection of the trinitarian concept of grace.[33]

Easter and Pentecost are real events in past time. The history of Jesus is summed up in these two events. Belief in the triune nature of God is based on these two events.[34] And the Christian life is grounded "only on the basis of these two factors" (Barth).[35] This triune revelation of God's history with humanity can be summed up in this way:

1.   creation is the manifestation of God as Father (I Cor. 8:6);

2.   the resurrection is the manifestation of Jesus as the Son of God (Rom. 1:4);

3. the event of Pentecost is the manifestation of the Holy Spirit as the third person of the Trinity, who was sent by the Father and Son (John 14:26; 15:26).[36]

As Father, God is creator; as Son, God is redeemer; as Holy Spirit, God is sanctifier (I Peter 1:2; II Thess. 2:13). Torrance, in a concise manner, has shown the significance of a trinitarian concept of grace: "Our human nature is now set within the Father-Son relationship of Christ. Through faith in Christ and union with him we share brotherhood with him and so share with him the Fatherhood of God, and in and through him we share in the one Spirit of the living God."[37]

Creation, redemption, and sanctification are three distinct but related events which constitute the revelation of God and the salvation of humanity. Hence, the successive manifestations of God as Father, Son, and Holy Spirit are the decisive events in the history of salvation and correspond to the three distinct but coordinate moments within "God's eternal essence as well" (Pannenberg).[37] This means that God's revelation as creator, redeemer and sanctifier is a reflex of his triune being.[39] Abraham Kuyper, the nineteenth century Dutch reformed theologian, describes the salvific significance of God's triune revelation this way:

> While these operations — creation, redemption, and sanctification — are hidden in the thoughts of His heart, His counsel, and His Being, it is Father, Son and Holy Ghost who creates, Father, Son, and Holy Ghost who redeems, Father, Son, and Holy Ghost who sanctifies, without any division or distinction of activities. The rays of light hidden in the sun are indivisible and indistinguishable until they radiate; so in the Being of God the indwelling working is one and undivided; His personal glories remain invisible until revealed in His outgoing works.[40]

This triune distinction of God's being and the corresponding saving activity of the divine persons is incorporated widely in the liturgy and catechism of the Christian tradition. The Heidelberg Catechism expresses it this way:

Question 24. How are these Articles divided? Into
three parts: the first is of God the Father, and our
creation; the second, of God the Son, and our redemption; the third, of God the Holy Spirit, and our sanctification.[41]

In defense of this triune concept of grace, the Heidelberg
Catechism particularly calls attention to I Peter 1:2: "Chosen
and destined by God the Father and sanctified by the Spirit
for obedience to Jesus Christ and for sprinkling with his
blood."

In "The Great Litany" of the Anglican *Common Book of
Prayer*, this triune distinction is carefully worded: "O God the
Father, Creator of heaven and earth, Have mercy upon us. O
God the Son, Redeemer of the world, Have mercy upon us.
O God the Holy Ghost, Sanctifier of the Faithful, Have
mercy upon us."

Roman Catholic theology has also maintained a distinction
between the Resurrection and Pentecost in defining the nature
of the Christian life — baptism is a participation in Jesus'
resurrection, while confirmation is the participation in the
Pentecostal gift of the Spirit.[42] The purpose of the coming of
the Pentecostal Spirit was for the sanctification of believers.
This is affirmed in *The Documents of Vatican II*: "When the
work which the Father gave the Son to do on earth (cf. Jn.
17:4) was accomplished, the Holy Spirit was sent on the day
of Pentecost in order that he might continually sanctify the
Church."[43] For Catholic theology, the Resurrection and
Pentecost must be personalized in the life of each person.
Hence, there are two distinct acts of initiation before one is
truly Christian and can participate in the Lord's Supper.[44]

Wesleyan theology holds a similar position, except these
two decisive events for the Christian life are understood in
evangelical rather than sacramentalist terms.

That the history of theology acknowledges a distinction of
activities among the three persons of the Trinity is not a
tritheism. Nor does the distinction between the Resurrection
and Pentecost intend to suggest that the Spirit is not operative

in the Resurrection, or that the coming of the Spirit in his sanctifying work on the day of Pentecost was something in addition to the history of Jesus. It should be also emphasized that when Roman Catholic and Anglican theology differentiate between receiving Christ at baptism and subsequently receiving the Spirit in confirmation, it is not being suggested that the Spirit is an essentially different reality from Jesus. Nor is it being suggested in Wesleyan theology that the Spirit is not operative in conversion when Christian perfection is defined as a subsequent experience. Rather, conversion is the birth of the Spirit; sanctification is the fulness of the Spirit.[45] Nor should it be thought the divine acts of Creation, Redemption, and Sanctification are exclusive of each other. From the moment of one's birth (creation), there are redemptive and sanctifying influences affecting his life. When one experiences justifying faith in Jesus Christ, sanctifying grace in a unique sense begins. Fletcher points this out:

> When I say that pious Jews and our Lord's disciples, before the day of Pentecost, were strangers to the great outpouring of the Spirit, I do not mean that they were strangers to his directing, sanctifying, and enlivening influence, according to their dispensation. . . . Nevertheless, they were not fully baptized. The Comforter that visited them did not properly dwell in them. Although they had already wrought miracles by his power, 'the promise of the Father was not yet fulfilled to them.' They had not yet been 'made perfect in one,' by the assimilating power of the heavenly fire.[46]

While there is a unique reception of the Spirit in the life of the believer subsequent to the new birth, nonetheless, it is the same Spirit whom we receive at conversion. Devotionally speaking, there is no difference between Christ and the Holy Spirit, for the Spirit is the exalted Christ (Acts 2:33; II Cor. 3:18). Theologically speaking, there is a real differentiation among the Father, Son, and Holy Spirit, but it is a differentiation-in-unity. This triunity of God's being means that whatever unique function one of the divine persons has, the other divine persons also share in the same activity (*opera trinitatis ad extra sunt indivisa*).

The concept of the Trinity does not mean three independent centers of consciousness within the divine life. Nor do the progressive stages of Christian experience lend itself to the notion that one can have the Son without the Spirit, as if the Christian life were made up of disjointed events. Terminologically, we can speak of the deeper Christian life as the fulness of the Spirit without depreciating the reception of Christ in conversion; even as we can speak of the unique coming of the Spirit on the day of Pentecost as a deeper revelation of God without depreciating the person of Jesus Christ in his earthly ministry. The Spirit of Pentecost is the continuation of the earthly Jesus. Even as there were stages in salvation in which God was progressively known as Father, Son, and Holy Spirit; so there may be stages in one's personal history of salvation in which one may know God successively as Father, Son, and Holy Spirit. Yet it is the one God who is known.

In this respect, creation serves as the framework of God's covenantal promise to Abraham. The Exodus and Conquest brought about the actualization of that promise. The significance of the Exodus (Redemption from bondage) and Conquest (which brought about the sanctifying of the Promised Land through rooting out idolatry) was their New Testament counterparts — the Resurrection and Pentecost. Hence, the history of Jesus consummated the history of Israel. God in his revelation is known as Father (Creation), Son (Redemption-Easter), and Holy Spirit (Sanctification-Pentecost). These three historical events, reflecting the three personal distinctions of the triune God, have a threefold corresponding significance for the history of each believer in his physical birth (Creation), his redemption (Resurrection life), and his sanctification (Pentecostal gift of the Spirit). Just as Creation, Redemption (Resurrection), and Sanctification (Pentecost) are continuous events, though extended in time; even so, the believer's Christian life is a single complex reality, though extended in time.

This trinitarian concept of grace which is reflected in the

historical acts of creation, redemption, and sanctification is a conceptual framework for understanding the Wesleyan doctrine of two works of grace. Easter is the ground of justification (Rom. 4:23-24); Pentecost is the ground of sanctification (I Peter 1:2; Acts 15:8,9; Rom. 5:5). As Easter and Pentecost are distinguished in time, even so, they may be in one's own personal history of salvation.

### 3. Time-Space and the Idea of a Second Work of Grace

It is a matter of dispute within the larger Christian tradition whether or not righteousness can be fully imparted while one is living within the framework of fallen space-time. Yet the Wesleyan tradition carries as one of its theological distinctives the teaching that Christian perfection ought to be the norm of the Christian life. This experience of imparted righteousness is to be received by faith alone. Wesley, in a sense, rediscovered this evangelical doctrine of inherent righteousness by faith alone, even as Martin Luther had rediscovered the doctrine of justification by faith alone.[47] Wesley's concept of inherent righteousness was a further development of the evangelical doctrine of justification by faith alone.

Yet Wesley was in basic agreement with the Reformation doctrine of justification. This can be seen in his sermon, "The Lord Our Righteousness." Wesley says a believer is "invested or clothed with the righteousness of Christ."[48] More specifically, Wesley means that the human (not the divine) righteousness of Christ is imputed to the believer. That is, in justification the image of God (including every "holy and heavenly temper" which is "without any defect, or mixture of unholiness") is imputed to the convert "as soon as he believes."[49]

It can be seen from this that Wesley did not interpret justification by faith solely in terms of "forgiveness of sins." Paul Tillich's comments are apropos in this regard. He has warned against making the mistake of equating "forgiveness of sins" with justification. He speaks of justification as "the experience of the New Being as Paradox."[50]  He writes: "Justification in the objective sense is the eternal act of God by which he accepts as not estranged those who are indeed estranged from him by guilt and the act by which he takes them into the unity with him which is manifest in the New Being in Christ."[51]  In this objective sense, justification is "identical with Sanctification"; whereas, subjectively, sanctification is the experience of real transformation.[52]  Hence justification relates to the believer's *standing* before God and his being considered holy, whereas sanctification is the process of *really* becoming holy.  It is in this respect that Tillich cautions against merely equating justification with "forgiveness of sins."  In his discussion of justification, he writes: "The symbol of forgiveness has proved dangerous because it has concentrated the mind on particular sins and their moral quality rather than on the estrangement from God and its religious quality."[53]  While Tillich's existentialist-panentheistic interpretation[54] of theology is hardly compatible with historic Christianity, the point which Tillich is rightly making is that justification has to do with man's total being (not just his outward acts) and that man's total salvation is "by faith through grace alone."[55]

Karl Barth also in describing what it means for the believer to be "in Jesus Christ" says: "He cannot in any sense declare to himself that he is righteous and holy."[56]  Rather, Jesus Christ "alone is the Word of God that is spoken to us. There is an exchange of status between Him and us: His righteousness and holiness are ours, our sin is His."[57]  Barth further says that it is because of our participation in "his human nature" that "the righteousness and judgment of God" are satisfied.[58] Justification "denotes the unification of the eternal divine Word with the nature of man, and therefore with the rectification of that human nature, notwithstanding and in spite of its natural perversion, to humility and obedience to God."[59]

Because Wesley was engaged so much in antinomian controversies, he at times was thought to have denied "imputed righteousness" which comes at justification. Wesley intends in his sermon on "The Lord Our Righteousness" to show that he was in basic agreement with Luther[60] and Calvin.[61] Neither Luther nor Calvin believed merely in imputed righteousness. Like Wesley, they also stressed the actual change which occurred in the justified person. What Wesley wished to guard against, however, was the antinomian belief (a hyper-Calvinism) that one could be holy in Christ and yet be devoid of all actual righteousness.[62] Wesley insisted upon "inherent righteousness" as being "consequent upon" imputed righteousness.[63]

Though Wesley was in basic agreement with Luther and Calvin in regard to the doctrine of justification by faith alone, Wesley went beyond them in insisting upon the full appropriation of Christ's righteousness. In this respect, the time factor is a crucial part of Wesley's concept of perfection. Wesley believed that the full appropriation of righteousness was a present possibility under the New Covenant of grace. While Luther and Calvin emphasized the eschatalogical appropriation of full righteousness, rather than its present actuality in the life of the justified believer; Wesley believed that the full appropriation of personal righteousness could be had here and now, subsequent in time to the experience of justification. Wesley agreed with Luther and Calvin on the eschatological aspect of righteousness (justification by faith), yet he taught that subsequent to justification the believer should go on to experience the full appropriation of righteousness.

Unfortunately, the concept of the perfection of the believer's righteousness as being subsequent to justification has often been interpreted strictly in accord with the modern concept of linear time. Consequently, the doctrine of perfection as a second work of grace has often been discredited, through the static notion that there are only two absolute crisis points in which righteousness is appropriated. To be sure, Wesley stressed *the second work* of sanctifying grace, but it would be a misunderstanding to think of "two works of grace" as disjointed and absolute events. It has already been pointed out that the biblical concept of salvation history presupposed a view of time which was a synthesis of the "circular view" and a "linear view." Hence, the biblical view of time is neither purely sequential, nor circular; rather, the biblical concept of the flow of time presupposes both the idea of crisis points and an ongoing process. The past event in the flow of time is never merely past, but is constantly relived and updated in the present. The events in time constitute both crisis and process. Any view which eliminates the dynamics of this tension between process and crisis is inadequate. To speak of two works of grace in absolutist terms, or to speak of two works of grace in mere fluid terms is a misconception of Wesley's understanding.

John Fletcher speaks with cogency to this point. He shows that the life of perfect love has both a crisis and process aspect. It may be that some believers will have a number of crisis points before the experience of perfect love becomes a habit of life. In fact, he testified from his own personal life that he had a number of experiences of perfect love before it became a daily habit of his Christian life.[64] Fletcher uses the metaphor of the Israelites crossing the Jordan River on several occasions before becoming settled in the land of Canaan, to illustrate the progressive aspect of sanctification.

> For we assert, that as a carnal professor may occasionally cross Jordan, take a turn into the good land, and come back into the wilderness, as the spies did in the days of Joshua; so a spiritual man, who lives in Canaan, may occasionally draw back, and take a turn in the wilderness, especially before he is "strengthened, established, and settled" under his heavenly vine, in the good land that flows with spiritual milk and honey.[65]

Fletcher here shows that one may have a number of experiences with the Holy Spirit in his sanctifying grace before the life of holiness becomes a habit of life.

While keeping in mind this flexibility of the meaning of a "second" work of grace, one can appeal to two Old Testament themes which prefigure the sanctifying experience of the Pentecostal kerygma which is subsequent to the justifying experience of the Resurrection kerygma, as support for Wesley's concept of Christian perfection. These two themes are the crossing of the Jordan River into Canaan Land, and the circumcision of Abraham. In fact, both of these themes appear in Wesley's and Fletcher's writings as descriptive of the doctrine of perfect love. The concept of circumcision will be discussed in the next chapter. The focus of the following discussion will be upon the crossing of the Jordan River.

Possession of the Promised Land completed the redemption which was begun with the Exodus from the land of bondage. The goal of being "led forth" from Egypt was to be "led into" the Promised Land (Ps. 105:43-45). Hence, the Israelites were frequently reminded: "I . . . brought you out . . . [to] bring you in" (Exod. 6:7-8).

After the crossing of the Jordan River, "all the people that were born on the way in the wilderness after they had come out of Egypt" (Josh. 5:5) were circumcized. "And the Lord said to Joshua, 'This day I have rolled away the reproach of Egypt from you' " (Josh. 5:9). The crossing into Canaan Land thus *perfected* their deliverance from Egypt, for they had been set free from Egyptian bondage in order to be established in the land "flowing with milk and honey."

As it will be pointed out in the next chapter, circumcision was the "guarantee" (seal) that the Israelites would possess the Canaan Land. Now that Joshua had led them through the Jordan River into Canaan, it was indeed fitting that the event should be celebrated with the rite of circumcision (Josh. 5:9).

The "reproach" from which they had at last been totally liberated was their slavery in Egypt. John Bright comments on this passage in Joshua 5:9: "The rite [of circumcision] symbolically rolled away the reproach of their slavery in Egypt."[66] It was one thing to be taken out of Egypt; it was another thing for "Egypt" (uncleanness) to be taken out of them. That is, it was one thing for the Israelites to be saved from Egyptian bondage; it was another thing for them to be a completely free people to serve God in a land which was truly theirs.

The crossing of the Red Sea symbolized their deliverance from bondage, and it prefigures the New Testament concept of justification by faith. On the other hand, the crossing of

the Jordan River into Canaan Land symbolized the com-
pletion of their liberation which was begun with the Exodus,
and it prefigures the New Testament concept of sanctification
through the Spirit. Another way of expressing this theological
parallel is to say that the Exodus event corresponds to the idea
of "imputed righteousness," whereas the crossing of the
Jordan River into Canaan Land corresponds to the idea
of "imparted righteousness." That is, the Exodus event
pointed forward to the goal of the possession of Canaan Land,
whereas the crossing of the Jordan River was the appropriation of that goal.

As it has been previously shown, the Exodus and the
crossing into the Promised Land were the two decisive historical moments which brought into being the life of Israel as
a people. Likewise, the Resurrection of Jesus from the dead
and Pentecost were the two decisive historical events which
made possible the Christian life, giving rise to the Church as
the "holy people of God." Pentecost made possible the perfecting of grace begun with Jesus' resurrection. That is why
Barth speaks of Pentecost as "the confirmation of Easter."
The Resurrection and Pentecost are thus extended in time,
yet they form a single complex event.

The Resurrection means for the Christian life that believers
are taken out of Egypt; Pentecost means that the uncleanness
(reproach) of Egypt is taken out of the believer, so that he can
then meet the requirement of perfect love. The whole point
of God's rescuing the Israelites from Egypt and bringing them
into the Promised Land was "to the end that they should keep
his statues, and observe his laws" given at Sinai (Ps. 105:45).
Entrance into the Promised Land meant the Egyptian "reproach" (uncleanness) was removed and they could now
fully serve their Lord.

Yet, the Israelites were subsequently sent into exile and
their land taken away from them because they did not obey
God's commandments. It was not until the kingdom was to
be restored, when a New Covenant would be instituted, that
the ability to love God perfectly (Deut. 30:6) would render
them capable of obedience to God. This new reality was to

be made possible by a new Exodus (Jesus' resurrection) and a new Conquest (Pentecost). It is not enough, however, for these saving events to be in the historical past; rather, they must be updated in the life of every believer.

Edmond Jacob specifically calls attention to the decisiveness of the Exodus and the crossing of the Jordan River into Canaan Land as events of the past which were to be personalized (actualized) in the life of every Israelite in the present time. He writes:

> The invitation which we read in several places (Dt. 5.3: 26.16-19; Ps. 95.7ff.) to respond "to-day" to God's call is not explained solely by the solidarity which unites the people through successive generations, but supposes some definite act which was to make that solidarity evident: the insistence on the fact that it was not "with the fathers" that God concluded the covenant (Dt. 5.3), but with the present generation, proves that the stress was placed less on the solidarity and the historicity of facts in the strict sense than on their actualization.[67]

It was not sufficient to live with the meaning of what God had done for their fathers in the past; the same saving events of history were to be appropriated in the life of every Israelite.

Jacob further shows that the personalizing of the saving events of Israel's past history was accomplished through the Word of God. The whole point of worship was "the commemoration of events" in which God was praised as the mighty deliverer of his people. Both through liturgy, and possibly through, "dramatic representation of the great events of the past such as the Exodus from Egypt and the crossing of the Jordan," God's saving acts were to be a present realization. Jacob writes: "Whether by gesture or simply by word, the recalling of these events had as its object the overcoming of chronological and spatial distance and the real introduction of the onlookers into the presence of the God who not only acted there and then, but who still acts *hic et nunc*."[68]

The Exodus-Conquest sequence thus formed a pattern of

salvation for the individual Israelite. This can be especially seen in the liturgical use of the Psalms. "Remember me, O Lord, when thou showest favor to thy people; help me when thou deliverest them [Exodus theme] ; that I may see the prosperity of thy chosen ones, that I may rejoice in the gladness of thy nation, that I may glory with thy heritage [Conquest theme]" (Ps. 106:4-5; cf. 106:9,24; Ps. 66:5ff.; Ps. 105:37-45).

The possession of the Promised Land involved both a crisis and process. The two crisis moments came with the crossing of the Red Sea and the Jordan River. When Joshua led the people across the Jordan River, it marked the realization of God's promise to Abraham. They were commanded to take 12 stones (representing the 12 tribes of Israel, Josh. 4:8) from the Jordan River and erect them at Gilgal as a memorial of the day they set foot in the Promised Land, when the Lord "rolled away the reproach of Egypt" from them (Josh. 5:9). The decisive nature of these events were such that it would be apparent to everyone that God had done a mighty work. "When your children ask their fathers in time to come, 'What do these stones mean?' then you shall let your children know, 'Israel passed over this Jordan on dry ground.' For the Lord your God dried up the waters of the Jordan for you until you passed over, as the Lord your God did to the Red Sea, which he dried up for us until we passed over, so that all the peoples of the earth may know that the hand of the Lord is mighty; that you may fear the Lord your God for ever" (Josh. 4:23-24; cf. 5:6).

Yet it was not until the reign of David that the ideal boundary of the Promised Land (Deut. 11:24; Gen. 15:18-19; Acts 13:19 became an actuality. The Conquest came about only after much effort, lapses, and renewed trust (Josh 11:18; 13:1ff; 18:3). Likewise, the Christian life involves both crisis and process. The crisis moments were the Resurrection of Jesus and the Pentecostal outpouring of the Holy Spirit experienced anew in the life of the individual believer. The decisive nature of the Pentecostal event was such that it would be apparent to everyone that God had done a mighty work: "the rush of a mighty wind," and "tongues as of fire" (Acts 2:2). Yet the process of the Christian life is a life-long process. The book of Acts, as the record of the struggles, sufferings, and growth of the body of believers, is illustrative of this process.

A. C. Hervey, in his exposition of Acts 2:43 in *The Pulpit Commentary*, points out the similarity between the Pentecostal event and the Israelites' immediate arrival in Canaan Land (Deut. 11:25).

> This seems to be spoken of the fear which fell upon the whole people, and restrained them from interfering with the disciples. Just as at the first settlement of Israel in the land of Canaan God laid the fear of them and the dread of them upon all the land (Deut. xi. 25), so now the fear engendered by the events on the day of Pentecost, by the signs and wonders which followed and by the wonderful unity and holiness of the new-born Church, so wrought upon every soul at Jerusalem that all enmity was paralyzed, and the disciples had time to multiply and to consolidate and establish themselves before the storm of persecution fell upon them.[69]

Even as the fear of God united the Israelites in their conquest of the Promised Land (Josh 5:1), so the apostles were united in faith to conquer the world. They were thereby established in the Lord before the storm of persecution came upon them as they went forth to fulfill the Great Commission of making Pentecost a reality for the whole world. Though they experienced tension and setbacks (e.g., Paul's controversy with Peter and his dispute with John Mark; the tensions involving the ceremonial laws and the meaning of freedom in Christ), yet they remained firm in the faith and continually were filled with the Holy Spirit.

Wesley did not systematically develop the idea of "a second work of grace" in connection with the crossing of the Jordan River, though he did allude to it. However, he did defend the idea of a second work of grace largely on the grounds of "experience" and specific Scriptural references. In this respect, Wesley shows that the Christians at Corinth were "carnal Christians" not yet "Spiritual" Christians — "Their hearts were *truly*, yet not *entirely* renewed."[70]

Having sought to show that contemporary experience as well as Scripture teaches that some are justified but not entirely sanctified, Wesley believes that because of the promises of Scriptures,[71] the prayers for entire sanctification in Scripture,[72] the commands in Scripture for it,[73] and an example of one who had achieved it in Scripture,[74] entire sanctification is an experience to be achieved in this life. Hence he believes that the doctrine of entire sanctification is subsequent to justification both because of experience and Scripture. However, he says if experience refuted the doctrine, "I should be clearly convinced that we had all mistaken the meaning of those Scriptures."[75] Also, notice this progression: "(1) There is such a thing as perfection; for it is again and again mentioned in Scripture. (2) It is not so early as justification; for justified persons are to 'go on unto perfection' (Heb. vi.1). (3) It is not so late as death; for St. Paul speaks of living men that were perfect (Phil. iii.15)."[76]

Though Wesley taught the subsequent aspect of sanctifying grace, his writings stressed the dynamic and ongoing realization of the life of grace. The idea of a second work of grace is understandable only in the light of a dynamic processive view of time. The two critical moments in the history of our personal salvation are justification by faith and sanctification through the Spirit. They are being continuously appropriated through the preached Word, the sacraments, and a personal devotional life.

### 4. The Salvific Significance of the Distinction Between the "Jesus of History" and the "Christ of Faith"

In chapter three, we pointed out Bultmann's exposition of the Pauline distinction between the Spirit-endowed Christians as opposed to non-spiritual (i.e., not Spirit-endowed) Christians. This distinction is explicable in the light of "a doctrine of dispensations," which is not altogether unlike Fletcher's project of thought (discussed in Chapter VI).

This Pauline distinction between the Spirit-endowed Christian as opposed to the Christian who is not Spirit-endowed closely corresponds *experientially* to the historical distinction between the earthly Jesus and the Christ of faith. The debate over the relationship between the historical Jesus and the kerygmatic Christ is a commonplace in contemporary theological scholarship. But what has not received adequate consideration is its implication for interpreting the nature of Christian experience. If the decisiveness of Jesus' Resurrection from the dead and the outpouring of the Pentecostal Spirit for Christian experience is to be appreciated, then the historical distinction between the Jesus of Nazareth and the Christ of faith must be clearly kept in mind.

Bultmann has, in an important sense, rightly pointed out that there is a difference between the Jesus of history and the Christ of faith. The earthly Jesus is not simply the exalted Christ. In fact, Jesus did not become the Messiah until after his Resurrection: "Acts 2:36 and Rom. 1:4 . . . show that in the earliest Church, Jesus' messiahship was dated from the resurrection."[77] Hence, the Synoptic gospels speak of the coming of the Messiah, not of a return of the Messiah. This means that the earthly activity of Jesus "was not yet considered messianic by the earliest Church."[78] Calvin also maintained that "he truly inaugurated his Kingdom only at his ascension into heaven."[79] That is, "Christ was invested with lordship over heaven and earth" because he had conquered death and destroyed the power of Satan's kingdom and through his ascension to his Father he "entered into possession of the government committed to him."[80] This difference *in time* between his earthly and heavenly states must be interpreted in a realistic sense. A real and definitive action of God occurred in the process of time. Something really new occurred.

It is of paramount importance to distinguish between the exalted Christ ( = the Pentecostal Spirit) and the earthly Jesus. While this distinction has been exaggerated into a bifurcation for Bultmann, it is nonetheless an important distinction if the significance of Pentecost is to be fully appreciated. The Jesus Christ proclaimed in the apostolic kerygma is not simply identical to the Jesus of history. For the historical Jesus was not yet raised from the dead and exalted to the Father. There is a genuine transformation in the humanity of Jesus after his Resurrection and exaltation. This transformation from his earthly to his heavenly state is an essential aspect of salvation. His life without his Resurrection is not salvific. Nor is his Resurrection fully salvific without his exaltation to the Father and the consequent sending of his Spirit. The Jesus Christ of the apostolic proclamation is *functionally* and *devotionally* identical to the Holy Spirit, though ontologically there is a real differentiation between the Spirit and the Son within the triunity of God's essence.

Bultmann's denial, however, that there is any continuity between the earthly Jesus and the Christ of faith is surely unwarranted.[81] Likewise his refusal to allow for any real continuity between the Old Testament kerygma and the apostolic kerygma is unwarranted. It is indeed most surprising for him to call the Old Testament "the miscarriage of history." Yet his emphasis upon the radical newness of the Christian proclamation is not to be minimized. Surely the apostolic interpretation of the earthly Jesus is given in retrospect from the standpoint of the exalted Christ. The gospels make no attempt to give a mere biography of the earthly Jesus. Rather, the true significance of the earthly Jesus can be seen only from the standpoint of his Resurrection from the dead and exaltation.

Bultmann, in a qualified sense, is right to insist that the preaching of Jesus Christ (i.e., the exalted Christ) originated with the primitive Christian community rather than with the earthly Jesus. Yet Bultmann's denial that the exalted Christ can be accepted as the risen Jesus of Nazareth is a rejection of the essence of the apostolic preaching. The center of the apostolic preaching is seen in Peter's Pentecostal sermon that the exalted Christ, whose Spirit has now come into the world, is none other than the crucified Jesus (Acts 2:32-33).

The earthly Jesus had spoken of the disciples' inability to understand himself as the Christ. Only through the Pentecostal gift of the Spirit were they enabled to understand truly his life and teaching. Hence, all that is said about the earthly Jesus, while it is historically based, could be interpreted only from the standpoint of Easter and Pentecost. The clue for interpreting the history of Jesus, *as well as the history of Israel*, is the faith of the earliest Christians in the risen and exalted Lord. One can see the decisiveness of the Resurrection and Pentecost as the two determining events for the Christian revelation, as well as for the Christian life. Without the fact of the risen Lord, the history of Israel and the history of Jesus would have been an enigma.

The apostolic proclamation is clear in this regard. Without personal participation in the Resurrected life of Jesus Christ and in the Pentecostal gift of the Holy Spirit, there can be no true Christian life. With all literalness, Paul's statement that we no longer know Christ after the flesh should be accepted (II Cor. 5:16). The Christ who is worshipped is the one who died and rose again (vs. 15). This means that the believer is one who shares in his Resurrected life; because of this a new creation, even as the humanity of the exalted Christ is the new creation of God (vs. 16-17).

It can be said that all that Paul has to say about Jesus Christ is meant to be a statement about the risen and exalted Christ, not the Jesus of history per se. This is clearly seen in Romans 1:4, where Paul shows that Jesus Christ is the Son of God because of his Resurrection from the dead and the Pentecostal outpouring of his sanctifying Spirit. "The gospel concerning his Son, who was . . . designated Son of God in power according to the [Pentecostal] Spirit of holiness by his Resurrection from the dead [Easter], Jesus Christ our Lord."

Unlike Bultmann's interpretation, there is continuity between the earthly Jesus and the exalted Christ; for the exalted Christ is none other than the Jesus who died and rose again. Yet the exalted Christ is not identical to the earthly Jesus, for the Jesus who died also rose to a new kind of life. His resurrection was not a mere resuscitation of a dead body, but the transformation of the earthly body into a spiritual (heavenly) body (I Cor. 15:44). His Resurrection meant the restoration of humanity; hence the believer's salvation is dependent upon a participation in his redeemed human nature. To be in Christ is to share in his death and Resurrection (Romans 6:4). It also means to be "a dwelling place of God in the Spirit" (Eph. 2:22).

Further, the breaking of the bread and the drinking of the cup in Holy Communion is a real sharing in the redeemed humanity of Jesus Christ (I Cor. 10:16) Jesus did say: "Do this in remembrance of me" (I Cor. 11:24); but to remember involves more than mere intellectual recall. To remember is to share in *the same experience*. In order to protect this concept of participation from magical connotations, Calvin defined a sacrament as a sign. But to protect this sacrament from the idea of mere recollection, he defined it as a seal, i.e., an actual appropriation of grace through the physical signs of bread and wine.[82]

A presupposition for understanding the saving significance of the sacraments is the biblical concept of historical time. As it has already been seen, time is not circular, as is the Platonic thought; it is not the moving image of timeless-eternity; it is not a mirage. The idea of time presupposed in the biblical concept of salvation history is not merely sequential; it is not the ceaseless flow of "nows" which become a mere past, with the future being simply the unrealized present. Rather, the biblical idea of time is a synthesis of the circular and sequential concepts of time. Another way of defining the biblical idea of time is to point out that God is the basis of the continuity within the flow of time because he, as Creator *ex nihilo*, stands beyond all finite time. He is the power of the unbounded future (Pannenberg).[83] In this way it can be seen that the sacraments are a sign and seal. The past event of Jesus' Resurrection is really past and cannot be historically repeated. The Lord's supper is a "sign." Yet the believer today can *really* participate in the past event of Jesus' Resurrection. The Lord's Supper is a "seal," i.e., a *real* participation in the historical event.

This dynamic view of time helps to explain the continuity

between the exalted Christ and the earthly Jesus. It also explains how the Resurrection of Jesus and the sending of his Spirit are both historical events of the past, as well as living realities in the present. The risen and exalted Christ mediates salvation to us by allowing us to share in his redeemed humanity. This means that we are enabled to participate in his Resurrection and exaltation. Consequently, the Church is the extension of his incarnation. It is the collective body of those who have shared in his risen and exalted life — the fellowship of the Resurrection (Easter), which was brought into being through the Holy Spirit (Pentecost). The Church does not claim to be divine; it only claims to be truly human, because through the Holy Spirit the believer is completely renewed in the image of God by his participation in Christ's humanity.

The whole intent of the incarnation was for God to reconcile fallen humanity to himself. Yet only God could reconcile fallen humanity to himself, because the sinfulness of man precluded the possibility of his saving himself. Jesus Christ redeems us because he is identical to God *and* humanity. That is, God *really* joined himself (without compromising his deity) to fallen humanity, which he redeemed through Jesus' Resurrection and exaltation.

This means that the kingdom of God has already come, because Christ began to reign in his Church on the day of Pentecost when his Spirit was poured out upon believers. To be sure, the Church is not yet identical to the kingdom of God, since the coming kingdom will be consummated only in the eschaton. The Church now is the historical continuation of the incarnate and exalted Christ through the outpouring of the Spirit. It is the earthly setting of the body of Christ. It is the mystical body of the exalted Christ through which believers experience a new humanity (Eph. 2:15), because they really participate in the redeemed human nature of Jesus Christ. This is not to suggest a pantheistic identification with the exalted Christ; this is no mystical absorption into Christ's divinity, but rather a real participation in his glorified humanity.

However, it is entirely possible for one to be in the Church, through participating in Jesus' Resurrected life, without having appropriated the sanctifying fullness of his Holy Spirit. To be sure, the full righteousness of Christ is imputed to the believer at the moment of his incorporation into the Church, but each believer must come to appropriate for himself this full righteousness through the agency of the Pentecostal Spirit.

This interpretation of the Christian life is explicable only in the light of the biblical concept of historical time as a mediating synthesis between the circular and sequential notions of time. A believer may be experientially living as a pre-Pentecostal disciple. Subsequently, he may personally receive the fulness of the Pentecostal Spirit, even as the disciples did on the day of Pentecost. Further, believers in Christ have *proleptically* experienced the final hope of future glory in heaven, through the "earnest" of the Spirit (Eph. 1:14; 4:30).

The dynamic view of time as a synthesis between the circular and sequential concepts of time helps in understanding the Pauline differentiation between the dispensation of the Old Covenant and the New Covenant. The Old Covenant brings "death" and "condemnation," but the New Covenant bestows "life" and "righteousness" (II Cor. 3:6, 9). The Old Covenant was written "on tablets of stone" (II Cor. 3:3), but the New Covenant is "written not with ink but with the Spirit of the living God [Pentecost theme]" (II Cor. 3:3). Paul asks: "Will not the dispensation of the Spirit be attended with greater splendor? For if there was splendor in the dispensation of condemnation, the dispensation of righteousness must far exceed it in splendor. Indeed, in this case, what once had splendor has come to have no splendor at all, because of the splendor that surpasses it. For if what faded away came with splendor, what is permanent must have much more splendor" (II Cor. 3:8-11).

The decisive feature of the New Covenant is that the Pentecostal Spirit has brought about the "dispensation of righteousness." The superiority of the dispensation of the Spirit is the fact that the permanent and universal gift of righteousness has been realized and is now available in

Christ through his Spirit. "Now the Lord is the [Pentecostal] Spirit, and where the Spirit of the Lord is, there is freedom [from sin]" (II Cor. 3:17).

This freedom from sin, accomplished by the dispensation of the Pentecostal Spirit, is the corollary to being infused with the righteousness of Christ: "And we all, with unveiled face, beholding the glory of the Lord, are being changed into his likeness from one degree of glory to another; for this comes from the Lord who is the Spirit" (II Cor. 3:18). Paul does not belittle the Old Dispensation of the law. It had its own splendor, but it lacked the fulness of the dispensation of the Spirit with its permanent gift of righteousness.

The Old Covenant contained an offer of grace and glory typified in the brightness and splendor of Moses' face. However, it was not an experience of enduring grace, but a "fading" glory. God's sanctifying grace was certainly available to those under the Old Covenant, but the New Covenant ushered in the fulness of the dispensation of righteousness because the exalted Christ has sent His Spirit into the believers' hearts. The newness of the New Covenant ought not to be understood in such a way that the experience of grace was not available before the arrival of the New Covenant. Yet the radical newness of the New Covenant ought not to be obscured by thinking of it only in terms of an extension of the Old Covenant.

The radical newness of the Christ event means that something absolutely unique has occurred in history, comparable to the absolute uniqueness of the creation of the universe by God out of nothing (*creatio ex nihilo*). As a result of the Resurrection of Jesus from the dead and the Pentecostal gift of the Spirit, something absolutely new occurred. Something came into being which was not there before! That persons under the Old Covenant experienced grace is explicable only in the light of the absolute uniqueness of the Christ event. The Old had its splendor only because it anticipates the greater splendor of the New Covenant. Persons in the Old Covenant experienced grace through the event of Jesus Christ, because the death of Christ had retroactive significance. This illustrates the idea that time is not simply linear in a mechanical sense. God transcends time; hence there is continuity between the past and present, as well as the future. The future reality is also a part of God's knowledge, because He is the power of the unbounded future. Since he is transcendent, and as Creator *ex nihilo* stands above all finite reality (including the finite future), there is a continuity to time whereby the present includes the past and is moving toward the future of God's unbounded reality.

This means that the atonement of Jesus Christ was retroactively redemptive for those under the Old Covenant. But now that Jesus Christ has been raised from the dead for our justification and that he has sent the Holy Spirit for our sanctification, the permanent gift of righteousness is universally available to everyone. It can be seen from this passage in II Cor. 3:13ff. that Rahner rightly points out that the Pentecostal Spirit is not the same as the Spirit before Pentecost. The incarnate Spirit, i.e., the Spirit in believers who in their togetherness constitute the Church, is the exalted Christ. This passage further illustrates that Fletcher's doctrine of dispensations is generally in accord with the Pauline interpretation of the covenant. Of special significance is Fletcher's distinction between "babes in Christ" who are *experientially* disciples of John the Baptist or pre-Pentecostal followers of the earthly Jesus as opposed to the believers who have *experienced* the Spirit of the exalted Christ (See Chapter VI).

---

[1] *Space, Time, and Deity* (London: Macmillan, 1927), I, 91; cf. J. Alexander Gunn, *The Problem of Time* (London: George Allen and Unwin, Ltd., 1929) for a significant philosophical analysis of time.

[2] Edmond Jacob, *Theology of the New Testament*, p. 138.

[3] *Church Dogmatics*, I, Part II, 46-60.

[4] *Ibid.*, I, Part II, 46.

[5] *Ibid.*, I, Part II, 47.

[6] Karl Rahner, *Foundations of Christian Faith*, trans. William V. Dych (New York: Seabury Press, 1978), p. 78; cf. E. L. Mascall, *He Who Is* (1st ed. rev.; Hamden, Connecticut: Archon Books, 1966), pp. 97-98, 103; Jürgen Moltmann, *Theology of Hope*, trans. James W. Leitch (New York: Harper and Row, 1967), p. 179.

[7] E. L. Mascall, *He Who Is*, p. 25.

[8] Soren Kierkegaard, *Philosophical Fragments*, trans. David F. Swenson (Princeton University Press, 1962), p. 30.

[9] Kierkegaard, *A Concluding Unscientific Postscript*, trans. David F. Sevenson and Walter Lowrie (Princeton University Press, 1941), p. 122.

[10] *Foundations of Christian Faith*, p. 62; cf. Mascall, *He Who Is*, pp. 102ff.

[11] Kaufmann, *The Religion of Israel*, p. 298; cf. Barth, *Church Dogmatics,* I, Part I, 541f.

[12] B. W. Anderson, "Creation," *The Interpreter's Dictionary of the Bible,* A - D (1962), p. 727.

[13] Alan Richardson, "Salvation, Savior," *The Interpreter's Dictionary of the Bible*, R - Z (1962), p. 172.

[14] *Ibid.*

[15] *Ibid.*, p. 173.

[16] Oscar Gullmann, *Christ and Time*, trans. Floyd V. Filson (London: SCM Press Ltd., 1951), p. 37.

[17] Cullmann, *Salvation in History*, p. 57.

[18] "Creation," *The Interpreter's Dictionary of the Bible,* A - D, p. 727.

[19] *Ibid.*

[20] *Ibid.*

[21] *Church Dogmatics*, I, Part I, 472.

[22] Cf. Barth, *Church Dogmatics*, I, Part I, 447, 473.

[23]C. F. D. Moule, "God, NT," *The Interpreter's Dictionary of the Bible*, E - J, p. 432.

[24]*Ibid.*, p. 430; cf. Karl Barth, *Church Dogmatics*, I, Part I, 472.

[25]*Ibid.*, p. 433.

[26]*Ibid.*

[27]*Salvation in History*, pp. 103ff.

[28]Wolfhart Pannenberg, *Jesus – God and Man*, tran. Duane A. Priebe and Lewis L. Wilkins (Philadelphia: Westminster Press, 1968), p. 132; Barth, *Church Dogmatics*, I, Part II, 64, 111, 114.

[29]T. F. Torrance, *Space/Time and Resurrection* (Grand Rapids: Wm. B. Eerdmans, 1976), pp. 65-66.

[30]*Church Dogmatics*, I, Part II, 111; *ibid.*, I, Part I, 445, 447, 472; cf. Torrance, pp. 69-70.

[31]*Ibid.*, I, Part II, p. 114.

[32]*Ibid.*

[33]Cf. Torrance, pp. 64, 69-70; Barth, *Church Dogmatics*, I, Part I, 445, 517, 534.

[34]Cf. Torrance, pp. 64, 69-70.

[35]*Church Dogmatics*, IV, Part IV, 30.

[36]Cf. Barth, *Church Dogmatics*, I, Part I, 541-557.

[37]Torrance, p. 69.

[38]*Jesus – God and Man*, p. 180.

[39]Cf. Eberhard Jüngel, *The Doctrine of the Trinity* (Grand Rapids: Wm. B. Eerdmans, 1976), pp. 35-36 *et passim*.

[40]*The Work of the Holy Spirit*, trans. Henri De Vries (New York: Funk and Wagnalls, 1900), p. 15.

[41]*Heidelberg Catechism* (Cleveland, Ohio: Central Publishing House, 1907), revised ed., p. 37.

[42]Cf. Chapter VII.

[43]*The Documents of Vatican II*, ed. Austin P. Hannery (Grand Rapids: Wm. B. Eerdmans, 1975), pp. 351-352.

[44] Cf. Chapter VII.

[45] Fletcher, *Checks*, I, 590.

[46]*Ibid.*

[47]Lindström, *Wesley and Sanctification*, 11-18.

[48] *The Standard Sermons of John Wesley*, 433.

[49]*Ibid.*, 427-428.

[50]Paul Tillich, *Systematic Theology* (University of Chicago Press, 1953), III, 223.

[51]*Ibid.*, II, 178.

[52] *Ibid.*, II, 179.

[53]*Ibid.*, III, 225.

[54] *Systematic Theology*, I, 60-62; II, 27; III, 420-421.

[55]*Systematic Theology*, III, 224, 226.

[56]*Church Dogmatics*, I, Part II, 308.

[57]*Ibid.*

[58]*Ibid.*, I, Part II, 355.

[59]*Ibid.*

[60]*The Standard Sermons of John Wesley*, II, 425.

[61] *Ibid.*, II, 432-433.

[62]*Ibid.*, II, 438.

[63]*Ibid.*, II, 434.

[64] Paul Rees, *The Valiant Vicar of Madeley*, (University Park, Iowa: John Fletcher College, 1937), p. 21.

[65] Fletcher, *Checks*, II, 546.

[66] "The Book of Joshua," introduction and exegesis by John Bright, exposition by Joseph R. Sezoo, *The Interpreter's Bible* (Nashville: Abingdon Press, 1953), II, 585.

[67] Jacob, p. 266.

[68] *Ibid.*, p. 267.

[69] *The Acts of the Apostles, The Pulpit Commentary*, I, 55.

[70] *The Standard Sermons of John Wesley*, II, 371.

[71] *Plain Account of Christian Perfection*, p. 35.

[72] *Ibid.*, p. 36.

[73] *Ibid.*, p. 37.

[74] *Ibid.*

[75] *Ibid.*, p. 58.

[76] *Ibid.*, p. 106.

[77] *Theology of the New Testament*, I, 27.

[78] *Ibid.*, I, 33.

[79] *Institutes of the Christian Religion*, I, 522.

[80] *Ibid.*, I, 524.

[81] Bultmann, "The Primitive Christian Kerygma and the Historical Jesus," *The Historical Jesus and the Kerygmatic Christ*, trans. and ed. Carl E. Braaten and Roy A. Harrisville (New York: Abingdon Press, 1964), p. 18.

[82] *Institutes of the Christian Religion*, II, 1276ff.

[83] Wolfhart Pannenberg, *Theology and the Kingdom of God*, pp. 51-71.

# CHAPTER V.

## CIRCUMCISION OF THE HEART

In addition to the language of Canaan Land, Wesley also used the convenantal language of circumcision as descriptive of Christian perfection. Wesley defined the circumcision of the heart as "that habitual disposition of soul which, in the sacred writings, is termed holiness; and which directly implies, the being cleansed from sin, 'from all filthiness both of flesh and spirit'; and, by consequence, the being endued with those virtues which were also in Christ Jesus; the being so 'renewed in the spirit of our mind,' as to be 'perfect as our Father in heaven is perfect.' "[1] In May, 1765, he wrote to a friend: "January 1, 1733, I preached the sermon on the Circumcision of the Heart, which contains all that I now teach concerning salvation from all sin, and loving God with an undivided heart. . . . This was then, as it is now, my idea of perfection."[2]

This theological linkage between spiritual circumcision and Christian perfection can be exegetically defended by developing three implications of the rite of circumcision. It denotes cleansing, perfect love, and the appropriation (seal) of righteousness.

Since the rite of circumcision has fundamental significance for Wesley's idea of perfection, it is most important to point out the generally accepted consensus in Old Testament scholarship that the rite of circumcision essentially implies the idea of cleansing. More specifically, the (inherited) flesh excised in the formal rite of circumcision prefigured the New Testament concept of being cleansed from original (inherited) sin "by putting off the body of flesh in the circumcision of Christ" (Col. 2:11).

Even before Abraham, circumcision "was a well known and already understood *symbol of purity*."[3] Kaufmann Kohler, a Jewish scholar of Hebrew Union College, has shown that *'arelin* (uncircumcised) is "used synonymously with 'tame' (unclean) for heathen (Isa. 1ii.1)" and that in other instances it "is also employed for 'unclean' " (Lev. xxvi.41, Ezek. xliv. 7, 9).[4] Walther Eichrodt also shows that circumcision and cleansing form a single theme and that the rite of circumcision was altogether replaced with its spiritual meaning of cleansing in the prophets.[5] As Kohler shows, it can be seen that circumcision symbolized "an indispensable act of national consecration and purification."[6] Likewise, J. P. Hyatt has shown that "circumcision represented the removal of impurity, and thus was an act of purification" and that this is further attested indirectly by the fact that "one of the words used by Arabs for circumcision is *tuhr*, 'cleansing.' "[7]

The origin of the practice of circumcision is unknown, but its theological significance is first given to Abraham in Genesis 17. While his own circumcision was understood primarily in a formal sense, it did have at the same time an ethical signification. G. F. Oehler writes: "It binds him to obedience to God, whose covenant sign he bears in his body and to a blameless walk before Him (cf. Gen. xvii.1). Thus it is the *symbol of the renewal and purification of heart*."[8] Later on this spiritual significance is set forth by Moses (Deut. 10:16); 30:6) and the prophets (Jer. 4:4; 9:25; Ezek. 44:7).[9] Hence, von Rad points out that this spiritualizing interpretation is based on a prior belief that the idea of circumcision was "an act of bodily purification and dedication."[10] In this respect, Immanuel Benzinger shows that "not only among the Jews, but also among the Egyptians and most other peoples by whom circumcision is practiced, the uncircumcised are regarded as unclean."[11] This bodily purification by which the inherited "unclean" flesh is excised thus became a symbol of a spiritual circumcision by which the impurity of sin is cleansed.

Through the practice of circumcision antedated Abraham, its theological significance given in the Old Testament was unique. Oehler has pointed out that "the *historical origin* and the *religious import* of circumcision must be carefully distinguished."[12] That circumcision was understood as signifying cleanness must be understood first and foremost in the light of Israel's absolutely unique concept of God's holiness and transcendence and man's sinfulness. Circumcision was "a symbol of the purification and sanctification of the whole life" because it symbolized living in the presence of God.[13] In this respect, excising the flesh in circumcision symbolized a removal of "the inborn guilt and impurity of human nature."[14] To enjoy a covenantal relationship with a transcendent, holy God "presupposes that the natural life" which "is tainted by impurity" is removed.[15] Because God was holy, it was required that Israel be holy (Lev. 11:44). Circumcision typified this holiness (Gen. 17:1).

That the rite of circumcision implied sanctification is clearly enunciated in the Jewish ceremony in which the following prayer is said immediately before and after the act of circumcision: "Blessed art Thou, O Lord our God, King of the Universe, who hast sanctified us by Thy commandments, and hast enjoined us to perform the commandment of circumcision."[16] The *flesh* thus circumcised represented an act of sanctification.[17]

It is highly significant that Paul links this concept of the flesh ($\sigma \acute{\alpha} \rho \xi$) with the idea of original sin, i.e., inherited sin (Col. 2:13). The sin of Adam which has been passed on to every person (Rom. 5:12-19) is labelled the "flesh" (Rom. 7:14).[18] As S. J. De Vries shows, Paul identifies "the flesh" with "the principle of sin which lies within the heart" and is thus "responsible for the unruliness of these desires"(Rom. 13:14; Gal. 5:16-21).[19]

Rudolf Bultmann has probably given more attention to the Pauline concept of the flesh than other recent New Testament scholars. His exposition is especially illuminating for seeing the relationship between the rite of circumcision and Paul's use of the word σάρξ. This present discussion will draw freely from his exegesis, but it will do so without intending to imply his agreement with the general thrust of the theological position being embraced here.

Bultmann shows that for Paul the original sin of Adam (Rom. 5:12-19) is an attitude of pride and self-sufficiency. He writes: "At the base of the idea of inherited sin lies the experience that every man is born into a humanity that is and always has been guided by a false striving."[20] He further shows that this "ultimate sin reveals itself to be the false assumption of receiving life not as the gift of the Creator but procurring it by one's own power, of living from one's self rather than from God."[21]

This Pauline concept of the flesh is in no way associated with Greek dualistic thought, as if he were implying that the physical flesh is sinful while the immaterial spirit is holy.[22] Rather, when Paul speaks of the flesh as sinful it is a *metaphor* derived from the Old Testament practice of the circumcision of the flesh. Hence the Pauline interpretation of the sinful flesh is not unique with him. As it has already been pointed out, "the outward appearance of the rite was early compared by Moses (Deut. 10:16) and later by prophets such as Jeremiah and Ezekiel to the inward purification" which they called heart-circumcision.[23] In particular, purification of the heart is symbolically represented in the rite of circumcision as a cleansing from the foreskin (Jer. 4:4).[24] Rudolf Meyer in *Kittel's Theological Dictionary of the New Testament* further attests to this association of original sin with the concept of the flesh: "Thus the spiritualizing of the ancient rite, which is found from the time of Jeremiah and is attested in Deuteronomistic circles, is mentioned in the [Qumran] Manual of Discipline, 5,5: 'And men of truth are to circumcise in the community the foreskins of desire and obduracy.'"[25]

De Vries has also shown that "very prominent in Paul's harmartiology is the concept of 'the flesh' " and that this concept of "evil in man . . . almost certainly has affinities with the ideology of the Qumran sect."[26] This is not to suggest that Paul directly borrowed from the Qumran beliefs, but only to acknowledge that the concept of the flesh as a symbol for sin was a widely held idea in the first century A.D.[27]

It can at least be said that during the intertestamental period a highly developed theological concept of inherited sin had taken shape which was nonetheless firmly rooted in the Old Testament.[28] As De Vries has shown, the Old Testament had a very strong sense that "sin's essence lies, not in isolated acts of transgression, but in the depth of man's being."[29] Particularly De Vries points out that Job 14:1; 15:14; Psalm 51:5; Jer. 17:9; Gen. 6:5; Jer. 11:8; 16:12; 18:12; 23:17; Isa. 6:10; 63:10 testify to "a depth of iniquity in the human heart" which is a consequence of Adam's sin in the Garden.[30] De Vries writes:

> As the Hebrew mind held to the solidarity of the race, it also believed in the essential unity of the life and being of the individual man. Therefore, as has been pointed out, a man's whole being and activity, beginning in his sinful heart and reaching out to all his thoughts, words, and deeds, are affected by sin. This also means that man is a sinner from his conception. It is said that
>> The wicked go astray from the womb,
>>> they err from their birth, speaking lies
>>>> (Ps. 58:3 — H 58:4).

Another psalmist applies this to himself:

> Behold, I was brought forth in iniquity,
>> and in sin did my mother conceive me
>>> (Ps. 51:5 - H 51:7).*

---

*The New Bible Commentary contains this comment about David's confession in Psalm 51:5: "He confesses the true depth of his sinfulness as being the natural state of man from birth. . . . This is the Old Testament's greatest statement of the doctrine of original sin, and it is not pleaded as an excuse but called as a witness to the depth and extent of man's need as a sinner." (Leslie S. McCaw and J. A. Motyer, "Psalms," The New Bible Commentary: Revised [Grand Rapids: Eerdmans, 1970], p. 483).

Thus the Old Testament contains the elements of a doctrine of original sin. It does not theorize about the process by which humanity has become corrupt: all it knows — and it knows this for sure, through painful experience — is that all of mankind since Adam has been sinful, that the whole man is sinful, that man's entire life is sinful from its beginning.[31]

That the foreskin excised in circumcision was widely accepted prior to the New Testament as symbolic of *inherited sin* is also indicated in *Hasting's Dictionary of the Bible*:

Among the Jewish teachers circumcision was regarded as an operation of purification, and the word foreskin has come to be synonymous with obstinacy and imperfection. The rite was regarded as a token in the flesh of the effect of Divine grace in the heart, hence the phrases used in Deut. 30[6]. Philo speaks of it as a symbolic inculcation of purity of heart, and having the advantage of promoting cleanliness, fruitfulness, and avoidance of disease.[32]

The interpretation of circumcision as a symbol of heart-purification is also suggested by the translators of the Septuagint (the Greek translation of the Old Testament which was made in 200 B.C. in Alexandria and widely used by Palestinian Jews in Jesus' day). The word "cleansing" ($\pi\epsilon\rho\iota\kappa\alpha\theta\alpha\rho\acute{\iota}\zeta\epsilon\iota\nu$) is substituted for "circumcision" (*mûl*) in Deut. 30:6.[33] Thus, according to the Septuagint, it is through the *cleansing* of the heart that one is enabled to love God perfectly. It is probably not too much to say that on many, if not on most, occasions in Scripture the concept of moral cleansing carries with it the idea of spiritual circumcision.

Gerhard von Rad has shown in this regard that the circumcision of heart in Deut. 30:6 and Jer. 4:4 is directly connected with the idea of cleanness in Jer. 31:31ff.; 32:29-41, and Ezek. 36:24ff.[34] The formal rite of circumcision, like the sacrificial rites in general, was of no interest to the prophets, but they nonetheless stressed its spiritual implication for cleanness of heart which was to be achieved through the outpouring of the Spirit under the New Covenant.

This prophetic concept of the outpouring of the Spirit as effecting the cleansing of the heart is the meaning of Pentecostal grace. This can be seen both in Acts 15:8-9 and Rom. 2:28f. where the cleansing (circumcision) of the heart is the result of the gift of the Holy Spirit.[35] It is also significant that sanctification is identified with the work of the Holy Spirit (I Peter 1:2). As Benzinger puts it, the prophets "gave the first impetus to the later symbolical interpretation of the rite [of circumcision] as an act of purification."[36]

In the light of this spiritualizing of the rite of circumcision in Deuteronomy and the prophets, it is clear that the Pauline concept of the sinful flesh has nothing at all to do with the Greek notion of matter as evil. In fact, it is clear that the Pauline attitude toward matter is quite Hebraic. In this respect, Paul does not limit his use of the word "flesh" to sin. He may use it to mean physiological flesh ($\dot{\epsilon}\nu$ $\sigma\alpha\rho\kappa\dot{\iota}$, Rom. 2:28). It may be used to designate earthly-natural human life (Philemon 16). Yet the concept of flesh as inherited sin is an important metaphor for expressing the Pauline understanding of fallen human life. As Wesley put it, "The flesh, in the usual language of St. Paul, signifies corrupt nature."[37] Paul is not borrowing Greek categories when he personifies "sin" as a being. Rather, his personification of sin as a being (cf. Rom. 5:12, 21; 6:6, 13, 17ff., 23; 7:8, 11, 13, 14, 20) harks back to the Old Testament (cf. Ps. 51:5).

This is seen especially in the concept of the circumcision of heart which denotes cleansing from all impurity. Jeremiah specifically writes: "Circumcise the *foreskins* of your hearts" (Jer. 4:4). Borrowing this flesh-concept of the covenantal rite of circumcision, which was also used in contemporary Judaism of his day, Paul speaks of sin as a being. Yet, Bultmann has clearly shown that this being-language is figurative, not literal.[38]

The Pauline concept of sin is clearly anti-Greek in character. For Paul is not at all employing the metaphysical category of being, but rather he is using the concrete-functional categories which is characteristic of the Hebrew mindset when he speaks of sin as a being. On the other hand, classical Christian theology, in borrowing the Greek philosophical category of being, defines sin as *nonbeing*. To personify sin as a *being* is quite out of keeping with a strictly philosophical framework.

The difference between the concrete-functional categories of the Bible as opposed to the abstract-ontological categories of philosophical-theological thought in the classical tradition is that the biblical categories are largely *metaphorical*, whereas philosophical categories are *metaphysical*. The concept of substance (being) in the Bible is to be interpreted *metaphorically*, whereas in philosophical-theological thought it is to be interpreted *metaphysically*. For example, to speak biblically, sin is metaphorically described as a being; to speak theologically, sin is metaphysically described as nonbeing (i.e., the distortion of true being). (See appendix to this chapter.)

The Pauline concept of the being of sinful flesh is the very opposite of the Spirit-filled life (Rom. 8:9).[39] The flesh is all that is contrary to the will of God (Gal. 5:19). The flesh is the course of sinful deeds. Hence Paul differentiates between the flesh as a spiritual defect in one's character on the one hand, and sinful deeds as the manifestation of that spiritual defect on the other hand (cf. Gal. 5:17, 19, 24). In Col. 2:13, Paul speaks of this twofold nature of sin as "dead in *trespasses*" (sinful actions) and "the uncircumcision of your *flesh*" (original sin as the source of sinful actions). This twofold distinction between "sins" (actions) and "the sin"* (the source of sins) is the theological basis for a distinction between justification (forgiveness of sins) and sanctification (cleansing from the principle of sin and empowering with perfect love for God).

The essence of the life dominated by the flesh is pride — worshipping oneself instead of God. In this respect, Bultmann shows that while for Paul the flesh first of all means "simply the physiological flesh on which circumcision is performed,"[40] yet it also can denote "carnality."[41] It is pride and

---

*In the Greek text, original sin is usually denoted by the definite article ( ἡ ἀμαρτία) See Rom. 6-7.

arrogance.[42] It is "the attitude of sinful self-reliance."[43] It "is the self-reliant attitude of the man who put his trust in his own strength and in that which is controlled by him."[44] It is the attitude of "turning away from the Creator, the giver of life, and a turning toward the creation — and to do that is to trust in one's self as being able to procure life by the use of the earthly and through one's own strength and accomplishment."[45]

Paul particularly employs the metaphor of flesh to account for the bondage of the will in Romans 7:14: "I am carnal (σαρκικός), sold under [the] sin" (ἡ ἁμαρτία)." Here flesh is identified with the *being* of inherited sin, even as the physiological flesh which is excised in the rite of circumcision represents the being of inherited impurity.[46] To be sure, Paul's description of the flesh as "the sin which dwells within me" is a personification. He does not think of the being of sin (or the flesh) in literal terms, but as "figurative, rhetorical language."[47]

Bultmann points out that for Paul the self is "inwardly split."[48]

> That self which in Rom. 7:17, 20 distinguishes itself from the "sin which dwells within me," is flatly labeled in v. 14 as "carnal" [σαρκικός] and "sold under sin" — just as the first person is used throughout vv. 14-24 both in regard to willing and to doing. Therefore "I" and "I," self and self, are at war with each other; i.e., to be innerly divided, or not to be at one with one's self, is the essence of human existence under sin.[49]

Hence the "flesh" or the being of sin is a metaphorical description of man's "inner dividedness" and "self-reliant" attitude which prevents his true self from experiencing the life of God.[50]

Bultmann further shows that this concept of the flesh is linked by Paul to the universality of sin which originated with Adam's sin.[51] That one lives "according to the flesh" means that "in man — because his substance is flesh — sin slumbers from the beginning."[52]

145

The "flesh" is a "substance," not in a physical and literal sense, but only in the spiritual and metaphorical sense that sin is an inherent condition of man's fallen situation. That "sin slumbers from the beginning" is an apt way of personifying the Pauline concept of original sin.

It must be stressed again, in order to avoid any possible misunderstanding, that the idea of sin as a substance is a metaphorical way of describing an ontological situation. To speak of the being (substance) of sin is a conceptual abstraction utilizing metaphorical language to speak of man's inner disorientation and his godless self-reliant attitude. Bultmann's exposition has clearly shown that this Pauline substantialist concept of sin does not in any sense stand in contradiction to a covenantal-relational interpretation of sin.[53]

It is difficult to know why some have considered a metaphorical, substantialist interpretation to denote the idea that sin is a literal, physical-like "thing." E. H. Sugden accuses Wesley of this confusion, but such an accusation seems altogether unwarranted. Wesley's reference to the being[54] of sin is simply drawing from the language of Paul. However, Sugden's own conception of sin as an evolutionary hang-over in which man's alleged bestiality is the theological meaning of original sin comes dangerously close to a materialistic interpretation of sin.[55]

One would expect a philosophical materialist such as Bertrand Russell to define sin as man's evolutionary hangover resulting from "the instinctive and emotional makeup by which he had survived through previous ages" in his non-human stage of development.[56] To be sure, this evolutionary concept of evil became largely influential in theology through the writings of Schleiermacher. However, such a materialistic understanding of sin is hardly compatible with the doctrine of *creatio ex nihilo*. If God created the world out of nothing and if his creation was good, then sin inevitably must be interpreted as a "Fall."[57] On the other hand, if sin is the inevitable consequence of an evolutionary development in which man's biological development has progressed slower than his moral and spiritual development, then it hardly seems possible to speak of the goodness of God's original creation. It is surely understandable that the split between man's biological and spiritual makeup is a consequence of the Fall, but if one is to take seriously the concept of *creatio ex nihilo* this split can hardly be the *cause* of sin.

For Wesley — like Augustine, Luther, and Calvin — the being of sin is essentially perversity of will which expresses itself as pride. To charge that Wesley thought of sin as a materialistic substance is unfair. For Wesley's conception of sin is in fundamental agreement with Pauline language. In this respect, Bultmann has shown that the Pauline "substantialist" concept of the flesh is linked with original ("inherited") sin, and it is in no way connected with the idea of a literal, material-like substance.[58]

Bultmann further shows that for Paul inherited sin is not something for which he is responsible *per se*, but "by his concrete 'transgression' " he becomes "jointly responsible" with Adam for his sin.[59] John Fletcher, in reference to Rom. 5:18, also writes: "We are *no way* accountable for our moral infection, yet it cannot be denied that we are answerable for our obstinate refusal of relief, and for the *wilful neglect* of the means found out by Divine mercy for our cure."[60] This distinction between original sin (for which we are not directly responsible) and actual sins (for which we are directly responsible) is an important distinction for Wesley's and Fletcher's concept of salvation. In justification one is liberated from the dominion of sin and his sins are forgiven; in sanctification one is freed from the being of sin and enabled to love God perfectly.[61]

Inasmuch as one can be freed from all sin, Fletcher insists that it is incumbent upon the justified believer to avail himself of the fulness of Pentecostal grace ("a sanctifying baptism").[62]

That the Pentecostal Spirit frees the believer from the sinful flesh is the meaning of the Pauline concept of "walking in the Spirit."[63] In this respect the Pentecostal gift of the Spirit releases one from inherited sin. Bultmann shows that the Pauline concept of the life of the Spirit means the believer no longer is under "the *compulsion* of sin."[64] He shows that this "sinlessness" means "freedom from the power of sin."[65] "To have received the Spirit means to be standing in grace (Rom. 5:2)."[66] The Pentecostal Spirit is given to the believer in order to establish him in Christ and to free him from the power of inherited sin.

The Pauline emphasis is thus not upon justification ("forgiveness of sins") but upon sanctification ("freedom from sin"). Paul focuses his attack upon the *source* of sins – the inherited flesh. Bultmann writes: "His avoidance of the term 'forgiveness of sins' (which is connected with his avoidance of the term 'repentance' . . . ) is evidently due to the fact that 'forgiveness of sin' is insofar ambiguous as it seems to declare only release from the guilt contracted by 'former sins,' whereas the important thing for Paul is release from *sinning*, release from the power of sin."[67]

Krister Stendahl has termed Paul's sense of his freedom from the power of sin "a robust consciousness." He has shown that Paul felt himself to be a person whom Christ had truly made holy and free from sin. Paul's attitude about himself shows no indication of a troubled conscience.[68] Stendahl also shows that Luther's struggle with conscience has been wrongly interpreted as typical of Paul.[69] Stendahl's exposition of the following passage substantiates his emphasis that Paul felt himself to have been made a truly good and holy person through Jesus Christ, Acts 23:1; 24:16; I Cor. 9:27; Rom. 9:1; II Cor. 1:12; II Cor. 5:10f.; I Cor. 4:4; II Cor. 12:9-10. In this respect, Stendahl writes:

> The famous formula "simul justus et peccator" – at the same time righteousness and sinner – as a description of the status of the Christian may have some foundation in the Pauline writings, but this formula cannot be substantiated as the center of Paul's conscious attitude toward his personal sins. Apparently, Paul did not have the type of introspective conscience which such a formula seems to presuppose. This is probably one of the reasons why "forgiveness of sins" is the term of salvation which is used least of all in the Pauline writings.[70]

This emphasis upon the actual possibility of freedom from sin is intelligible only if the distinction between the ethical and the legal ideas of sin is kept in mind. Wesley speaks of this distinction in terms of voluntary (ethical) and involuntary (legal) transgressions. He interprets the concept of sinning in Scripture to denote voluntary transgressions of the known will of God.[71] However, Wesley also allowed for the validity of a legal definition of sin which meant that involuntary transgressions are also serious and need the atonement of Christ.[72] Wesley writes: "The most perfect have continual need of the merits of Christ, even for their actual transgressions, and may say, for themselves, as well as for their brethren, 'Forgive us our trespasses.'" [73] Hence he can say that "many mistakes may consist with pure love," but not any sin.[74]

That the ethical definition of sin is the normal meaning of sin in Scripture can easily be tested. For example, Wesley shows that the idea that sin is the transgression of the will of God (I John 3:4) is not the same as saying that every transgression is a sin. Otherwise, John's assertion that everyone who sins is of the devil becomes unintelligible (I John 3:8).[75] For example, if I John 3:8 is interpreted to mean, "Everyone who both voluntarily and involuntarily transgresses the will of God is of the devil," then everyone presumably must be condemned, since it is apparent that no one can claim that his actions are altogether perfect. It does not lessen the force of this conclusion to argue that John was only speaking of those who habitually transgress, since everyone does in fact habitually, involuntarily transgress the will of God. Only if the biblical demand to cease from sinning is interpreted ethically (i.e., refrain from voluntary transgressions) can it be made intelligible.

This distinction between the ethical and legal definitions of sin is implicit in the Levitical sacrificial system. If one committed an involuntary sin and it became known, he was to offer immediately a sacrifice as an atonement (cf. Lev. 4:13-15). Yet once a year on the Day of Atonement the high priest offered up a sacrifice to atone for involuntary sins of ignorance

(Lev. 16; cf. Heb. 9:7). Sins, whether voluntary or involuntary, need to be atoned for; but voluntary sins carry a special degree of ethical seriousness about them because of one's willful involvement in what is contrary to God's will.

The circumcision of the heart, which releases one from the being of sin, means that one is enabled to live a life of obedience and perfect love to Christ, even though one can never achieve in this life perfect behavior. That is, one can have perfect intentions but not perfect conduct. The Levitical law which clearly distinguished between those transgressions which are committed "wittingly" and "unwittingly" is illustrative of this distinction between perfect intention and perfect performance.

This level of ethical living was especially implied in the initial institution of the formal rite of circumcision. In Genesis 17:1, God commands Abraham "to walk before me and be perfect." The word "perfect" (*tāmîn*) does not mean faultless behavior. Von Rad shows that it denotes perfect intent of the heart. It implies a perfect relationship to God. "It signifies complete, unqualified surrender."[76] Hence circumcision was a "typological correspondence" (von Rad's term) to perfection of heart. As von Rad puts it, this perfection symbolized in his circumcision means: "It is the constraint of his whole life which is henceforth to be lived in the presence of this revealed God (life is a 'walk,' a 'walking about')."[77]

This understanding of circumcision as a symbol of a perfect heart is precisely in accord with Wesley's insistence that under the New Covenant it is required of every believer in Christ to be made perfect in love — which he defined as the circumcision of the heart. Christian perfection signifies a perfect relationship to Christ, though not a life of perfect behavior. It is a perfection of intent, not performance.

This circumcision which enables one to walk blamelessly before the Lord is accomplished through the Spirit (Rom. 2:28-29).[78] This is particularly seen in Acts 15:8-9: "And God who knows the heart bore witness to them, giving them the Holy Spirit just as he did to us; and he made no distinction between us and them, but cleansed their hearts by faith."

This cleansing of the Gentile Cornelius (Acts 10) recalls the rite of circumcision. That Cornelius was uncircumcised meant that he was unclean under the Old Covenant. Peter would have nothing to do with an uncircumcised Gentile, just as he would have nothing to do with the eating of food which was considered unclean (Acts 10:12-14). However, Peter was made to realize through a vision that under the era of Pentecostal grace physical circumcision did not count (Acts 10:9-16). The only circumcision which mattered was of the heart, through the Spirit. So Peter reported to the Apostolic Council in Jerusalem (Acts 15:3-21) that physical circumcision amounted to nothing, since the Holy Spirit had already circumcised the Gentiles' hearts, i.e., their hearts were cleansed by the Holy Spirit.[79] Hence there was no need to put "a yoke upon the neck of the disciples which neither our fathers nor we have been able to bear" (Acts 15:10).

Alford also shows that the cleansing referred to in Acts 15:9 is a spiritual circumcision:

> The allusion is throughout to *spiritual circumcision*, as the purification of the *heart*. God, who saw deeper than the mere fleshly distinction between Jew and Gentile, who knows that the hearts of *all* are unclean, and that the same all-sufficient sacrifice can cleanse them *all*, if applied by faith (compare the remarkable parallel, I Pet. i.18-22 incl.), put no difference between us and them, but has been pleased to render them spiritually clean.[80]

John Fletcher specifically relates this cleansing in Acts 15:9 to Wesley's concept of Christian perfection. He points out that Cornelius, as well as the disciples on the day of Pentecost, experienced the cleansing from all sin (spiritual circumcision) through the fulness of the Holy Spirit.[81]

That Cornelius' *cleansing* implied total deliverance from original sin is seen through its equation with the idea of circumcision (Acts 10:1-11:18; 15:1-11). Even as circumcision symbolized sanctification through the excision of the physiological flesh, so the cleansing of the Holy Spirit meant for Cornelius the total purification of his heart from the sinful flesh. We pointed out earlier that the Septuagint substituted cleansing (περικαθαρίζειν) for circumcision (mûl). This interchangeability of cleansing and circumcision is most evident in this particular context in Acts 15:9. Hence it seems particularly appropriate for John Fletcher to link the Pentecostal language of the baptism with the Spirit with Wesley's concept of entire sanctification, since Peter in this passage identified his own experience of the fulness of the Spirit, as well as the experience of Cornelius, with the circumcision of the heart. (This will be discussed in the next chapter.)

That Wesley understood Acts 15:8-9 to imply full purity of heart is stated in *The Poetical Works of John and Charles Wesley*, in which the following verses are given as an interpretation of the phrase in Acts 15:8-9, "God . . . giving them the Holy Ghost . . . purifying."

> God of grace, vouchsafe to me
> That Spirit of holiness,
> Sighs my heart for purity,
> And pants for perfect peace;
> Spirit of faith, the blood apply,
> Which only can my filth remove,
> Fill my soul, and sanctify
> By Jesus' heavenly love.
>
> By Thy Spirit's inspiration
> Bid my evil thoughts depart,
> All the filth of pride and passion,
> Purge out of my faithful heart:
> Then I shall with joy embrace Thee,
> Meet to see Thy face above,
> Then I worthily shall praise Thee,
> Then I perfectly shall love.[82]

That this cleansing of Acts 15:8-9 is a total and not a partial cleansing is supported by John Calvin's interpretation of this passage in his *Commentary on the Book of Acts.*[83] To be sure, for Calvin this total cleansing is *imputed* to the believer and only progressively realized in his actual life until its full appropriation at death.

A parallel conception to spiritual circumcision is the Pauline imperative to walk by the Spirit. Bultmann shows that Paul makes a careful distinction between "living in the Spirit" (indicative mood) and "walk in the Spirit" (imperative mood).[84] To *live in* the Spirit is the meaning of justification; to *walk in* the Spirit is the actual appropriation (sanctification) of the righteousness imputed to the believer in his justification. The indicative mood denotes what has happened in principle; the imperative mood denotes what has happened in actuality. "What has happened in principle must be brought to reality in practice."[85]

The Pentecostal gift of the Spirit is thus the foundation of a life of obedience to Christ which is freed from the bondage of "the flesh." Bultmann expresses this sanctification of the believer's life in a way which warrants a long quotation in his own succinct words.

> Therefore, the *imperative*, "walk according to the Spirit," not only does not contradict the *indicative* of justification (the believer is rightwised [i.e., justified]) but results from it: "Cleanse out the old leaven that you may be fresh dough, as you really are unleavened" (I Cor. 5:7f.). In a certain sense, then, "Become what thou art!" is valid — but not in the sense of idealism, according to which the "idea" of the perfect man is more and more closely realized in endless progress. In this idealistic sense the transcendence of "perfection" is conceived as the "idea's" transcendence, and man's relation to it is regarded (Stoically expressed) as a "progressing" or a "tending" toward it. Rather, "sinlessness" — i.e. freedom from the power of sin — is already realized in the "righteousness of God." . . . Its transcendence is that of the divine verdict, and man's relation to it is that of "obedience of faith." The way the believer becomes what he already is consists there-

fore in the constant appropriation of grace by faith, which also means, in the concrete, "obedience," which is henceforth possible in his "walking": "for sin will have no dominion over you, since you are not under law but under grace" (Rom. 6:14).[86]

From Bultmann's exposition of Paul's thoughts, it can be seen that the imperative of walking in the Spirit is what constitutes the perfection (sanctification) of the Christian life. This imperative of sanctification is what completes the "indicative of justification." This perfection is a "cleansing out the old leaven," and it does not correspond to a philosophical notion of perfectionism in which "the perfect man is more and more closely realized in endless progress." Rather, the perfection of the Christian life is a "freedom from the power of sin" which is achieved only by "the constant appropriation of grace by faith." Though Bultmann's "existentialist pre-understanding" forces his theological interpretation of Christian faith in a direction altogether different from the historic confession of the Church, his exegetical interpretation of Pauline thought is most incisive.

In the light of these exegetical-theological considerations, it is not without biblical warrant that Wesley speaks of entire sanctification as the cleansing of the heart from "all inbred sin," and being "saved from all sin."[87] He further describes original sin metaphorically as "leprosy," "the evil root," "the carnal mind."[88] The essence of original sin is carnal pride; the essence of Christian perfection is *agape* love. Christian perfection is "the circumcision of the heart from all filthiness, all inward as well as outward pollution. It is a renewal of the heart in the whole image of God, the full likeness of Him that created it."[89]

As we have already pointed out, it is important to keep in mind that Wesley's language of cleansing goes back to the covenantal language of circumcision. As such, the being of sin — or the flesh — symbolizes an attitude of rebellion and pride. In this respect, holiness is being in proper relationship to God, whereas sin is being out of fellowship with God because one has made his own will the motivation of his life.

When Wesley speaks of being cleansed from all sin, such language ought not to be interpreted in a static sense. Rather, the holy life is an ongoing dynamic relationship to God that presupposes continual growth and further increase in love. As we are "renewed from moment to moment, we are every whit clean."[90] Wesley further points out that even in eternity the believer will continue to grow in love.[91] Christian perfection involves both the realization of (crisis), and increase in (process), love.[92]

Wesley also shows that to walk by the Spirit is to have the righteousness of Christ fulfilled in the believer (Rom. 8:3-4).[93] Bultmann's exposition of "walking in the Spirit" provides exegetical warrant for Wesley's use of this phrase to describe the perfect life. This metaphor of walking suggests "the constant appropriation of grace by faith."[94]

This walking by the Spirit recalls the same imagery in Genesis 17 where Abraham's circumcision typified a blameless walk before God.[95] As von Rad shows in that context, to walk before the Lord implied living continually in the full presence of God.[96] Likewise, to walk by the Spirit means living constantly in the full presence of God. It suggests perfect consecration to the will of God.

Bultmann has shown that this Pauline concept of "walking according to the Spirit" is "not a decisionless capacity henceforth to do the good only. . . . 'Sinlessness' is not a magical guarantee against the *possibility* of sin . . . but release from the compulsion of sin."[97] Likewise, Wesley insists that Christian perfection is "purity of intention."[98] It is not a static perfectionism, but a dynamic perfection of continual love — a compulsion! Even as Wesley's idea of a second work of grace is not a mere quantitative numerical notion, even so "cleansing from inbred sin" is not literalistic-quantitative language. Rather, such metaphorical language as "cleansing" suggests a life lived in continual obedience to God with a perfect love.

Hence the imperative of walking according to the Spirit (Gal. 5:25) is to appropriate righteousness (Gal. 5:5). To walk by the Spirit is to possess the fruit of the Spirit (vs. 22). To walk by the Spirit is to belong wholly to Jesus Christ

(Gal. 5:24). To walk by the Spirit is to have "crucified the flesh with its passions and desires" (v. 24). It can thus be seen that the rite of circumcision of the flesh prefigured the Pauline idea of "walking in the Spirit," and of being freed from the dominion of the flesh.

In this respect, Bultmann has shown that "in the flesh" (Rom. 7:5;  8:8f.) is the antithesis of "in the Spirit" (Rom. 8:9). This antithesis is based in Paul's contrast between "flesh-circumcision" and "heart-circumcision" (Rom. 2:28f.).[99] Flesh-circumcision is ineffective in achieving righteousness. Rather, heart-circumcision supersedes flesh-circumcision, since the Holy Spirit is now the gift of righteousness to the believer and transforms him into a new creation.[100] It is the Holy Spirit who grants "freedom from sin."[101] Heart-circumcision means the cleansing of the flesh through the Holy Spirit.[102]

To practice flesh-circumcision under the New Covenant is, ironically, to perpetuate the attitude of pride and self-sufficiency. While the rite of circumcision under the Old Covenant was the seal of righteousness, since it represented Israel's purification, it is replaced in the New Covenant with the circumcision of the heart through the Spirit (Rom. 2:28f.). To practice flesh-circumcision is to evidence pride and self-righteousness which was the very opposite of the intent of the rite's original signification. Hence, flesh-circumcision (like possession of the Promised Land) is significant primarily because of what is prefigured — the cleansing of the heart through the Pentecostal Spirit.

It would surely seem from these exegetical-theological considerations that Wesley's equation of Christian perfection with circumcision of heart as well as with the idea of the possession of Canaan Land is well-founded. It would also seem appropriate for John Fletcher to equate Christian perfection with the Pentecostal Spirit, since it is the full presence of the Holy Spirit who effects cleansing and enables one to love God perfectly.

Another parallel covenantal concept to spiritual circumcision is the Pauline concept of being "*sealed*" with the promised Holy Spirit" (Eph. 1:13). An exposition of circumcision as a seal will indicate this relationship.

Circumcision was the seal of the covenant with Abraham that his posterity would become a nation and that they would occupy Canaan Land (Genesis 12:2, 7). In this respect, circumcision as a seal pointed to the fact that a holy God, a holy people, and a holy land would form "an indissoluble triad."[103]

Circumcision as a seal was more than a mere symbol of the future actualization of the promise of Canaan Land. Rather, the future reality of the promise had become a present appropriation. Von Rad thus speaks of Abraham's circumcision as an "act of appropriation."[104] He points out that the covenant which Abraham entered into fourteen years earlier constituted the offer of divine salvation; circumcision was Abraham's subsequent appropriation of that divine offer of salvation.[105] Paul in particular interprets Abraham's circumcision as "the seal of his righteousness" (Rom. 4:11).

What is further significant is that Paul specifically argues that Abraham's justification came prior to his circumcision. The implication of this time lapse between Abraham's justification and his subsequent circumcision, which symbolized his appropriation of the righteousness imputed to him at his earlier justification, is most significant for Wesley's idea of Christian perfection as a second work of grace. To be sure, the Pauline concern in this passage is to show that Abraham's faith which justified him was altogether independent of the formal rite of circumcision; hence any Jewish ceremonial restriction placed upon true believers is not valid. Yet the Pauline interpretation of circumcision as a seal (appropriation) of righteousness with its temporal distinction from his justification is in accord with Wesley's perception that the cleansing of the heart from all sin comes *after* justification. Abraham is a paradigm of one who experienced both justifying faith and sanctifying faith.

A seal is a confirmation; it is an imprint of the reality; it is the reality realized in a provisional way.[106] Circumcision as a seal was thus the pre-actualization of the promise of

Canaan Land.* It was the proleptic event of the crossing of the Jordan River into Canaan Land.

In the light of this linking of circumcision and the Promised Land, it becomes highly significant that upon the Israelites' immediate crossing of the Jordan River into Canaan, circumcision was performed upon all uncircumcised males. This crossing into Canaan Land accompanied by the rite of circumcision meant "the reproach of Egypt was removed." Not only had they been taken out of Egypt, but Egypt had now at last been taken out of them. Circumcision was the symbolic appropriation of possession of the Promised Land; it spiritually denoted actualized righteousness and perfect love.

The circumcision of Abraham denoted, in a figurative way, the sanctifying grace under the Pentecostal era of the New Covenant. To be sealed with the Pentecostal Spirit (Eph. 4:30) is to be stamped with the righteousness of Christ; it is to experience the actual and total righteousness of Christ. Wesley interprets Ephesians 4:30 this way:

> The being 'sealed by the Spirit' in the full sense of the word I take to imply two things: first, the receiving the whole image of God, the whole mind which was in Christ, as the wax receives the whole impression of the seal when it is strongly and properly applied; secondly, the full assurance of hope, or a clear and permanent confidence of being with God in glory.[107]

In Ephesians 5:18-19, Paul shows that being "filled with the Holy Spirit" enables one to love God with all the heart: "Be filled with the Spirit, addressing one another in psalms and hymns and spiritual songs, singing and making melody to

---

*Gerhard von Rad shows that the Abrahamic covenant was threefold: (1) a promise that Abraham's posterity would become a nation; (2) a promise of a new relationship to God, "I will be your God"; (3) a promise to possess the land of Canaan. The first promise was fulfilled in Egypt; the second promise was fulfilled at Sinai; the third promise was fulfilled when Joshua led Israel into Canaan (*Old Testament Theology*, I, 134-135).

the Lord *with all your heart*," i.e., worshipping the Lord with all the heart. This is the essence of being filled with the Spirit — being wholeheartedly devoted to God and worshipping the Lord with all the heart. Being filled with the Spirit is the essence of perfect love. This passage is perhaps the most direct statement in the New Testament which clearly shows that being filled with the Spirit means loving, i.e., worshipping the Lord with all the heart.

The concept of being Spirit-filled corresponds to the Pauline definition of a "real Jew" whose circumcision is of the Spirit (Rom. 2:29). Circumcision signified entire devotion to God (Gen. 17:1) and perfect love (Deut. 30:6), and under the New Covenant of Pentecostal grace heart-circumcision became a living reality through the outpouring of the Holy Spirit. Heart-circumcision, perfect love, and being filled with the Spirit are conceptually identical in Pauline thought.

This imperative to be filled with the Spirit parallels the imperative to walk by the Spirit (Gal. 5:16). It is also a parallel idea to being sealed with the Spirit (cf. Eph. 1:13; 4:30; 5:18). To walk by the Spirit, to be sealed with the Spirit, to be filled with the Spirit (Eph. 5:18-19), to be circumcised by the Spirit (Rom. 2:28-29) are equivalent phrases which denote the appropriation of the complete righteousness of Christ.

A further covenantal concept which parallels the theme of circumcision is the "fruit of the Spirit" (Gal. 5:22). The rite of circumcision signified that Abraham's posterity would enjoy the *fruit* of the Promised Land. Under the New Covenant, the fruit of the Spirit belongs to those who have experienced a spiritual circumcision (cf. Gal. 5:5, 6, 22). Hence to walk by the Spirit (Gal. 5:16), to possess the fruit of the Spirit (Gal. 5:22), to experience spiritual circumcision (Gal. 5:5, 6, 24), to live in love (Gal. 13-15) constitutes a single theme.

Likewise, being sealed with the Spirit is the same in meaning as "the fruit of the Spirit." Even as "to be sealed with the Spirit" is drawn from the covenantal language of circumcision, so likewise with "the fruit of the Spirit." The seal of circumcision was a faith-act symbolizing the appropriation of the fruit of Canaan Land. Even so, the seal of the Spirit, i.e., mark of the Spirit, is the fruit of the Spirit — love, joy, peace, patience, kindness, goodness, faithfulness, gentleness, self-control (Gal. 5:22-23).

We have already pointed out that Wesley used the Promised Land motif as descriptive of Christian perfection. We have also shown that he defined Christian perfection as being sealed with the Spirit. It is only natural that he would also equate "the fruit of the Spirit" with Christian perfection.[108] For Wesley, the fruit of the Spirit is the witness of being made perfect in love, in contrast to justified believers who are not "perfect Christians.[109] Wesley shows that the whole fruit of the Spirit is restricted to entirely sanctified believers.[110] That is, only the children of God "in the highest sense" can be said to possess "the fruit of the Spirit."[111]

Wesley thus shows that the "fruit of the Spirit," "being sealed with the Spirit," "being renewed in love" are phrases which denote Christian perfection. He writes: "Some [of the Christians spoken about in London] . . . . I believe, are renewed in love, and have the direct witness of it; and they manifest the fruit [of the Spirit] above described, in all their words and actions. Now, let any man call this what he will, it is what I call perfection."[112]

In conclusion, the concern of this chapter has been to show that the circumcision of the heart corresponds in meaning to Wesley's doctrine of perfect love. In this respect, the covenantal language of circumcision prefigures the Pentecostal language of the New Covenant. Hence the essence of the Spirit-filled life is perfect love. To be filled with the Spirit, to be circumcised by the Spirit, to be sealed with the Spirit, to possess the fruit of the Spirit, to walk by the Spirit denote the fulness of the sanctifying Spirit of Pentecost.

# AN APPENDIX
## ON
## THE CONCEPT OF SUBSTANCE

The biblical concept of sin as a being (substance) is certainly not a philosophical category derived from classical Greek philosophy. The Hebrew mindset expressed truth in a concrete and functional manner, rather than in abstract and philosophical terms. Yet very early in the history of Christian tradition it became necessary to translate the concrete-functional categories of the Bible into the abstract-ontological categories of Greek thought because of the rapid conversion of the Greco-Roman world to Christianity. In the light of this development, the concept of substance became especially significant.

The concept of substance (Latin: *substantia*) as a philosophical category was first of all expressed in the Greek word, οὐσία which is formed from ὤν, the participial form of εἰμί.[113]   Plato was the first significant writer to use this concept of being in a philosophical sense.[114]

In the history of classical thought the word substance normally refers to immaterial being rather than to material being, and it is equated with what is true and good. Platonic and neo-Platonic philosophy in particular identified true being with immaterial reality, while the material world was only a copy or a mere appearance of true being. Evil was also identified with resistant matter; hence the Greek notion that the body is evil (cf. Plato's *Phaedo*). The material world as inherently evil is thus the realm of nonbeing.

The meaning of nonbeing comes from the Greek words *mē on* (μη ὄν) which means "that which does not yet have being but which can become being if it is united with essences or ideas."[115]   This concept of nonbeing means that it is inherent in matter to resist union with reality (i.e., the Platonic ideas or essences). Hence this tension between the realm of matter and the realm of immaterial being "represents the dualistic element which underlies all paganism and which is the ultimate ground of the tragic interpretation of life."[116]

This concept of nonbeing is also labelled *me-ontic* matter. It stands in sharp contrast to the Christian concept of *creatio ex nihilo* (creation out of nothing). The *nihil* out of which God created is in Greek termed οὐκ ὄν. It is "the undialectical negation of being."[117] It is undialectical in the sense that it is not a tension between what is true being (*ousia*) and what is less than true being ($m\bar{e}$ *on*). The concept of *ouk on* means the sheer absence of being. Hence the Christian doctrine of *creatio ex nihilo* stands in opposition to the notion of *me-ontic* matter. In Christian thought, creation — including its material and spiritual elements — is inherently good, while evil is the deprivation of good.

In Christian thought, evil is always parasitic; it has no absolute existence of its own. Only the good has true being. Evil is nonbeing, in the sense that it is the deprivation, i.e., the distortion, of true being.[118]

It seems that the logic of this philosophical-theological analysis of being (goodness) and nonbeing (evil), which in Augustine is given its classical formulation, is inescapable. When Augustine employed the Platonic category of nonbeing to define sin, he, of course, did not intend to suggest that evil was sheer nothing (*ouk on*). Nor did he intend the idea that evil is physical nor that the body is evil. His stress is that what has true being comes from God who is ultimate Being; whatever is evil is a perversion ($m\bar{e}$ *on*) of true being.[119] In this respect, the devil as the source of evil is theologically interpreted as a fallen being (Luke 10:18; I Tim. 3:6; Isa. 14:12-15). He is the ultimate distortion of true being.[119]

While the concept of substance has different meanings in classical Greek thought, it was generally used to denote a static and immaterial reality. What changes was interpreted to be less than true being. Hence knowledge related to the truth of immaterial being, which was eternal and absolutely unchanging. The world was unknowable because it was always changing, hence it lacked true being. In this respect, most Western philosophers have interpreted the divine substance in a static sense (beginning with Plato and Aristotle and continuing through the post-sixteenth century philosophers as Descartes, Spinoza, Kant). However, classical Christian theology should not be confused with classical philosophy. While employing the Greek concept of substance, classical theology did not give substance a static interpretation. God is the ultimate substance who is the source of all finite reality, yet he is in himself a tri-personal being. He is always the same, but not in a static, immovable sense.[120]

Paul Tillich has shown that not until the nineteenth century was God ever defined as a person; rather, He is called substance.[121] This can be seen in the thought of Tertullian, who gave the first systematic statement on the doctrine of Trinity which he defined as a unity-in-trinity. His basic formula was *tres personae, una substantia.*[122]

However, Tillich's observation could be misleading unless it is also pointed out that in classical thought the concept of substance also implied the idea of individual personality. Christopher Stead shows that for Aristotle "human beings, and deities, were stock examples of substances."[123] Karl Barth has shown that the concept of substance in classical theology very definitely implies that God is a personal Lord:

> We may unhesitatingly equate the concept of the lordship of God, with which we found the whole Biblical concept of revelation to be related, with what in the language of the ancient church is called the essence of God, the *deitas* or *divinitas*, the divine οὐσία, *essentia, natura,* or *substantia.* The essence of God is the being of God *qua* divine being. The essence of God is the godhead of God.[124]

In Greek thought, the ultimate substance was often an impersonal principle; whereas, in classical Christian theology God as substance is a highly personal, living reality. With Thomas Aquinas the concept of substance especially lost its basic similarity to classical Greek thought when he defined God's substance in terms of *actus purus* (pure act).[125] God is not an unmoved mover; but God's fundamental nature is to act, since he is the tri-personal God of Christian revelation.

Tillich has also pointed out that while the word substance was used to specify the nature of God, the word person was reserved for the three hypostases of the Trinity.[126] This observation could also be misleading if it is not pointed out that the word person does not function in our modern period as it did during the formative years of Christian theology. The concept of person comes from the Greek word *prosōpon*, "facing towards," and the Latin word *persona*, which could designate a mask worn by an actor when he confronted the audience as a certain character. So the concept of person did not originally designate "subjective self-consciousness" as it does in our modern psychological sense. Rather, it meant "objective confrontation."[127] That the word person carries with it this subjective selfhood today is why Barth has proposed that it would be better to speak of three *eternal* modes of God's being rather than speak of a trinity of persons.[128]

Since the biblical categories are largely concrete and functional and not abstract and ontological except in an implied sense, the relational framework of the Covenant of the Old Testament is expressed in analogical terms. God is a living being, yet this *being* of God is a functional category, not a philosophical concept *per se*. In the New Testament, God's being is defined largely in Christological terms. This can be seen especially in the functional categories in which Jesus is designated by specific titles, such as prophet, priest, king, Son of man, Son of God, Messiah, etc. (Cf. Oscar Cullmann's *The Christology of the New Testament*).

It has been the traditional task of theology to translate these functional categories into philosophical language. This task was necessitated by the cultural fact that very early the Church was made up of Greek-thinking Christians rather than Jewish Christians. Appropriating neo-Platonic categories, Augustine defined God as the Eternal Now. Thomas Aquinas adopted Aristotelian categories in speaking of God as Pure Act. Process philosophers today speak of God as Energy Event or the Concrete Universal. Classical theology defines

God as a changeless, infinite, tri-personal being. Process theology defines God as absolutely related, including his being dependent upon, the actual world, and he is its all-inclusive unity (cf. Charles Hartshorne, *The Divine Relativity*).

The concept of relation in process thought is defined in a literal and univocal sense.[129] It thus denies the doctrine of *creatio ex nihilo*, and its concept of God lacks "subjective selfhood," i.e., God is not an *actual\** person. The concept of relation in classical Christian theology is used in an analogical sense inasmuch as God is a transcendent, personal Creator who brought the world into being from nothing (Heb. 11:3; Rom. 4:17). This God of Christian theism is a person in the analogical sense that he has subjective selfhood, but is not a mere person alongside other finite persons.

The concept of relation in classical Christian theology presupposes that the God of the covenant is a living personality. Yet classical Christian theology adapted the Greek concept of substance to show that the ontological implication of the covenantal God of the Bible is that He is an actual being who has no unrealized possibilities. Stead points this out:

> What is the point of stating that God is an *ousia* in the categorical sense, a substance? . . . Its principal function, as I see it, is to claim that God is not limited or prescribed by our experience of him, but exists in his own right. . . . To characterize God as a substance is to stake a claim against reductionist theories which in effect represent God as dependent on the human experience which he is invoked to explain."[130]

---

*The word *actual* for Hartshorne is used as a technical term to denote any reality which has specificity and individuality, in contrast to the word *existence* which denotes the abstract-conceptual side of actuality. God's existence is a conceptual abstraction, whereas God's actuality is the concrete world in its empirical all-inclusiveness. Cf. *Philosophers Speak of God* (University of Chicago Press, 1948), pp. 71, 72, 97, 98; *The Logic of Perfection* (La Salle, Ill.; Open Court, 1962), p. 109f.

Finally, the significance of this discussion on the concept of substance has been to show that it would be misleading to think that one could embrace a relational theology as if he could dispense with the concept of substance. Augustine's synthesis between the relational and substantial ("substantial relations") has shown that Christian theology must employ both philosophical concepts. The current debate in contemporary theology over the priority of relation (process) or being is not new, but harks back to the earliest Christian centuries of theological formulation, with such theologians as the Cappodician Fathers, Athanasius, Arius, and Augustine.[131]

In this respect, the ontological debate over the priority of substantialist categories or relational categories is only indirectly a concern within Scripture. While this philosophical-theological debate is terribly important, what is even more important in this regard is to avoid a confusion between Hebrew and Greek concepts. God is concretely talked about in Scripture as having arms and hands, and sin is personified as a concrete being. Yet such concrete-functional language is metaphorical, not philosophical and abstract. It would be misleading to refer to this anthropomorphic language as being an example of substantialist-philosophical categories. Hence in the technical language of theology, God is defined as *una substantia, tres personae*, and sin is defined as nonbeing. In the functional-concrete language of the Bible, God is defined in anthropomorphic terms, and sin is personified as a being. It can thus be seen that the biblical language of *relation* and *being* does not carry the explicit technical meanings of theology. To be sure, classical theology presupposes that the functional categories of Scripture have an implied ontology, but it is, nonetheless, most important to distinguish the technical language of theology from the phenomenal language of the Bible. This is especially true if the theological language about God's being (substance) and the nonbeing of sin is to be intelligible.

At the same time, to recognize the distinction between Hebraic and Greek concepts is not to suggest that one can simply dispense with ontological categories. Even a biblical

theologian when he speaks of the covenantal concept of relationship does not simply repeat the concrete-functional
language of the Bible; rather, he necessarily involves himself
in an abstract conceptualization of what the word means. If
one is to speak with clarity of meaning, the use of abstract
(ontological) categories is a must. The alternative is a strictly
existentialist methodology in which theological terms are
given only a non-cognitive, existential meaning with no
objective frame of reference.

In contrast to Rudolf Bultmann's existential theology,
Barth's *Church Dogmatics* is an impressive demonstration
that the task of theologizing is to interpret the language of
the Church in the light of the language of the Bible, as well
as to translate the meaning of the Bible into contemporary
thought patterns. He shows that biblical language has theo-
logical-ontological implications which must be made explicit. There is no escaping, then, the responsibility of
translating the concrete-functional language of the Bible into
abstract-ontological categories if the contents of Holy Scripture are to be made intelligible for the Church today. And
every theologian, preacher, and layman who reads the Bible
does this despite any denials to the contrary!

As Barth has put it, "we might very well be of the private
opinion that it would be better and nicer if God had not
spoken and did not speak with such deliberate 'intellectual-
ism.' "[132] Barth shows also that it does not help matters to
accuse one of "scholasticism" (in a pejorative sense) because
he gives the language of the Bible an objective, cognitive interpretation.[133] He further shows that while biblical exegesis
provides the basis for theologizing, "dogmatics as such does
not inquire what the Apostles and Prophets have said, but
what we ourselves must say 'on the basis of the Apostles and
Prophets.' "[134] That is, the task of theologizing is to set forth
"what Christian language ought to say and should say today."[135] In this respect, Barth points out that "all dogmatic
formulae are rational and so is every dogmatic procedure, so
far as general concepts, i.e., human *ratio*, are employed in
it."[136] In this respect, Barth has shown that ontological

concepts such as *substantia* and *essentia* have been indispensable ways of expressing what the Church has understood to be the message of the Bible.[137]

The real intent of this appendix has been to show that it is a confusion of categories to think that Wesley believed that sin was a physical-like substance which was extracted through the circumcision of the heart (entire sanctification). E. H. Sugden's criticism of Wesley at this point is certainly wide of the mark (see above). Wesley was simply using the metaphorical language of Paul when he described in a concrete-functional way that the *being* of sin was cleansed in entire sanctification. Sugden's rejection of the idea of sin as a *being* since such language allegedly denotes a material-literal type of substance is curious. Neither Wesley, Calvin, Luther, or Augustine thought of sin in such a naive way.

(For an in-depth study of how the concept of substance has functioned in the history of philosophical and theological thought, Christopher Stead's *Divine Substance* [London: Oxford Press, 1977] is one of the best works available).

---

[1] *The Standard Sermons of John Wesley*, I, 267-268.

[2] *Ibid.*, I, 265.

[3] *The Popular and Critical Bible Encyclopedia and Scriptural Dictionary*, ed. Samuel Fallows (Chicago: The Howard-Severance Co., 1906), p. 428. Cf. Immanuel Benzinger, "Circumcision," *Encyclopaedia Biblica*, ed. T. K. Cheyne and J. Sutherland Black, A - D (1899), pp. 829-833.

[4] Kaufmann Kohler, "Circumcision," *The Jewish Encyclopedia*, IV (1907), p. 92.

[5] Walther Eichrodt, *Theology of the Old Testament*, trans. J. A. Baker (Philadelphia' The Westminster Press, 1961), I, 138f. Cf. Gustov Friedrich Oehler, *Theology of the Old Testament*, trans. George E. Day (New York' Funk and Wagnalls, 1883), p. 194.

[6] Kohler, p. 92. Cf. David Jacobson, *The Social Background of the Old Testament* (Cincinnati: Hebrew Union College Press, 1942), p. 301.

[7] "Circumcision," *The Interpreter's Dictionary of the Bible*, A - D (1962), p. 630. Cf. David Jacobson, p. 301.

[8] *Theology of the Old Testament*, trans. George E. Day (New York: Funk and Wagnalls, 1883), p. 194..

[9] *Ibid.*; cf. *The Encyclopedia of the Bible* (Englewood Cliffs: Prentice-Hall, 1965), p. 48.

[10] Gerhard von Rad, *Genesis, A Commentary*, tran. John H. Marks (Philadelphia: Westminster Press, 1972), p. 201; cf. von Rad, *Deuteronomy, A Commentary*, trans. Dorothea Barton (Philadelphia: Westminster Press, 1966), p. 84.

[11] *Encyclopaedia Biblica*, p. 831.

[12] Oehler, p. 191.

[13] *Ibid.*, p. 194.

[14] *Ibid.*

[15] *Ibid.*, p. 193.

[16] *Jewish Encyclopedia*, p. 95.

[17] *Encyclopaedia Biblica*, p. 831.

[18] Bultmann, I, p. 249ff.

[19] S. J. De Vries, "Sin, Sinners," *The Interpreter's Dictionary of the Bible* (1962), R - Z, p. 373.

[20] Bultmann, I, 253.

[21] *Ibid.*, I, 232.

[22] *Ibid.*, I, 233.

[23] *The Encyclopedia of the Bible*, p. 48; cf. *Encyclopaedia Biblica*, pp. 831-832.

[24] *Encyclopaedia Biblica*, p. 831; cf. von Rad, *Genesis, A Commentary*, p. 201; von Rad, *Deuteronomy, A Commentary*, p. 84.

[25]*Kittel's Theological Dictionary of the New Testament*, VI (1968), p. 79.

[26]*The Interpreter's Dictionary of the Bible*, R - Z, p. 373.

[27]*Ibid.*, p. 370.

[28]*Ibid.*, pp. 370ff.

[29]*Ibid.*, p. 364.

[30]*Ibid.*

[31]*Ibid.*, p. 365.

[32]A. Macalister, "Circumcision," *A Dictionary of the Bible*, ed. James Hastings (New York: Charles Scribner's Sons, 1903), p. 443.

[33]*Kittel's Theological Dictionary of the New Testament*, VI (1968), p. 74.

[34]*Deuteronomy, A Commentary*, pp. 183-184.

[35]*Kittel's Theological Dictionary of the New Testament*, VI (1968) p. 83.

[36]*Encyclopaedia Biblica*, A - D, p. 832.

[37]*The Standard Sermons of John Wesley*, I, p. 164.

[38]Bultmann, I, 245; cf. Arndt-Gingrich, *A Greek-English Lexicon*, pp. 42f.

[39]Bultmann, I, 243, 235, 241, 334.

[40]*Ibid.*, I, 234.

[41]*Ibid.*

[42]*Ibid.*, I, 240.

[43]*Ibid.*, I, 243.

[44]*Ibid.*, I, 240.

45*Ibid.*, I, 239.

46*The Interpreter's Dictionary of the Bible,* R - Z, p. 373.

47Bultmann, I, 245.

48*Ibid.*

49*Ibid.*

50*Ibid.*, I, 245ff.

51*Ibid.*, I, 249ff.

52*Ibid.*, I, 249; cf. I, p. 25.

53*Ibid.*, I, 238.

54*The Standard Sermons of John Wesley*, II, 364, 373.

55*Ibid.*, II, 459; I, 112ff., 164.

56Bertrand Russell, *Has Man a Future?* (Baltimore: Penguin Books, 1961), p. 9.

57Paul Tillich, *Systematic Theology* (University of Chicago Press, 1957), II, 29ff.; cf. Paul Tillich, *A History of Christian Thought*, ed. Carl E. Braaten (New York: Simon and Schuster, 1967), pp. 409f.

58Bultmann, I, 251.

59*Ibid.*, I, 253.

60*The Works of the Reverend John Fletcher*, ed. John Gilpin (Salem, Ohio: Schmul Publishers, 1974), III, 320-321.

61*The Standard Sermons of John Wesley,* II, 366ff.

62Fletcher, *Checks*, II, 646-647.

63Bultmann, I, 330ff.

64*Ibid.*, I, 332.

65*Ibid.*

[66]*Ibid.*, I, 335.

[67]*Ibid.*, I, 287.

[68]Krister Stendahl, *Paul Among Jews and Gentiles*, (Philadelphia: Fortress Press, 1976), p. 90.

[69]*Ibid.*, pp. 82ff.

[70]*Ibid.*, p. 82.

[71]*Plain Account of Christian Perfection*, p. 45.

[72]*Ibid.*, pp. 44-45.

[73]*Ibid.*, p. 43.

[74]*Ibid.*, pp. 45-46, 42-43.

[75]*The Standard Sermons of John Wesley*, I, 44-45, 304ff.

[76]*Genesis, A Commentary*, p. 198.

[77]*Ibid.*

[78]*Kittel's Theological Dictionary of the New Testament*, VI, (1968) p. 83.

[79]*Ibid.*

[80]Henry Alford, *The New Testament for English Readers* (Chicago: Moody Press, n.d.), p. 752.

[81]Fletcher, *Checks*, II, 645.

[82]*The Poetical Works of John and Charles Wesley* (London: Wesleyan-Methodist Conference Office, 1971), IXX, 298-299.

[83]John Calvin, *Commentary upon the Book of Acts* (Grand Rapids: Eerdmans, 1949), II, 51. Edited from the original English translation of Christopher Fetherstone by Henry Beveridge.

[84]Bultmann, I, 330-340.

[85]*Ibid.*, I, 101.

[86]*Ibid.*, I, 332-333.

[87]*A Plain Account of Christian Perfection*, p. 36.

[88]*The Standard Sermons of John Wesley*, II, 390-391.

[89]*A Plain Account of Christian Perfection*, p. 109.

[90]*The Standard Sermons of John Wesley*, II, 393.

[91]*A Plain Account of Christian Perfection*, p. 53.

[92]*Ibid.*, pp. 80-81.

[93]*Ibid.*, p. 36.

[94]Bultmann, I, 332.

[95]Oehler, p. 194.

[96]*Genesis, A Commentary*, p. 198.

[97]Bultmann, I, 332.

[98]*A Plain Account of Christian Perfection*, p. 109.

[99]Bultmann, *Theology of the New Testament*, I, 234ff.

[100]*Ibid.*, I, 330.

[101]*Ibid.*, I, 337.

[102]*Ibid.*, I, 330-339.

[103]John Skinner, *Genesis, The International Critical Commentary*, ed, S. R. Driver, A. Plummer, and C. A. Briggs (Edinburgh' T. & T. Clark, 1963), p. 290.

[104]*Genesis, A Commentary*, p. 201.

[105]Gerhard von Rad, *Old Testament Theology*, trans. D. M. G. Stalker (New York: Harper & Row, 1962), I, 134.

[106]Bultmann, I, 138.

[107]*The Letters of John Wesley*, ed. John Telford (London: Epworth Press, 1960), 280.

[108]Harald Lindström, *Wesley and Sanctification*, pp. 131, 155.

[109]*A Plain Account of Christian Perfection*, pp. 78-79.

[110]*Ibid.*, p. 80.

[111]*Ibid.*, pp. 80-81; cf. Harald Lindström, p. 131.

[112]*Ibid.*, pp. 82-83.

[113]Christopher Stead, *Divine Substance* (Oxford: Clarendon Press, 1977), p. 1.

[114]*Ibid.*, p. 25.

[115]Paul Tillich, *Systematic Theology* (Chicago: University of Chicago Press, 1951), I, 188.

[116]*Ibid.*, I, 188. Paul Edwards' analysis of nonbeing in the thought of Paul Tillich reflects a basic misunderstanding of the way this concept has functioned in classical theology. His philosophical positivism is most evident in his giving the concept of nonbeing a purely logical function to denote the sheer absence of being and his disallowance of any metaphysical concept of reality at all. (Cf. "Professor Tillich's Confusion," *Philosophy of Religion*, ed., Norbert O. Shedler [New York: Macmillan, 1974], pp. 202ff.). His attempted *reductio ad absurdum* of Tillich's concept of nonbeing is seen in his comparing the quite meaningless categories of *and*-being and *or*-being with nonbeing (*ibid.*, p. 205). If Edwards had paid close attention to Tillich's distinction between the concepts of a logical non-being (*ouk on*) and an ontological nonbeing (*mē on*), Tillich's "bombastic redescription" (*ibid.*, p. 199) might not have seemed so absurd. Edwards' concept that an "irreducible metaphor" which cannot be translated into universal language is "devoid of cognitive meaning" (*ibid.*, p. 193) is also another instance of his extreme positivism. Michael Polanyi's concept of the *tacit* dimension of knowledge is a much needed corrective to a positivistic interpretation of language (*Personal Knowledge* [University of Chicago Press, 1958], p. 95).

[117]*Ibid.*

[118]Cf. C. S. Lewis, *Mere Christianity* (New York: Macmillan, 1972), pp. 48f.

[119]Cf. Frederick Copleston, *A History of Philosophy*, Vol. II: *Medieval Philosophy*, Part I (Garden City, New York: Image Books, 1962), pp. 99-100.

[120]Cf. R. G. Collingwood, *The Idea of History* (London: Oxford University Press, 1956), pp. 46ff.; H. Orton Wiley, *Christian Theology* (Kansas City, MO- Beacon Hill Press, 1964), I, 335-339.

[121]Tillich, *Systematic Theology*, I, 245.

[122]Georgia Harkness, *The Fellowship of the Holy Spirt* (Nashville: Abingdon Press, 1966), p. 108ff.; Karl Barth, *Church Dogmatics*, trans. G.T. Thomson (Edinburgh: T. & T. Clark, 1963), I, 1, 408.

[123]Stead, p. 267; cf. Barth, *Church Dogmatics*, I, Part I, 400-401.

[124]Barth, *Church Dogmatics*, I, Part I, 401.

[125]Collingwood, p. 47.

[126]*Systematic Theology*, I, 245.

[127]Harkness, p. 110. Barth, *Church Dogmatics*, I, Part I, 408.

[128]Barth, *Church Dogmatics*, I, Part I, 407.

[129]Charles Hartshorne, *The Divine Relativity* (New Haven: Yale University Press, 1967), p. X.

[130]Stead, p. 273.

[131]*Ibid.*, pp. 164-165.

[132]*Church Dogmatics*, I, Part I, 150.

[133]*Ibid.*, p. X.

[134]*Ibid.*, p. 16.

[135]*Ibid.*, P. 17.

[136]*Ibid.*, p. 340.

[137]*Ibid.*, pp. 400ff., 408ff.

# CHAPTER VI.

## JOHN FLETCHER'S CONCEPT OF
## CHRISTIAN PERFECTION

The writings of John Fletcher have had a significant bearing upon the development of holiness theology within the Wesleyan movement. They were standard reading for the Methodist preachers in the eighteenth century and have also had a significant influence upon the development of nineteenth century holiness theology in America.[1]

Fletcher is Methodism's first systematic theologian. After graduating from the University of Geneva he did further studies at Lentzburgh in the canton of Berne, and at Nyon.[2] He came to England in 1752 where he came into contact with the Methodists.[3] Fletcher soon came to look upon Wesley as his "spiritual guide."[4] Throughout the remaining years Fletcher and Wesley were bosom friends. In his biography of Fletcher, Wesley writes:

> I was intimately acquainted with him for thirty years. I conversed with him morning, noon, and night, without the least reserve, during a journey of many hundred miles; and in all that time I never heard him speak an improper word, or saw him do an improper action. To conclude: Within fourscore years, I have known many excellent men, holy in heart and life: but one equal to him I have not known; one so uniformly and deeply devoted to God. So unblamable a man, in every

respect, I have not found either in Europe or America. Nor do I expect to find another such on this side eternity.[5]

In writing of Fletcher's *Checks to Antinomianism*, Wesley recommends them in glowing terms: "One knows not which to admire the most, the *purity* of the language: (such as scarce any foreigner wrote before) the *strength* and *clearness* of the arguments: or the *mildness* and *sweetness* of the spirit that breathes throughout the whole."[6]

Wesley's admiration for Fletcher, as well as his being "a great favourite" among the Methodists,[7] led him to designate Fletcher as his successor of the Methodist movement. Though Fletcher declined the invitation, his untimely death would have prevented him from assuming that responsibility.

John Wesley spoke of himself, Charles Wesley, and John Fletcher as an "Exposed triumvirate."[8] Luke Tyerman, one of the earliest scholars to provide a biography of Wesley and Fletcher, speaks of the relationship among the three leaders of Methodism this way:

Among the Wesleyan Methodists, he settled forever all the questions of the Calvinian controversy. For many a long year, Methodist preachers drew their arguments and illustrations from his invaluable "Checks." . . . He did for Wesley's theology what no other man than himself, at that period, could have done. John Wesley traveled, formed Societies, and governed them. Charles Wesley composed unequalled hymns for the Methodists to sing: and John Fletcher, a native of Calvinian Switzerland, explained, elaborated, and defended the doctrines they heartily believed.[9]

John Knight, a recent interpreter of John Fletcher, writes:

Fletcher's writings gave the Methodist Revival an intellectual and theological foundation which today is almost universally accepted as matter of course. After he finished what he had to say on predestination, election, free will, good works, and Christian perfection, there was little left to be said — save for the perennial task of adapting to continuously changing cultural conditions.[10]

Knight also points out that there has been a growing recognition in recent years of "the importance of Fletcher to the development of Wesleyan theology."[11]

In the light of the recent resurgence of interest in the doctrine of the Holy Spirit within the Church as a whole, Fletcher's writings are highly relevant. In this respect, this chapter will focus upon the two main aspects of Fletcher's theology — his doctrine of dispensations and his equation of Pentecostal language with Christian perfection.

## 1. Fletcher's Doctrine of Dispensations

The writings of John Wesley and John Fletcher presuppose degrees of faith corresponding "to the different manifestations of Father, Son, and Holy Spirit."[12] Though John Wesley did not develop a trinitarian concept of grace in a systematic way like Fletcher, Fletcher believed his concept of the degrees of faith was in agreement with Wesley's sermons. It also is apparent that Wesley agreed in general with Fletcher's interpretation of Christian perfection along the lines of a doctrine of dispensations.

Since Fletcher's writings so heavily emphasized the doctrine of dispensations, it would hardly have been likely for Wesley to have remained silent if he disagreed with it. In fact, Wesley designated Fletcher to be his successor as leader of the Methodist movement because of his scholarly learning and "clear understanding" of "Methodist doctrine."[13] Wesley's selection of Fletcher in January, 1773, comes well after his "doctrine of dispensations" and his equation of Pentecostal language with Christian perfection.

In his *Third Check to Antinomianism* (February, 1772), Fletcher distinguished among the six degrees of spiritual life. Of special significance are the fifth and sixth degrees of faith:

(5.) The life of the feeble Christian, or disciple of John, who is "baptized with water unto repentance for the remission of sins," and believing in "the Lamb of God," immediately pointed out to him, enjoys the blessings of the primitive Christians before the day of pentecost. And, (6.) The still more abundant life, the life of the adult or perfect Christian, imparted to him when the love of God, or power from on high, is plentifully shed abroad in his believing soul, on the day that Christ "baptizes him with the Holy Ghost and with fire, to sanctify him wholly, and seal him unto the day of redemption."[14]

In making these six distinctions, Fletcher stresses that there is only one kind of faith, though varying degrees of this one faith. The one faith is always faith in "the mercy of God in Jesus Christ," though it be "the saving faith peculiar to the sincere disciples of Noah, Moses, John the Baptist, and Jesus Christ."[15]

Fletcher appeals to Wesley's sermons as support for his doctrine of varying degrees of faith according to the different manifestations of the Trinity. He quotes from Wesley's sermons, "Salvation by Faith,"[16] "Christian Perfection,"[17] and "Scriptural Christianity"[18] to substantiate his equation of the Pentecostal dispensation with Christian perfection. His reference to Wesley's sermons was intended to show that Wesley also differentiated among the various degrees of faith and that Wesley himself identified the possibility of Christian perfection with the Pentecostal outpouring of the Spirit. Fletcher particularly cites Wesley's sermon on "Scriptural Christianity" to show that he linked Christian perfection with being "filled with the Spirit."[19] Whether or not Fletcher's interpretation of Wesley's sermons is valid is another matter; yet in referring to Wesley, Fletcher was defending himself against the charge that he was the first to "set forth the doctrine of the dispensations."[20]

If Wesley thought that Fletcher's "doctrine of dispensations" was not representative of "Methodist doctrine," he nowhere rejects it. Nor does it seem that he would have spoken of Fletcher's "clear understanding" of what Methodists believe if he disagreed with it. Wesley did express a mild reservation about Fletcher's terminological use of "receiving the Spirit" as descriptive of Christian perfection, but he does not indicate any reservations about his idea of dispensations.[21] In one instance Wesley implied strong agreement with Fletcher's doctrine of dispensation. This agreement is expressed in a letter in which he recommends Fletcher's doctrine of dispensation for helping one to understand the nature of his own Christian experience: "You should read Mr. Fletcher's *Essay on Truth*. He has there put it beyond all doubt that there is medium between a child of God and a child of the devil — namely, a servant of God."[22] It is this "Essay on Truth"* where Fletcher specifically articulates his doctrine of dispensations and appeals to Wesley's sermons for support. If Wesley had thought that Fletcher had quoted him out of context or had misinterpreted his thought, he would hardly have recommend it as means for helping someone to understand the state of his Christian experience.

The intent of Fletcher's doctrine of dispensations was to show the theological basis for Wesley's concept of two works of grace. For example, there are those who have faith in God as Father who is Creator. Others have faith in Christ as Son who is Redeemer. Still others have faith in God as Holy Spirit who is Sanctifier. Fletcher interprets the Apostles' Creed to imply these three degrees of faith:

(1.) Faith "in God the Father Almighty, who made heaven and earth," which is the faith of the heathens.
(2.) Faith in the Messiah, or "in Jesus Christ, his only begotten Son, our Lord," which is the faith of pious Jews, of John's disciples, and of imperfect Christians, who, like the apostles before the day of pentecost, are yet strangers to the great outpouring of the Spirit:

---

* Wesley assumed responsibility for publishing Fletcher's *Works*, as he indicated at the end of the preface to Fletcher: *Works* (London: printed by G. Paramore, 1795), III, viii.

and (3.) Faith "in the Holy Ghost;" faith of the operation of God, by which Christians complete in Christ believe "according to the working of God's almighty power," and are "filled with righteousness, peace, and joy in [thus] believing.[23]

Fletcher's distinction among the dispensations is similar, though not equivalent to the thought of Wesley who also points out "that there are several stages in Christian life, as in natural [life]."[24] Some are "babes," others are "young men." The highest stage of the Christian life is that of "fathers," who know "the Father, and the Son, and the Spirit of Christ, in your inmost soul. Ye are 'perfect men,' being grown up to 'the measure of the stature of the fulness of Christ.'"[25]

In his sermon, "On Faith," Wesley quotes extensively from Fletcher's "Essay on Truth." Wesley indicates his fundamental agreement with "Mr. Fletcher, in his Treatise on the various Dispensations of the Grace of God."[26] He shows that Fletcher teaches "that there are four dispensations [actually, Fletcher usually spoke of three dispensations, though he distinguished among many degrees of faith] that are distinguished from each other, by the degree of light which God vouchsafes to them that are under each." Wesley's entire sermon consists of his explication of this doctrine of dispensations in which he shows that there are degrees of faith varying from the faith of a servant to the faith of one made perfect in love.[28]

In *Plain Account of Christian Perfection*, Wesley equates perfect love with "full of His Spirit."[29] Wesley also speaks of the possibility of Christian perfection because there has "been a larger measure of the Holy Spirit given under the Gospel than under the Jewish dispensation."[30] In yet another place in *Plain Account*, Wesley equates Christian perfection with "receiving a high degree of the Spirit of holiness."[31]

He further equates "the fruit of the Spirit" in its entirety with Christian perfection.[32] It is the "fruit of the Spirit" which is the witness of the children of God "in the highest sense" (i.e., those entirely sanctified) in contrast to the children of God "in the lowest sense" (i.e., the justified believer).[33] In response to the question, "Have we not all the fruit of the

Spirit when we are justified?" Wesley denies "all who are justified do."[34] Only the children of God "in the highest sense" can be said to possess completely "the fruit of the Spirit."[35] Wesley also equates "being sealed with the promised Holy Spirit" in Eph. 1:13, Eph. 4:30 and II Cor. 1:22, with Christian perfection.[36]

It is clear that Wesley associated Christian perfection with Pentecostal reality. This is further attested in a letter to a Miss March (March 14, 1768). Wesley wrote:

> There are innumerable degrees, both in a justified and a sanctified state, more than it is possible for us exactly to define. I have thought the lowest degree of the latter [i.e., the sanctified state] implies the having but one desire and one design [i.e., perfect love]. I have no doubt but in that general outpouring of the Spirit [Pentecostal language] God did give ____ [ an unnamed person] this degree of salvation . . . the threshold of Christian perfection.[37]

In yet another place Wesley relates sanctification to the baptism with the Holy Spirit:

> Many years ago my brother frequently said, 'Your day of Pentecost is not fully come; but I doubt not it will: And you will then hear of persons sanctified, as frequently as you do not of persons justified.' Any unprejudiced reader may observe, that it was now fully come. And accordingly we did hear of persons sanctified, in London, and most other parts of England, and in Dublin, and many other parts of Ireland, as frequently as of persons justified.[38]

Though Wesley located the basis of Christian perfection in Pentecostal *reality*, it is a matter of dispute whether he allowed for the equation of Pentecostal *language* and Christian perfection in the same way that Fletcher did. This is an issue to be discussed later, but the point to be made in this present discussion is that Wesley believed that the reality of Pentecost made available for the first time fully sanctifying grace. Yet it was Fletcher who gave the doctrine of dispensations its clearest systematic statement. Fletcher largely defended the doctrine on the basis of his exposition of Scripture, yet he did indicate its basis in the broader context of the history of Christian thought and especially in the theology of the Anglican Church.

It can also be seen that the doctrine of dispensations is similar to Roman Catholic theology, with its emphasis upon the various stages of the Christian life. As Ives Congar, a Roman Catholic theologian, puts it, the two stages of the Christian life are based in Easter and Pentecost.[39] He further writes: "With the help of the Bible we can (as the early Fathers did) apportion the various parts of God's work among the divine persons of the Blessed Trinity; and we then see what can be called, in human terms, an ever-deepening and closer concern of God with his creatures."[40] He shows that the purpose of the resurrection of Jesus from the dead was to effect our justification through Christ our Redeemer and the Pentecostal gift of the Spirit was to effect our sanctification. Our salvation corresponds to the three moments of God's revelation.[41] Hence, what happened in the history of salvation for the sake of the redemption of the whole world is to be repeated in the individual lives of believers, with the two decisive salvific events being Easter and Pentecost.[42]

Though there is this real differentiation within the Trinity among Creator, Redeemer, and Sanctifier, it should not be thought that Catholic theology teaches that there are separate persons within the trinity. Nor should it be thought that the two stages of the Christian life means that one could experience the Son without the Spirit. As Congar has expressed it, there is a "duality," yet there is a "unity" of the Christian life.[43] To speak of the unique grace of God which has become effective after Pentecost is not to suggest the Spirit and grace were inoperative before Pentecost. What Congar is suggesting seems to correspond closely with Fletcher's doctrine of dispensations.

*In language* one makes a distinction in his experience with

God as Father, Son, and Holy Spirit; yet *in reality* the three persons of the Trinity are together in their activity even though there is also a differentiation in their activities as Creator, Redeemer, and Sanctifier. Fletcher has succinctly pointed out this distinction between the eternality of the Father, Son, and Holy Spirit on the one hand, and their successive manifestations in saving history on the other hand.

> These three dispensations have one common end. They mutually tend to manifest the different perfections of the Supreme Being, to raise man from his present low estate, and to perfect his nature. This three-fold design is apparent under the dispensation of the Father; it unfolds itself more clearly under that of the Son; and shines out with increasing lustre under that of the Holy Spirit. As it is one and the same sun that animates every thing in the natural world, so it is one and the same God who operates every thing in the kingdom of grace. He, whom we address as our heavenly Father, in that sacred form of prayer which is common among Christians, is the very God in whose name the ancient patriarchs were accustomed to bless their children. The Word, through which we address him, is no other than that "Light of the world," by which the antediluvian fathers were illuminated in their several generations: and the Holy Ghost, by which the souls of the faithful are divinely regenerated, is the same Spirit that primarily "moved upon the face of the waters," Gen. i,2; of which also it was said in the days of Noah, "My Spirit shall not always strive with man," Gen. vi,3.
>
> There never was a time in which the Son and the Spirit were not occupied in completing the salvation of believers. But there was a time when the Son became manifest upon the earth, making a visible display of his astonishing labours; and then it was that his particular dispensation had its commencement. So likewise there was a time when the Holy Ghost, more abundantly shed forth by the Father and the Son, began to work his mysterious operations in a more sensible manner, and at that time commenced the particular dispensation of the Spirit, which serves to perfect the dispensation of

the Son, as that of the Son was given to perfect the dispensation of the Father.[44]

It can thus be seen that for Fletcher, his doctrine of dispensations is not a variation of the trinitarian heresy of Modalism, nor is it a tritheism. Rather, the Father, Son, and Holy Spirit have always had a *togetherness* in their activities because they in their threeness constitute one single essence. Yet there are three *eternal* distinctions within the triune being of God and these three distinctions within God correspond to three unique activities of creating, redeeming, and sanctifying. Likewise, each believer may find himself progressing in accordance with this threefold stage of salvation history.

There is, however, a serious weakness in Fletcher's theology of dispensations. His concept of an evangelical fulness of the Spirit needs to be balanced by a corresponding emphasis upon the objective, worldly reality of the Church as the body of Christ. In so doing, his equation of Pentecostal language (e.g., "filled with the Spirit") and Christian perfection could have been made without at the same time equating the whole dispensational reality of Pentecost with the doctrine of Christian perfection. That Fletcher equated the reality of the Church in a narrow, subjectivistic manner with those made perfect in Christian love can be seen in his call to believers to enter the dispensation of the Spirit:

If we will attain the full power of godliness, and be peaceable as the Prince of Peace, and merciful as our heavenly Father, let us go on to the perfection and glory of Christianity; let us enter the full dispensation of the Spirit. Till we live in the pentecostal glory of the Church: till we are baptized with the Holy Ghost; till the Spirit of burning and the fire of Divine love have melted us down, and we have been truly cast into the softest mould of the Gospel: till we can say with St. Paul, "We have received the Spirit of love, of power, and of a sound mind;" till then we shall be carnal rather than spiritual believers; we shall divide into sects like the Jews, and at best we shall be like the disciples of John and of Christ before they had received the gift of the Holy Ghost.[45]

Fletcher thereby maintains that if one fails to possess "the first love of the Church" he ceases to be a "spiritual" Christian and becomes like "carnal believers, even as . . . babes in Christ." Though he is still a believer he is no longer part of "pentecostal Christianity."[46]   Hence, "the kingdom in the Holy Ghost" is composed of those who are "partakers of so great salvation" through "the promise of the Father"; it is made up of those who know the love of Christ which "perfects believers in one."[47]   In a letter to Miss Perronet (January 19, 1777), Fletcher defines the "pentecostal Church" as "the kingdom" of believers made perfect in love.[48]

While Fletcher is quite generous in allowing that the heathen, Jews, and imperfect Christians are not in "a damnable state" if they are faithful to the measure of the light of natural reason which God the Father has in nature and grace given to them;[49] he is, on the other hand, quite restrictive in permitting others to be called Christians even though they may have experienced forgiveness of sins through "faith in Christ." In this respect, John the Baptist "saw the kingdom of heaven: he was not far from it. But yet he did not enter into it. He died 'a just man, made perfect,' according to his own incomplete dispensation, but not according to the dispensation of Christ and his Spirit."[50]   Yet John the Baptist was kept from participating in the "baptism with the Holy Ghost" because "the Holy Ghost was not yet given in the Christian measure."[51]   Fletcher then concludes that it is still possible for one today, though wrongly, to "rest satisfied with the inferior manifestations of the Spirit which belong to the baptism of John or to infant Christianity" instead of becoming a member of "the kingdom of the Holy Ghost" and of "perfect Christianity."[52]   Hence Fletcher maintains a sharp distinction among "faith in God," "faith in Jesus Christ" (pious Jews, disciples of John the Baptist and "imperfect Christians," i.e., "babes in Christ"), and "faith in the Holy Ghost" (perfect Christians).[53]   To have faith in the Holy

Ghost is to be made a true member of the kingdom of God. While a disciple of John the Baptist experiences faith in Christ as the one who takes away the sins of the world, "perfect Christians" alone are those who are established in the "kingdom of righteousness, peace, and joy in the Holy Ghost" through the baptism with the Holy Spirit.[54]

As an illustration of these three stages, Fletcher cites the experience of those hearers of Peter's sermon on the day of Pentecost who "passed from faith in the Father to an explicit faith in the Son,"[55] after which Peter exhorted them "to believe the great promise concerning the Holy Ghost."[56] Hence, for one to experience "this dispensation of the Holy Ghost" is to become a member of "Christ's spiritual kingdom."[57] Fletcher thus excludes those believers such as disciples of John the Baptist and "babes in Christ" from membership in the "pentecostal Church," even though they have "faith in Christ." Only those who are perfect in love are members of Christ's "spiritual kingdom" and the "pentecostal Church."*

What is further surprising is that Fletcher defines Christian perfection in terms of "the Spirit of adoption" and "the birth of the Spirit." For example, in his "Essay on Truth" to be an awakened sinner is to have "faith in Christ"; it is to experience the "Spirit of bondage unto fear." In contrast to this penitent believer is the perfect believer who has received "full assurance — the faith of Christianity in its state of perfection."[58] This perfect Christian, in contrast to the penitent believer, possesses "the Spirit of adoption."[59] Likewise, Paul became an awakened sinner on the road to Damascus. During the three-day period which followed, he experienced "the spirit of bondage unto fear," which corresponds to the experience of the penitent believers who are "faithful to the grace of their inferior dispensation." Paul's deliverance from blindness

---

*John Knight says that Fletcher "came close to asserting that one is not a true Christian until he is filled with the Holy Spirit," *The Wesleyan Theological Journal*, XIII (Spring, 1978), 27. In fact, that is *exactly* what Fletcher meant.

under the ministry of Ananias corresponds to the experience of the apostles who received "power from on high . . . after our Lord's ascension,"[60] which made them perfect in love.

In his *Last Check*, Fletcher further equates "the Spirit of adoption" with "this glorious liberty . . . under the perfection of the Christian dispensation," whereas one who has "received the spirit of bondage again to fear" is one who is a "disciple of Moses, a poor, carnal Jew, and remains still a stranger to the glorious privilege of the Christian dispensation."[61] Children of God under the Jewish dispensation are classified "servants" [62] – "such children as were in a stage of nonage and bondage."[63] The Christian dispensation refers to those "true Christians" who know "the glorious liberty of the *adult* sons of God."[64] For Fletcher, living in the Christian dispensation thus always denoted the adulthood faith of perfect Christians in contrast to the "infant Christianity" of pre-pentecostal believers and pious Jews.

In his sermon on the "State of the Natural Man," Fletcher further illustrates these threefold stages in reference to Paul's conversion. In becoming "a real Christian," Paul moved from the natural state of "an unawakened, unregenerate man" (who had "faith in God" and was thus not in "a damnable state")* to "an awakened and returning sinner" ("faith in Christ" like a disciple of John the Baptist or babe in Christ) on the road to Damascus, to a "true believer" when he received the "Spirit of adoption" in the house of Ananias. These three stages successively experienced constituted his "new birth."[65]

In this respect, Fletcher maintains that entrance into "the kingdom of the Holy Ghost" (i.e., into perfect Christianity) is made by the "new birth."[66] In a letter to Mary Bosanquet (who later became his wife), dated on March 7, 1778, Fletcher writes:

---

*As it will be pointed out subsequently, regeneration for Fletcher is identical to sanctification. Hence to be *unregenerate* for Fletcher does not necessarily imply that one is living a life of sin.

> If you ask me what I think to be the truth with respect to Christian perfection, I reply, my sentiments are exposed to the world in my essay on 'Christian Perfection,' and in my essay on 'Truth,' where I lay the stress of the doctrine on the great *promise of the Father,* and on the *Christian fulness of the Spirit.* This I have done more particularly in a treatise on the "Birth of the Spirit."[67]

Fletcher goes on to say in this same letter that it is "the Birth [of the Spirit] by which we enter into the Kingdom in the in the Holy Ghost [ = Christian perfection, for Fletcher]."[68]

In this respect, one may not have the Spirit of Christ (Rom. 8:9), yet he is not lost if he is "a disciple of Moses."[69] Hence it is possible for one to be an imperfect Christian; yet a perfect Christian is one who is "fully baptized" with the Holy Spirit. These perfect Christians are the only ones who, in the strict sense, can be said to "live in the kingdom of God."[70] One may be a pious Jew, or have "faith in Christ" as the disciples of John the Baptist, yet he is not truly a member of the kingdom of God until he has received the gift of the Holy Spirit. Fletcher writes in his sermon on the new birth, which was mentioned in his letter to Mary Bosanquet cited above, that the new birth is to be defined as "an entire change of our souls." He writes:

> He declares that your righteousness, which does not exceed that of the Pharisees, will never introduce you into the kingdom of God. Yes, were you a second Cornelius, a devout man, fearing God with all your house, giving much alms to the people, seeking God with fasting and continual prayer, if God hath not accepted you in the Beloved; if by faith in the name of Jesus you have not received remission of your sins; if the Holy Spirit have not descended upon you; if God, who knoweth the heart, beareth not witness to you as to him, purifying your heart by faith; your baptism has not saved you. And although you may not be far from the kingdom you are not yet possessed of it, you are not yet regenerated. You have the fear of the Lord, but not

his love. You are not yet a child of God. You still want the Spirit of adoption in order to be a Christian; for in Christ Jesus neither circumcision nor uncircumcision availeth any thing, but a new creation; *an entire change* [italics mine] of our souls, as well as of our life. In a word, "a new heart, a right spirit: the kingdom of God within us."[71]

In this sermon on the new birth, Fletcher further defines regeneration or the new birth as consisting both of justification and sanctification. The new birth begins in justifying faith, but is not completed until the work of sanctification is finished. He writes:

We, therefore, define sanctification to be that powerful work of the Holy Spirit upon the heart of a pardoned sinner, by which he receives power to go on "from faith to faith;" by which, illuminated more and more "to see the glory of God in the face of Jesus Christ," and "renewed day by day" in the image of his Saviour, which he had lost in Adam, he feels himself internally "changed from glory into glory," until he be "filled with all the fulness of God;" until he "loves the Lord his God with all his heart, and with all his soul, and with all his strength, and his neighbour as himself," even as Christ loved him. This is the highest point of the sanctification of a believer, and consequently, *his regeneration is complete* [italics mine].[72]

In this same context, Fletcher equates regeneration with being "baptized by the Holy Ghost."[73]

In his sermon, "The Nature of Regeneration," Fletcher speaks of the new birth as constituting one's total renewal to the image of God. It is the "mighty change" of becoming "a spiritual, or new man,"[74] who is an "adult" Christian as opposed to a "babe in Christ."[75]

The work of grace, whereby we are thus born again, is so great that St. Paul calls it *a new creation*; and it deserves that name, for thereby the soul of man is renewed throughout, with all the powers and faculties thereof; his carnal, sensual earthly disposition is turned into a spiritual and a heavenly one; his blind understanding is enlightened with the knowledge of God and Jesus Christ . . . Thus is he restored to that happiness, to that image of God, wherein he was at first created, though before, on account of his corruption through the fall, he was altogether destitute of it. O! how great, how inconceivably great must man's depravation be by nature, since God cannot fit him for glory by mending or repairing the Divine image in which he first made him; but must thus, as it were, create him a second time, and cause him to be born again, and made anew.[76]

Until one has entered into the state of "faith in the Holy Ghost," he is still in "the pangs of the new birth,"[77] even as Paul was until he had passed from the natural state of an unawakened Jew (faith in God) and the awakened state of a penitent sinner (faith in Christ) on the road to Damascus to the state of "a true believer, who loves God above all persons and things" (faith in the Holy Ghost). Paul thus became a true believer when he received "the Spirit of adoption" at the house of Ananaias.[78]

In his essay, "The Portrait of St. Paul," Fletcher's equation of regeneration with Christian perfection is further apparent. In this essay he urges the faithful pastor to become acquainted with the three dispensations in order to advance believers into the Kingdom of the Holy Spirit. "Converted sinners, or believers, are either under the dispensation of the Father, under that of the Son, or under that of the Holy Ghost, according to the different progress they have made in spiritual things."[79] He further says: "Under the dispensation of the Father, believers constantly experience the fear of God, and, in general, a much greater degree of fear than love. Under the economy of the Son, love begins to gain ascendancy over fear. But under the dispensation of the Holy Spirit, 'perfect love casteth out fear,' I John vi, 18."[80]

He distinguishes the three dispensations in the following manner, which limits "the Spirit of adoption" to those who have entered the dispensation of the Spirit (i.e., those made perfect in love):

> Under the economy of the Father, the *believer* [italics mine] is frequently heard to exclaim, "O wretched man that I am! who shall deliver me from the body of this death?" Rom. vii, 24. Under that of the Son, he gratefully cries out, "I thank God," who hath effectually wrought this deliverance, "through Jesus Christ our Lord," Rom. vii, 25. But under the perfect Gospel, which is the dispensation of the Spirit, all believers are enabled to say with one voice, "We have not received the spirit of bondage again to fear; but we have received the Spirit of adoption, whereby we cry, Abba, Father! The Spirit itself beareth witness with our spirit, that we are the children of God, and joint heirs with Christ," Rom. viii, 15-17.[81]

Thus, for Fletcher, those who have "the spirit of bondage and fear" are nonetheless "converted sinners, or believers" in contrast to "the unbelieving and impenitent who are to be considered as without God and without hope" and who live "without any symptom of fear."[82] Yet those believers who have not entered the dispensation of the Spirit "are still carnal and unrenewed by the Spirit of God."[83] Only those who have entered into the dispensation of the Spirit are Christians in the full sense of being perfected in love, so far as Fletcher was concerned.

In his *Last Check*, Fletcher also equates being "born of God" with being a "partaker of God's holiness, according to the perfection of the Christian dispensation."[84] He also in the *Last Check* speaks of Christian perfection as the "birthday of the Spirit of love in our souls."[85]

Fletcher thus defines the new birth (i.e., regeneration) in a way radically different from Wesley. For Wesley, regeneration was the gateway to holiness; it is only the beginning of the human heart; it is not coextensive with the meaning of full salvation. For Wesley, through justification by faith one experiences the Spirit's work of regeneration, thereby making

*193*

him a member of the family of God. Yet Wesley says that "the new birth is not the same with sanctification."[86] While regeneration marked a real change in the justified believer, sanctification is distinguished from regeneration. Hence Wesley says that it is an error to speak of "regeneration as a progressive work, carried on in the soul by slow degrees, from the time of our first turning to God." He thus writes that "this is undeniably true of sanctification; but of regeneration, the new birth, it is not true."[87] Wesley further writes:

> When we are born again, then our sanctification, our inward and outward holiness begins; and thenceforward we are gradually to 'grow up in Him who is our Head.' This expression of the Apostle admirably illustrates the difference between one and the other, and farther points out the exact analogy there is between natural and spiritual things. A child is born of a woman in a moment, or at least in a very short time: afterward he gradually and slowly grows, till he attains to the stature of a man. In like manner, a child is born of God in a short time, if not in a moment. But it is by slow degrees that he afterward grows up to the measure of the full stature of Christ. The same relation, therefore, which there is between our natural birth and our growth, there is also between our new birth and our sanctification.[88]

Sanctification is thus the process whereby one who is already born again (i.e., regenerated) is progressively changed into the likeness of Christ. Further, for Wesley the regenerated man is a babe in Christ and a member of the Church through the imputation of Christ's righteousness, as he makes plain in his sermon, "The Lord our Righteousness."

Though Fletcher described the state of pious Jews, righteous heathen, disciples of John the Baptist, and babes in Christ as not being *regenerate* in the full Christian sense, since they had not received the pentecostal fulness of the Spirit, he insisted that they nevertheless possessed the "directing, sanctifying, and enlivening influences" of the Holy Spirit "according to their dispensation."[89] Hence, instead of

Fletcher's having a low view of the state of grace among those who have not been made perfect in love under the dispensation of the Spirit, he held a high view of the possibility of sanctifying grace under the dispensations of the Father and of the Son. He thus writes:

> Some of my opponents . . . will probably think that to beat me and the doctrine of the dispensations out of the field of truth, they need only laugh at my "inventing" different sorts of faith "by the dozens."

> To nip this witticism in the bud, I declare, once more that I make no difference between the faith of a righteous heathen, and the faith of a father in Christ. . . . That the light of a sincere Jew is as much one with the light of a sincere Christian, as the light of the sun in a cold, cloudy day in March, is one with the light of the sun in a fine day in May. And, that the difference between the saving faith peculiar to the sincere disciples of Noah, Moses, John the Baptist, and Jesus Christ, consists in a variety of *degrees*, and not in the diversity of *species*; saving faith under all dispensations agreeing in the following essentials: (1.) It is begotten by the revelation of some saving truth, presented by free grace, impressed by the Spirit, and received by the believer's prevented free agency. (2.) It has the same original cause in all, that is, the mercy of God in Jesus Christ. (3.) It actually saves all, though in various degrees. (4.) It sets all upon working righteousness; "some bearing fruit thirty, some sixty, and some a hundred fold." And (5.) Through Christ it will bring all that do not make shipwreck of it, to one or another of "the mansions," which our Lord is gone to prepare in heaven for his believing, obedient people.[90]

Fletcher's insistence upon saving faith being a possibility among non-Christian believers is indeed an arguable position. Here Wesley was also in full agreement. To be sure, Fletcher points out that non-Christian believers usually lack the inner assurance of salvation, as J. N. D. Anderson also shows in his contemporary treatment of this complex issue.[91] Nevertheless, Fletcher's understanding of the dispensation of the Spirit tends toward a subjectivistic narrowing down of the Church. Surely "babes in Christ" are not second-rate Christians; nor are they to be placed in the same category of "pious Jews"[92] who are in "a state of nonage and bondage."[93] Wesley was surely right to insist that they were sons of God and possessed the witness of the Spirit. Their sonship is centered in Jesus Christ; hence they are truly Christians. Also, righteous heathen and pious Jews are surely members of the kingdom of God, even though not members of the Church. Fletcher's doctrine of dispensations needs to be developed more in line with an understanding of the all-inclusive nature of the kingdom of God on the one hand, and the nature of the corporate structure of the Church on the other hand. In so doing it would be appropriate to speak of the degrees of faith according to which it can be said that "babes in Christ" are *experientially* at the level of a disciple of John the Baptist, yet they are nonetheless members of the Church which was established at Pentecost and, thus, are "adopted sons of God."

Here it is to be recognized that the actual status of many believers who are already incorporated into the Church corresponds *experientially* with pre-Pentecostal believers, such as "the disciples of John the Baptist." Yet these believers are really members of the Church and not simply to be dubbed as pre-Pentecostal believers. Though they may not have personally appropriated the sanctifying fulness of the Spirit for themselves, they are nonetheless "holy in Christ" by virtue of their faith and incorporation into the Church. This means that every believer is living within the dispensation of Pentecostal reality even if he has not experienced a personal "filling with the Spirit." This distinction between the whole dispensation of Pentecostal reality on the one hand and a personal infilling of the Spirit on the other hand is essential, if the concept of the Church is to be saved from a subjectivistic and individualistic interpretation. Hence the "corporate" nature of the Church ( = "in Christ" motif) corresponds to the whole dispensation of Pentecostal reality; while the holiness of the body of Christ is to be appropriated by each believer through his own personal, Pentecostal infilling of the Spirit. This means that one truly becomes a member of the Church through his justification by faith and regeneration of the Spirit. Yet he is to appropriate in a personal manner the sanctifying fulness of the Spirit which is already imputed to him "in Christ."

From the distinction between the corporate body of Christ on the one hand and individual members on the other hand, it can be seen that there may be a tension between what a believer is *in Christ* and what he is experientially. Oscar Cullmann has shown in this regard that Paul uses two metaphors in describing the Church. The Church is the *body* of Christ, yet Christ is the *Head* of the Church (Eph. 1:22-23). Cullmann shows on the one hand that Christ's righteousness is given to the Church through the Spirit of Pentecost. Hence the Church is the body of Christ. Yet he shows that Paul acknowledges believers do not measure up to the standard of Christ's righteousness; hence Christ is the head of the Church in the sense that he is the pattern and basis of all righteousness.[94]

It is therefore not appropriate to interpret the whole Pentecostal dispensation in an individualistic manner, as if the Church were a mere amalgamation of believers. In this regard, one should not simply equate Pentecostal reality with entire sanctification. To do so would be to ignore that Pentecost had to do primarily with the rise of the Church. In this respect, Fletcher's doctrine of dispensations too unqualifiedly equated Christian perfection with the Pentecostal dispensation. What is lacking in Fletcher is the clear distinction between the Church as the corporate body of Christ on the one hand, and the individual members on the other hand.

While the Church as the corporate body of Christ is holy, individual members may not have fully appropriated sanctifying grace. In this respect, it is one thing to be holy "in Christ"; but it is another thing for Christ to be formed in us. To be sure, to be "in Christ" by virtue of our incorporation into the body of Christ involves an actual change (regeneration and initial sanctification), but individuals in the Church do not usually fully appropriate sanctifying grace until some time subsequent to their conversion-initiation into the Church.

## 2. Pentecostal Language and Sanctifying Grace: Fletcher's Contribution to Wesley's Theology

James D. G. Dunn in his book, *Baptism in the Holy Spirit*, which argues against the Wesleyan concept of two works of grace, has rightly pointed out that John Wesley held the view that Saul was not converted until his arrival in Damascus.[95] In Acts 9:9, where it is said that Saul was blind for three days, Wesley comments in his *Explanatory Notes on the New Testament*: "So long as he seems to have been in the pangs of the new birth." In another context, Wesley specifically says Paul did not have a "sudden conversion" on the road to Damascus; rather, the Lord worked gradually in Paul's soul until Ananias' ministry brought him into a state of conversion.[96]

However, Dunn implies that Wesley equated Paul's conversion with being filled with the Pentecostal Spirit. Yet Wesley nowhere explicitly makes this equation. Wesley locates the place of Paul's conversion to be in Damascus at the house of Judas, but his interpretation of Paul's "filling with the Spirit" is unclear. Nor is it exegetically required to date Paul's actual infilling with the Spirit with his contact with Ananias, though one may well infer this to be the case.*

---

*It is also quite possible that Paul's filling with the Spirit denoted his prophetic preparation rather than his experience of sanctifying grace. It will be pointed out in Chapter VIII that being filled with the Spirit may denote an ethical fullness *or* a prophetic fullness. Only the context can determine the meaning, and it is not altogether clear in this context. Though I am inclined to the former interpretation in this case, F. F. Bruce thinks Paul's filling with the Spirit denoted "the indispensable qualification for the prophetic and apostolic service," *Commentary on the Book of Acts, The New International Commentary on the New Testament* (Grand Rapids: Eerdmans, 1974), p. 201.

In contrast to Wesley it should be noted that even Bengel, whose *Gnomon* Wesley's *Explanatory Notes* are in large part based on, identifies Saul's conversion on the road to Damascus.[97]  John Calvin dates Saul's conversion on the road to Damascus when he "is suddenly changed into a new man"; he is "a new man framed by the Spirit of God."[98]  *The Interpreter's Bible* calls his conversion sudden, whereas it was Ananias who "was the interpreter of the experience."[99]  The preponderance of scholarly opinion is clearly against Wesley and Dunn on this point.[100]

Does Wesley's isolated interpretation of Paul's conversion mean that he did not relate the Pentecostal gift of the Spirit to entire sanctification?  Is the "baptism with the Spirit – entire sanctification" equation typical only of John Wesley's colleagues – John Fletcher, Adam Clarke, Charles Wesley – and not of himself?  In attempting to answer this question, it will be worthwhile to recall the previous discussion in Chapter V, in which it was pointed out that Wesley taught that the basis of Christian perfection was rooted in Pentecostal reality.

Wesley restricted the appropriation of perfect love to the Pentecostal era of grace.  In his sermon on "Christian Perfection," Wesley points out that there is a "wide difference . . . between the Jewish and the Christian dispensation" because prior to Pentecost "the Holy Ghost was not yet given in His sanctifying graces" in full measure.*  Because of the Pentecostal outpouring of the Spirit, the Holy Spirit has been sent "into the hearts of all true believers" to enable them to be "holy in all manner of conversation."  In this respect, Wesley

---

*That in this context "sanctifying graces" denotes entire sanctification is suggested by his emphasis upon being "more than conquerors over sin" and by his use of the phrases: "This great salvation from sin," and "the glorious salvation."  He also directly links the coming of the Pentecostal Spirit with Christian perfection in this immediate context.  Harald Lindström (*Wesley and Sanctification*, p. 135) and Lycurgus M. Starkey, Jr. (*The Work of the Holy Spirit*, pp. 21, 33) also interpret Wesley's use of "sanctifying graces" in this context to denote full sanctification.

says that "when the day of Pentecost was fully come, then *first it was* [italics mine], that they who 'waited for the promise of the Father' were made more than conquerors over sin by the Holy Ghost given unto them." Hence, "this great salvation from sin was not given till Jesus was glorified." Wesley thus says that David is far "from being the pattern or standard of Christian perfection" because "the kingdom of heaven is now set up on earth" and everyone is capable of receiving "the great salvation of God." That is, the Christian dispensation does not look forward to a political restoration of the Davidic kingdom, but rather through the Holy Spirit God now reigns supremely in the hearts of all true believers.[101]

In this particular context it should be noticed that Wesley uses the following equivalent phrases as descriptive of Christian perfection:

1. "more than conquerors over sin,"
2. "this great salvation from sin,"
3. "the great salvation of God," and
4. "the kingdom of heaven is now set up on earth."

The phrase, "the great salvation," is used frequently by Wesley (and Fletcher) to denote Christian perfection.[102] Harald Lindström has shown in this regard that Wesley's normal use of the word "salvation"* is limited to present salvation, i.e., justification and full sanctification, with an emphasis on the latter.[103] This can be seen in his sermon, "Salvation by Faith." Wesley writes:

> *Ye are saved* (to comprise all in one word) from sin. This is the salvation which is through faith. This is that great salvation foretold by the angel. . . . "Thou shalt call His name *JESUS*; for He shall save His people from their sins." And neither here, nor in other parts of holy writ, is there any limitation or restriction. . . . He will

---

*It is to be noticed that Wesley did not distinguish between being "saved" and being "sanctified." Rather, he carefully distinguished between being justified and sanctified, but not between salvation and sanctification.

save from all their sins; from *original* [italics mine] and actual, past and present sin.[104]

Even though Wesley taught that Pentecostal reality was the basis for Christian perfection, he did not develop "a doctrine of dispensations" in a systematic way like Fletcher. Nor did Wesley normally equate Pentecostal language with Christian perfection in the explicit manner in which Fletcher did. Perhaps Fletcher's philosophical and systematic-theological orientation accounts in part for this, whereas Wesley's writings were primarily sermons. Yet it would be most problematic to try to altogether disassociate John Wesley's thought from his very close associate, John Fletcher (who was Methodism's first systematic theologian), as well as from his brother, Charles Wesley (Methodism's hymn writer) — both of whom equated Pentecostal language with perfect love.

In what way, then, is Fletcher's doctrine of dispensations in agreement with John Wesley's thought? This is a most important historical question which deserves careful consideration for any contemporary effort to interpret Wesley's idea of perfection; especially since Pentecostal language has been traditionally used in the Wesleyan tradition to describe the nature of perfect love. We shall now give more detailed attention to this question.

It has already been seen that Fletcher's doctrine of dispensations means that there are three basic stages of the Christian life. First, some believers know God only as Father-Creator. This stage corresponds to the faith of those who have not heard of God incarnate in Jesus Christ but who, nonetheless, have an experience of saving grace in their hearts (e.g., Abraham, Noah, Cornelius).[105] Second, some know God as Son-Redeemer. This second stage corresponds to the faith of "pious Jews" and "disciples of John the Baptist" ("babes in Christ")[106] who have not experienced "the great outpouring of the Spirit." Third, some know God as Holy Spirit-Sanctifier. This third stage corresponds to the faith of those who have experienced the sanctifying fulness of the Holy Spirit and who are "filled with righteousness."[107]

It has already been pointed out that Wesley distinguished among the varying degrees of faith, but not in the theologically precise manner in which Fletcher did. However, it was also pointed out that Fletcher appealed to Wesley's writings to substantiate his doctrine of dispensations.[108] It was also shown that Wesley spoke approvingly of the general idea of Fletcher's doctrine of dispensation. This can be further seen in a letter written by Wesley to Elizabeth Ritchie in London, January 17, 1775:

> Mr. Fletcher has given us a wonderful view of the different dispensations which we are under. I believe that difficult subject was never placed in so clear a light before. It seems God has raised him up for this very thing.[109]

It is also significant that in his "Essay on Truth" Fletcher repeatedly addressed himself to the charge that his doctrine of dispensations was "singular" to himself alone.[110] He also had to defend himself against the accusation that his doctrine of dispensations encouraged a kind of "lukewarm" spiritual life, since it presupposed one could have saving faith while not living experientially in the Pentecostal era. By setting up a supposedly double standard, believers might opt for the lesser demanding life.[111] In the light of the apparently well-known objections to Fletcher's equation of Pentecostal fulness and Christian perfection, it is all the more significant that Wesley approved of Fletcher's writings and selected him to lead the Methodist movement.

Not only did Fletcher's doctrine of dispensations classify the Christian life along the lines of a trinitarian understanding of grace, but he also specifically equated Pentecostal language and perfect love. In urging believers on to the experience of Christian perfection, Fletcher exhorts them to pray in the following fashion:

> Lord, I want a plentitude of thy Spirit, the full promise of the Father, and rivers which flow from the inmost

souls of the believers, who have gone on to the perfection of their dispensation. I do believe that thou
canst and wilt thus "baptize me with the Holy Ghost
and with fire:" help my unbelief; confirm and increase
my faith, with regard to this important baptism. . . .
O, baptize my soul, and make as full an end of the
original sin which I have from Adam. . . . Give me thine
abiding Spirit, that he may continually shed abroad thy
love in my soul. Come, O Lord, with that blessed Spirit:
come thou, and thy Father, in that holy Comforter, —
come to make your abode with me. . . . Send thy Holy
Spirit of promise to fill me therewith, to sanctify me
throughout.[112]

Fletcher further shows in this same regard that "*a believer
completely baptized with the Holy Ghost and with fire*"
is one "in whom he that once visited as a Monitor now fully
resides as a Comforter. . . . The carnal mind and body of sin
are destroyed, and 'God is all and in all' to that just man
'made perfect in love.' "[113] Elsewhere he writes: "With
respect to adult perfect Christianity, which is consequent upon
the baptism of the Holy Ghost, administered by Christ himself, its perfection is described in the sermon on the
mount."[114]

He also shows that "social prayer is closely connected with
faith in the capital promise of the sanctifying Spirit: and
therefore I earnestly recommend that mean of grace, where it
can be had, as being eminently conducive to the attaining of
Christian perfection."[115] He cites the disciples' experience
of Pentecost as an example of Christian perfection being
received through social prayer. He also refers to the Samaritans in Acts 8 as an example of Christian perfection being
received through social prayer: "Thus also the believers at
Samaria were filled with the Holy Ghost, the Sanctifier,
while Peter and John prayed with them, and laid their hands
upon them."[116]

In regard to the question whether or not Christian perfection is received instantaneously or gradually, Fletcher says
that "both ways are good."[117] He shows that there is no

absolutely fixed manner in which God is prescribed to work in the life of the believer. Yet he encourages the believer to expect to receive the experience of perfect love instantly. *Pentecostal language suggests the instantaneous nature of Christian perfection.*

> May not the Sanctifier descend upon your waiting soul, as quickly as the Spirit descended upon your Lord at his baptism? Did it not descend "as a dove," that is, with the soft motion of a dove, which swiftly shoots down, and instantly lights? . . . . If the sun could instantly kindle a mote; nay, if a burning glass can in a moment calcine a bone, and turn a stone to lime; and if the dim flame of a candle can in the twinkling of an eye destroy the flying insect which comes within its sphere, how unscriptural and irrational is it to suppose that, when God fully baptizes a soul with his sanctifying Spirit and with the celestial fire of his love, he cannot in an instant destroy the man of sin, burn up the chaff of corruption, melt the heart of stone into a heart of flesh, and kindle the believing soul into pure, seraphic love![118]

In this same connection Fletcher shows that one may be *"gradually* perfected" in love.[119] That is, it may be that "by acts of feeble faith and feeble love so frequently repeated as to become strong, habitual, and evangelical natural to us" that one comes to live a life of perfect love.[120] Hence he says in this same context:

> Should you ask, how many baptisms, or effusions of the sanctifying Spirit are necessary to cleanse a believer from all sin, and to kindle his soul into perfect love; I reply, that the effect of a sanctifying truth depending upon the ardour of the faith with which that truth is embraced, and upon the power of the Spirit with which it is applied, I should betray a want of modesty if I brought the operations of the Holy Ghost, and the energy of faith, under a rule which is not expressly laid down in the Scriptures. . . . If one powerful baptism of the Spirit "seal you unto the day of redemption, and

cleanse you from all [moral] filthiness,' so much the better. If two or more be necessary, the Lord can repeat them"[121]

Fletcher then goes on to show that the whole body of believers in the early church may have been perfected in love through the giving of the Holy Spirit, including those who had just become believers in Christ on the day of Pentecost. He suggests that while those newly converted to Christ at Pentecost might have experienced perfect love, this does not seem to be the normal pattern because "God does not usually remove the plague of indwelling sin till it has been discovered and lamented."[122] Hence, "while many of them were perfect in love, many might have the imperfection of their love only covered over by a land flood of peace and joy in believing." Yet Fletcher allows:

However, it is not improbable that God, to open the dispensation of the Spirit, in a manner which might fix the attention of all ages upon its importance and glory, permitted the whole body of believers to take an extraordinary turn together into the Canaan of perfect love, and to show the world the admirable fruit which grows there, as the spies sent by Joshua took a turn into the good land of promise before they were settled in it, and brought from thence the bunch of grapes which astonished and spirited up the Israelites, who had not yet crossed Jordan.

Upon the whole, it is, I think, undeniable, from the four first chapters of the Acts, that a peculiar power of the Spirit is bestowed upon believers under the Gospel of Christ; that this power, through faith on our part, can operate the most sudden and surprising change in our souls; and that when our faith shall fully embrace the promise of full sanctification, or of a complete "circumcision of the heart in the Spirit," the Holy Ghost, who kindled so much love on the day of Pentecost, that all the primitive believers loved or seemed to love each other perfectly, will not fail to help us to love one another without sinful self seeking; and as soon as we do so, "God dwelleth in us, and his love is perfected in us," I John iv, 12; John xiv, 23.[123]

It is at this point that Fletcher says a believer might have a number of experiences of the sanctifying fulness of the Holy Spirit before he becomes settled and established in the habit of perfect love. That is, a believer might "take the extraordinary turn into Canaan Land" on several occasions before being settled in perfect love. It is significant to note here that Fletcher interpreted Acts 4:31-33 to be a deepening of Acts 2:1: "Some time after, another glorious baptism . . . carried the disciples of Christ farther* into the kingdom of grace which perfects believers in one."[124] That is, "once more" (Fletcher says) the disciples were filled with the Holy Spirit. Hence, Fletcher speaks of this second filling as the "kingdom" being "confirmed."[125] Yet he says that "if one outpouring of the Spirit . . . so empties us of self, so as to fill us with the mind of Christ, and with pure love, we are undoubtedly Christians in the full sense of the word."[126]

In summing up his discussion concerning the "instantaneous" or "gradual" appropriation of perfect love, Fletcher stresses the *present moment* of realization. While it may take awhile before believers are settled in the habit of pure love, the important thing is: "They now are *all love*. . . . They are all love today; and they take no thought for the morrow."[127]

That one may have a number of "effusions of the sanctifying Spirit" before he becomes settled in the habit of perfect love recalls Fletcher's own personal testimony, given on August 24, 1781:

My dear brethren and sisters, God is here! I feel Him in this place; but I would hide my face in the dust, because I have been ashamed to declare what He has done for

*Notice that Fletcher interprets Acts 4:31-33 as taking the disciples *deeper* into the kingdom, but they entered the kingdom on the day of Pentecost (Acts 2:1) when they were filled with the Holy Spirit (*Works*, II, 631).

*me.* For many years, I have grieved His Spirit; I am deeply humbled; and He has again restored my soul. Last Wednesday evening, He spoke to me by these words, *"Reckon yourselves, therefore, to be dead indeed to sin; but alive unto God through Jesus Christ our Lord."* I obeyed the voice of God: I now obey it; and tell you all, to the praise of His love, — *I am freed from sin.* Yes, I rejoice to declare it, and to be a witness to the glory of His grace, that *I am dead unto sin, and alive unto God, through Jesus Christ,* who is my Lord and King! I received this blessing four or five times before; but I lost it, by not observing the order of God; who has told us, *With the heart man believeth unto righteousness, and with the mouth confession is made unto salvation.* But the enemy offered his bait, under various colours, to keep me from a public declaration of what God had wrought.

When I first received this grace, Satan bid me wait awhile, till I saw more of the *fruits*: I resolved to do so; but I soon began to doubt of the *witness*, which, before, I had felt in my heart; and, in a little time, I was sensible I had lost both. A second time, after receiving this salvation, I was kept from being a witness for my Lord, by the suggestion, "Thou art a public character — the eyes of *all* are upon thee — and if, as before, by *any* means thou lose the blessing, it will be a dishonour to the doctrine of *heart-holiness.*" I held my peace, and again forfeited the gift of God. At another time, I was prevailed upon to hide it, by reasoning, "How few, even of the *children of God,* will receive this testimony; many of them supposing every transgression of the Adamic law is sin; and, therefore, if I profess to be *free* from sin, *all* these will give my profession the lie; because I am *not* free in *their* sense: I am not free from ignorance, mistakes, and various infirmities; I will, therefore, enjoy what God has wrought in me; but I will not say, *I am perfect in love.*" Alas! I soon found again, *He that hideth his Lord's talent, and improveth it not, from that unprofitable servant shall be taken away even that he hath.*

Now, my brethren, you see my folly. I have con-
fessed it in your presence; and *now* I resolve before you
all to confess my Master. I will confess Him to all the
world. And I declare unto you, in the presence of God,
the Holy Trinity, I am now *dead indeed unto sin.* I
do not say, *I am crucified with Christ*, because some of
our well-meaning brethren say, by *this* can only be
meant a *gradual dying*; but I profess unto you, *I am dead
unto sin, and alive unto God*: and, remember, all this is
*through Jesus Christ our Lord. He* is my Prophet,
Priest, and King — my indwelling Holiness — my *all
in all.* I wait for the fulfilment of that prayer, *That
they all may be one, as Thou, Father, art in me and I
in Thee, that they also may be one in us: and that they
may be one, even as we are one.* O for that pure baptismal flame! O for the fulness of the dispensation of
the Holy Ghost! Pray, pray, pray for this![128]

That Fletcher understood the real possibility of having a
number of sanctifying experiences before being established in
the habit of perfect love is also illustrated in his interpretation
of the Galatians who having begun in the Spirit were now
living under the law. Their having "fallen from grace" did not
mean that they were now living in "a damnable state." Rather,
they had fallen from the Christian dispensation of the Spirit
whose reception perfects the believer in love.[129]

There are two other significant selections which show
Fletcher's equation of Pentecostal language and Christian
perfection:

The still more abundant life, the life of the adult or
perfect Christian, imparted to him when the love of
God, or power from on high, is plentifully shed abroad
in his believing soul, on the day that Christ "baptizes
him with the Holy Ghost and with fire, to sanctify him
wholly, and seal him unto the day of redemption."[130]

. . . .

But if Christian perfection is (next to angelic perfection)
the brightest and richest jewel which Christ purchased
for us by his blood; if it is the internal kingdom of God

ruling over all; if it is Christ *fully* formed in our hearts, the *full* hope of glory; if it is the fulfillment of the promise of the Father, that is, "the Holy Ghost given unto us, "to make us abound in righteousness, peace, and joy, through believing;" and in a word, if it is the Shekinah, filling the Lord's human temples with glory; is it right, sir, to despise it as some do?[131]

Is there any indication that Wesley clearly rejected or approved Fletcher's equation of Pentecostal language and Christian perfection? An easy and direct answer to this question is not possible. It is just as misleading to say that he rejected this equation as it would be to say that he explicitly and fully endorsed it. However, I offer the following considerations to show that Wesley at least strongly implied a general agreement with it.

As we have already seen, this general approval of Fletcher's doctrine of dispensations is indicated in a letter in which he recommends Fletcher's "Essay on Truth" which shows "beyond all doubt that there is a medium between a child of God and a child of the devil — namely, a servant of God."[132] It is this essay in which Fletcher specially articulates the distinctions among those who have "faith in the Father," faith in the Son," and "faith in the Holy Spirit." We have already seen that Wesley's sermon, "On Faith," is his own explication of Fletcher's doctrine of dispensations. Yet did Wesley agree with the *specifics* of Fletcher's doctrine of dispensations? More exactly, did Wesley equate Pentecostal language — such as, "filled with the Spirit," "receive the Spirit," and "baptism with the Spirit" with Christian perfection? In 1771, Fletcher in a letter to Lady Huntington observed that if Wesley's writings were taken as a whole, his idea of Christian perfection could be called "the baptism of the Holy Ghost" among other descriptive phrases, including "the Spirit of adoption."

With regard to perfection itself, I believe that when Mr. Wesley is altogether consistent upon that subject, he means absolutely nothing by it but the full cluster of

Gospel blessings, which Lady Huntingdon so warmly presses the students to pursue; namely, Gospel faith, the immediate revelation of Christ, the baptism of the Holy Ghost, the Spirit of adoption, the kingdom that cannot be moved, the element of forgiving love, deep and uninterrupted poverty of spirit, and, in a word, a standing upon Mount Sion and enjoying its great and glorious privileges.[133]

In a letter to Charles Wesley November 24, 1771, Fletcher observed that John Wesley's doctrine of Christian perfection could be improved upon through its identification with the Pentecostal gift of the Spirit;

> I am busy about my third and last check. . . . I want sadly both your prayers and advice. I shall introduce *my*, why not *your* doctrine of the Holy Ghost and make it one with your brother's perfection. He holds the truth, but this will be an improvement upon it, if I am not mistaken. In some of your *pentecost hymns* you paint my light wonderfully. *If you do not recant* them we shall perfectly agree.[134]

Throughout his "Essay on Truth," published in 1774, Fletcher indicates that he believed Wesley's writings implied an agreement with him on this point. In responding to the charge that his doctrine of dispensations was a "novel" opinion peculiar to himself alone, Fletcher quotes extensively from Wesley's writings to show their fundamental agreement.[135] In particular, he shows that Wesley's sermon, "Salvation by Faith," distinguishes "Christian faith, properly so-called, or faith in Christ glorified, not only from the faith of a heathen, but also from the faith of initial Christianity, that is, 'the faith which the apostles, had while our Lord was upon earth.' " The faith of Christ glorified is "the great salvation" of Christian perfection.* The faith of a heathen is the saving faith of

---

*Fletcher thus presupposes that an experience of "Christ glorified" is equivalent to an experience of the fulness of the Pentecostal Spirit, since the Holy Spirit is the Spirit of the exalted Christ. On the other hand, a "Christian" who has not received the fulness of the Pentecostal Spirit is one whose experience corresponds to the disciples' pre-Pentecostal relationship to the earthly Jesus.

any non-Jew or non-Christian who lives up to the light of natural revelation. The faith of initial Christianity corresponds to one who is a pre-Pentecostal "Christian."[136] Accordingly, Fletcher argues that his doctrine of dispensations is contained in Wesley's writings.[137]

Fletcher also interprets Wesley's sermon on "Christian Perfection" as equating Pentecostal "fulness" with Christian perfection.[138] He quotes extensively from this sermon to show that "true believers" and "all real Christians" have experienced Christian perfection and thus belong to the "Kingdom of God on earth."[139]

It is evident throughout Fletcher's writings that he equated the experience of Christian perfection with the Pentecostal dispensation. This means that for one to be a member of the "kingdom of God on earth," and thus to be a true Christian, one must experience the sanctifying fulness of the Pentecostal Spirit. Hence, in a letter to John Wesley, March 18, 1771, Fletcher said: "I am not yet a Christian in the full sense of the word; but I follow after, if so be I may apprehend that for which I am apprehended of Christ."[140] Parenthetically, this is not altogether unlike the Roman Catholic and Anglican doctrine — that there are two initiatory events before one becomes a true and full member of the Church. These two initiatory events are baptism (justification) and Confirmation (the reception of the Pentecostal Spirit). When these rites have been completed one can participate in the Lord's Supper, since he is then a full member of the Church. In like manner Fletcher says perfect Christians are qualified to "enjoy the grace of both sacraments" of baptism and the Lord's Supper.[141]

In support of Fletcher's interpretation of Wesley's thought, it seems evident enough in his sermon on "Christian Perfection" that Wesley equated "true believers" and "real Christians" with "perfect Christians." He speaks of the justified state of "babes" and "young men" as those who do not commit sin, whereas only those who "have known both the Father, and the Son, and the Spirit if Christ, in your inmost soul" are "perfect Christians," in the sense that they are also free from evil tempers.[142] Wesley thereby refers to these perfect Christians as real Christians. Just as Christ had "no evil or sinful thought . . . hence it follows, that neither have *real Christians* [italics mine] ; for 'every one that is perfect is as his Master' (Luke vi. 40)."[143] Wesley further writes: "But his Master was free from all sinful tempers. So, therefore, is His disciple, even every real Christian."[144] He also refers to the perfect Christians as "true believers," in contrast to those believers who are not free from inward sin: "He, [Christ] therefore, who liveth in true believers hath 'purified their hearts by faith'; insomuch that every one that hath Christ in him, the hope of glory, 'purifieth himself, even as He is pure' (I John iii.3). He is purified from pride."[145]

This concept of "true believers" and "real Christians" further coincides with Wesley's distinction between "the Almost Christian" who has a low level of saving faith and "the altogether Christian" who has perfect love.

In a letter to Mary Stokes, March 17, 1771, Wesley commends her for her faith in Christ, yet he exhorts her: "The Sun of righteousness will rise upon you in quite another manner than you have hitherto experienced." He further asks her: "What hinders you from receiving Him now?" This further experience of the Spirit will make her and her friend, Molly Jones, "not almost but altogether Christians!"[146]

Hence the "altogether Christian" is one in whom the love of God "engrosses the whole heart, as takes up all the affections, as fills the entire capacity of the soul, and employs the utmost extent of all its faculties."[147] Wesley also distinguishes between "nominal Christians" and "real Christians," such as the apostles who were at "first filled with the Holy Ghost" on the day of Pentecost.*[148] To be sure, it cannot be argued that Wesley always — or even most of the time — equated "real Christians" with perfect Christians, though it is usually strongly implied.

When further showing in his "Essay on Truth" that the doctrine of perfect love is identified with the Pentecostal

---

*In his *Explanatory Notes on the New Testament*, Wesley says the disciples were filled with the Spirit "afresh" in Acts 4:31.

experience of the disciples,[149] Cornelius' reception of the Spirit,[150] the Anglican doctrine of Confirmation,[151] and other Scriptural references (e.g., Acts 19:2; Acts 10:44; Rom. 5:5; Eph. 1:18), [152] Fletcher also quotes from Wesley's sermon on "Scriptural Christianity" to show that he equated "faith in the Holy Spirit" and perfect love. Fletcher writes: "This good old Gospel is far more clearly set forth in Mr. Wesley's sermon, called 'Scriptural Christianity,' and in his 'Hymns for Whitsunday,' which I earnestly recommend, as pointing out the 'one thing needful' for all carnal professors."[153] Fletcher particularly calls attention to the following passage in Wesley's sermon on "Scriptural Christianity." Wesley writes: "It was, therefore, for a more excellent purpose than this, that 'they were all filled with the Holy Ghost,' " He shows that "it was, to give them . . . the mind which was in Christ, those holy fruits of the Spirit, which whosoever hath not, is none of His; to fill them with 'love, joy, peace, long-suffering, gentleness, goodness' (Gal. v. 22-24) . . . to enable them to crucify the flesh, with its affections and lusts."[154] It is to be noted that each of these phrases of what it means to be "filled with the Holy Spirit" ( = the mind which was in Christ = holy fruits of the Spirit = fill them with love) corresponds to Wesley's usual descriptions of Christian perfection.

Fletcher's interpretation of this sermon has much to commend it. After all, Wesley had himself first published Fletcher's *Equal Check* containing the "Essay on Truth" in the summer of 1774,[155] which implies his approval of Fletcher's interpretation.

Wesley had also spoken approvingly of Fletcher's "Essay on Truth" — as well as all of his writings — and he made no attempt to correct him if he believed his sermon on "Scriptural Christianity" — along with his sermons on "Salvation by Faith" and "Christian Perfection" — had been misappropriated. It is further apparent in the sermon on "Scriptural Christianity" that Wesley strongly implied an equation being "filled with the Spirit" and the parallel concepts of perfect love and the fruit of the Spirit. This can be seen in the pointed question which he addressed to the clergy who were in the university audience at St. Mary's, Oxford, where the sermon was first preached:

> Ye venerable men, who are more especially called to form the tender minds of youth, to dispel thence the shades of ignorance and error, and train them up to be wise unto salvation, are you "filled with the Holy Ghost"? with all those "fruits of the Spirit," which your important office so indispensably requires? Is your heart whole with God? full of love and zeal to set up His kingdom on earth?[156]

Wesley, too, equated the Pentecostal gift of the Spirit with the work of sanctification (i.e., the fruit of the Spirit in his *Explanatory Notes* on Acts 2:38: *"The gift of the Holy Ghost* does not mean, in this place, the power of speaking with tongues; for the promise of this was not given *to all that were afar off*, in distant ages and nations; but rather the constant fruits of faith, even righteousness, and peace, and joy in the Holy Ghost [ = sanctification]."

In his *Explanatory Notes* on Acts 4:31 (which is the text for his sermon on "Scriptural Christianity" cited above), Wesley says the believers were filled with the Holy Ghost "afresh." Wesley obviously means that the disciples experienced the ongoing renewal of the fruit of the Spirit ( = sanctification) in their daily lives. In his *Explanatory Notes* on Acts 1:5, Wesley says that the baptism with the Holy Ghost is given to "all true believers" (a phrase used by Wesley on occasion to denote those made perfect in love). *Wesley thus does not equate "filled with the Spirit" with the new birth or justification.* Rather, he relates the phrase, "filled with the Spirit," with sanctification, i.e., with the fruit of the Spirit. Thus Wesley says, "the Holy Spirit is [given] to every believer, for his personal sanctification and salvation."[157] He further writes:

> The title Holy, applied to the Spirit of God, does not only denote that he is holy in his own nature, but that

he makes us so: that he is the great fountain of holiness to his church; the Spirit from whence flows all the grace and virtue, by which the stains of guilt are cleansed, and we are renewed in all holy dispositions, and again, bear the image of our Creator.[159]

Wesley further shows:

This likeness to God, this conformity of our will and affections to his will, is, properly speaking, holiness; and to produce this in us, is the proper end and design of all the influences of the Holy Spirit.[159]

Since Wesley equated the whole fruit of the Spirit with Christian perfection,* and since he equated being "filled with the Spirit" with the fruit of the Spirit in his sermon on "Scriptural Christianity" and in his *Explanatory Notes*, it seems appropriate for Fletcher to equate explicitly the Pentecostal fulness of the Spirit with Christian perfection. This equation according to Fletcher was not only an improvement upon Wesley's thought, but a consequence of making Wesley "altogether consistent upon that subject."[160]

In his *Third Check to Antinomianism* (February 3, 1772), where Fletcher earlier articulates his doctrine of dispensations and equates "baptism with the Holy Spirit" with "to sanctify wholly,"[161] it is significant that it was published one year prior to Wesley's full endorsement of Fletcher's theological "orthodoxy" and his choice of Fletcher as his successor to lead the Methodist movement.

Further, in *A Short Account of the Life and Death of the Reverend John Fletcher*, Wesley writes an extensive and glowing biography of his close friend and associate. In it Wesley cites Joseph Benson's report about Fletcher's distinctive emphasis upon the equation of Pentecostal language and Christian perfection:

---

*We have previously pointed out that Wesley equated Christian perfection with the "fruit of the Spirit" and with being "sealed with the promised Holy Spirit" (cf. Chapter V).

When he was able to converse, his favourite subject was, "the promise of the Father, the gift of the Holy Ghost," including that rich, peculiar blessing of union with the Father and the Son, mentioned in that prayer of our Lord which is recorded in the seventeenth chapter of St. John. Many were the sparks of living fire which occasionally darted forth on this beloved theme. "We must not be content," said he, "to be only cleansed from sin: we must be filled with the Spirit." One asking him, what was to be evidenced in the full accomplishment of the promise; "O," said he, "what shall I say? All the sweetness of the drawings of the Father, all the love of the Son, all the rich effusions of peace and joy in the Holy Ghost; — more than ever can be expressed, are comprehended here! To attain it, the Spirit maketh intercession in the soul, like a God wrestling with a God!"[162]

It could hardly have been the case that Wesley was not fully aware of Fletcher's equation of Pentecostal language and Christian perfection. It also seems fair to assume that Wesley's endorsement of Fletcher indirectly aligns him with his more systematic development of "a doctrine of dispensations" and the equation of Pentecostal language and Christian perfection.

Mildred Wynkoop has rightly insisted upon taking "the whole Wesley,"[163] and not just focusing upon segmented aspects of his multifarious thought. Surely his own admitted agreement with Fletcher's doctrine of dispensations and his own *carte blanche* approval of Fletcher's writings, along with his occasional use of "filled with the Spirit" as description of perfect love — especially as it is seen in some of his 16 Hymns of Petition and Thanksgiving for the Promise of the Father — must be a valid part of the "whole Wesley."

Though we have pointed out Fletcher's appeal to Wesley's writings as support for his doctrine of dispensations without Wesley's apparent objection, it must now be seen that Fletcher was aware that his formulation of a doctrine of dispensations was considered by some to be different from Wesley's concept of Christian perfection. Hence, Fletcher felt it necessary to defend himself against the charge of creating "a new doctrine." The following selection is taken from his specific discussion of Wesley's question in "The Scripture Way of Salvation": "But what is that faith whereby we are sanctified, saved from sin, and perfected in love?"[164]

> From this striking definition of faith [given in Wesley's sermon, "The Scripture Way of Salvation"], it is evident that the doctrine of this address exactly coincides with Mr. Wesley's sermon; with this verbal difference only, that what he calls faith, implying a twofold operation of the Spirit productive of *spiritual light* and *supernatural sight*, I have called faith, apprehending a sanctifying "baptism (or outpouring) of the Spirit." His mode of expression savours more of the rational divine, who logically divides the truth, in order to render its several parts conspicuous: and I keep closer to the words of the Scriptures, which, I hope, will frighten no candid Protestant. I make this remark for the sake of those who fancy that when a doctrine is clothed with expressions which are not quite familiar to them, it is a new doctrine, although these expressions should be as Scriptural as those of a "baptism, or outpouring of the Spirit," which are used by some of the prophets, by John the Baptist, by the four evangelists, and by Christ himself.[165]

This brings us to the only issue over which Wesley himself indicated his explicit disagreement with Fletcher. In March, 1775, Fletcher had given to John Wesley his manuscript entitled, *The Last Check to Antinomianism*, from which the preceding selection was quoted. Wesley wrote a letter to Fletcher within a week indicating his approval of it and utter delight with his forceful style of writing and logic. He particularly commended Fletcher for his addresses to the "Perfectionists" and "imperfectionists." Fletcher had said that his position "exactly coincides" with Wesley. Wesley apparently agreed with the general thrust of the manuscript, since he said to Fletcher that "this address to the Perfectionists and imperfectionists will be well bestowed."[166]

Yet he did show a slight difference of opinion with Fletcher on the general equation of "receiving the Spirit" and Christian perfection. It is significant that Wesley did not register disagreement with the equating of "filled with the Spirit," and Christian perfection. He only mildly disagreed with the phrase, "receiving the Spirit," as a general description of Christian perfection. Wesley wrote:

> It seems our views of Christian perfection are a *little
> different* [italics mine], though not opposite. It is
> certain every babe in Christ has received the Holy
> Ghost, and the Spirit witnesses with his spirit that he
> is a child of God. But he has not obtained Christian
> perfection. Perhaps you had not considered St. John's
> threefold distinction of Christian believers: little chil-
> dren, young men, and fathers. All of these had received
> the Holy Ghost; but only the fathers were perfected
> in love.[167]

After having received this letter from John Wesley, Fletcher then sent the manuscript in May, 1775, to Charles Wesley with permission for him to make any changes: "I give you *carte blanche* to add, or top off."[168] Then Fletcher sent the manuscript to Wesley again for him to review the changes. In response Wesley wrote him the following letter on August 18:

> I have now received all your papers, and here and there
> made some small corrections. . . . I do not perceive
> that you have granted too much, or that there is any
> difference between us. The Address to the Perfect I
> approve of most, and think it will have a good effect.[169]

As a "good" editor, Wesley then warns him: "But there may be some danger of growing too voluminous, for then the work will come into fewer hands."[170] In December of the same year (1775), John Wesley published Fletcher's manuscript under the title, *The Last Check to Antinomianism, A*

*Polemical Essay on the Twin Doctrines of Christian Imperfection and a Death Purgatory.*[171]

The puzzling question is why Wesley now says that there is no difference between the two of them in his correspondence of August 18, 1775. Did Fletcher cease to equate "receiving the Spirit" with Christian perfection? A careful reading shows that Fletcher persisted in this equation. Nor is there any difference in this regard between his "Essay on Truth" and *The Last Check* — the two main works in which Fletcher developed his doctrine of dispensations.

In the "Essay on Truth," Fletcher interpreted Acts 2:38 — "You shall receive the gift of the Holy Spirit" — to mean that "they all were filled with the Spirit" and that "their hearts overflowed with 'righteousness, peace, and joy in the Holy Ghost."[122] In this respect, the three thousand converts 'received the gift of the Holy Ghost' on the memorable day in which Christ opened the dispensation of his Spirit."[173] This same event was repeated some time later (Acts 4) in which "the multitude of them that believed . . . were of one heart and soul . . . having been made perfect in one."[174]

In *The Last Check*, Fletcher also interpreted "receiving the Spirit" (Acts 2:38) to denote "the perfection of the Christian dispensation."[175] He thus speaks of receiving the gift of the Spirit to mean the fulness of the Spirit. To receive the Spirit is "to enjoy the full blessings of the Christian dispensation, Acts ii.17, 33, 38," and to experience "pure love and unmixed holiness."[176] Hence, a believer can know Christ in the forgiveness of sins without having received the Pentecostal gift of the Holy Spirit.[177] Whereas John the Baptist was not able to experience "the promise of the Father" because "the Holy Ghost was not yet given in the Christian measure,[178] believers today "are culpable if we rest satisfied with the inferior manifestation of the Spirit which belong to the baptism of John or to infant Christianity."[179]

Fletcher also maintained his same interpretation of Acts 2:1 and Acts 4:31 in *The Last Check* as being parallel events. He calls Acts 4:24 a "confirmation" of Acts 2:1.[180]

In both treatises, Fletcher also equates Christian perfection with "filled with the Spirit,"[181] "outpouring of the Spirit,"[182] "baptism with the Spirit,"[183] "The Spirit being given,"[184] "The Spirit descending upon,"[185] "receiving the Spirit,"[186] and "the promise of the Father."[187]

In a letter to Thomas Rankin, June 25, 1781, six years after the publication of *The Last Check,* Fletcher limited the idea of "receiving the Spirit" to those who had experienced Christian perfection, in contrast to believers in Christ who have experienced forgiveness of sins:

> The work of justification seems stopped, in some degree, because the glory and necessity of the pardon of sins, to be *received* and *enjoyed now by faith*, is not pressed enough upon sinners; and the need of *retaining it* upon *believers.* The work of sanctification is hindered, if I am not mistaken, by the same reason, and by holding out the being *delivered from sin* as the mark to be aimed at, instead of being *rooted in Christ*, and *filled with the fulness of God*, and with *power from on high.* The dispensation of the Spirit is confounded with that of the Son, and the former not being held forth clearly enough, formal and *lukewarm believers in Jesus Christ suppose they have the gift of the Holy Ghost* [italics mine]. Hence the increase of *carnal* professors, see Acts viii.16. And hence so few *spiritual* men.[188]

Hence it can be seen that Fletcher persisted in his equation of "receiving the Spirit" and Christian perfection. Just why Wesley wrote Fletcher on August 18, 1775, that there is no difference between them is not altogether clear. Did this mean that Wesley had been won over to Fletcher's interpretation? Probably not. Rather, Fletcher possibly had reworded his statement about "little children," "young men," and "fathers" to Wesley's satisfaction — the specific issue which Wesley had mentioned.

There is only one paragraph of *The Last Check* in which Fletcher had specifically mentioned the three together — "little children," "young men," and "fathers."[189] It is possible that Fletcher in his first draft of the manuscript may have specifically denied that "little children" had "received the Spirit," and he may have said that they had not received "the Spirit of adoption." This would certainly have been in keeping with his doctrine of dispensations. As he maintained in his "Essay on Truth," a "babe in Christ" was the equivalent of a pre-Pentecostal disciple of John the Baptist who had not yet "received the gift of the Spirit."[190] He further maintained that "the Spirit of adoption" and the "full assurance" of faith is the privilege of those who share in "the faith of Christianity in its state of perfection."[191]

As we have seen, Fletcher consistently distinguished among the degrees of faith — faith in the Father, faith in the Son, and faith in the Holy Spirit. The dispensation of the Holy Spirit alone is inclusive of the kingdom of God. Thus only those who have personally been baptized with the Holy Spirit — i.e., who have received the gift of the Spirit — are "adopted sons of God," for they alone have "received the Spirit of adoption." Nonetheless, those living according to "inferior dispensations" have the faith of "servants" and live according to the "spirit of fear and bondage."[192] To have "faith in the Holy Ghost" is to be an "adult" son of God, which is the characteristic of all those who live in the Pentecostal dispensation.[193] "Babes in Christ," "disciples of John the Baptist," "pious Jews," and "righteous heathen,"[194] are also "children of God," since they too have experienced saving faith.[195] Yet their faith is imperfect, since they have not received the gift of the Spirit who "perfects believers in one."[196] Further, only "adult" Christians who have "faith in the Holy Ghost" have a "luminous faith" with a full assurance of their salvation, whereas "babes in Christ" and disciples of John the Baptist who have "faith in Christ," along with "pious Jews" and "righteous heathen" who have "faith in God," have at most only a low level and intermittent assurance of their salvation.[197] Hence, while believers of "inferior dispensations" have saving faith, they are not in the strict sense members of the kingdom of God, i.e., "the kingdom of the Holy Ghost."

It seems to me that Wesley's criticism in his letter to

Fletcher points to the fundamental weakness in Fletcher's doctrine of dispensation — an adequate doctrine of justification and regeneration whereby a penitent believer becomes a member of the Church is lacking. If one is justified by faith in Jesus Christ, then the righteousness of Christ's humanity is fully imputed to him and through his consequent regeneration of the Spirit the process of sanctification is begun. Hence Wesley insisted in his letter of March, 1775, that "every babe in Christ" has the witness of the Spirit "that he is a child of God." [198]

It is thus most likely that Fletcher reworded his statement about "little children," "young men," and "fathers" in *the one paragraph* which Wesley had referred to in order to bring it in line with Wesley's recommendation. Consequently, Wesley could now say that there was no difference between them, while reassuring Fletcher that he had not "granted too much" to the status of "babes in Christ." While Fletcher did not say *explicitly* in that paragraph that "babes in Christ" had "received the gift of the Spirit," and while he did not admit that they possessed the Spirit of adoption, he did not deny it in his revised manuscript — which must have apparently satisfied Wesley.

Yet it must still be seen that Fletcher himself understood that there continued to be a slight difference between him and Wesley. This is explicitly stated in a letter to Mary Bosanquet (March 7, 1778):

> You will find my views of this matter in Mr. Wesley's sermons on Christian Perfection and on Spiritual Christianity; with this difference, that I would distinguish more exactly between the believers baptized with the Pentecostal power of the Holy Ghost, and the believer who, like the Apostles after our Lord's ascension, is not yet filled with that power.[199]

The basic difference between them was that Fletcher made a *general* equation of "receiving the Spirit" and Christian perfection, whereas Wesley did not.

In 1771, when Fletcher was equating Wesley's concept of perfection with Pentecostal language, Wesley first called attention to his disagreement with Fletcher's terminological equation of "receiving the Spirit" and Christian perfection in a letter to Joseph Benson, March 9, 1771. Wesley cautioned against "Mr. Fletcher's late discovery" (a probable reference to Fletcher's equating "receiving the Spirit" and Christian perfection).* Wesley further commented about this terminological equation: "The Methodists in general could not bear this. It would create huge debate and confusion."[200]

Wesley thus cautioned against speaking of Christian perfection in general terms of "receiving the Spirit," since it is also true that all Christians have the Spirit: "If they like to call this 'receiving the Holy Ghost,' they may: only the phrase in that sense is not scriptural and not quite proper; for they all 'received the Holy Ghost' when they were justified."[201]

Yet in a letter addressed to Benson one week after he had warned Benson against equating "receiving the Spirit" with Christian perfection, Wesley specifically equated *"perfected in love"* with "filled with the Holy Ghost."[202] This would seem to substantiate the observation that Wesley disagreed with Fletcher's *general* equation of receiving the Spirit and perfection, while apparently agreeing with the terminological equation of "filled with the Spirit" and Christian perfection. However, it will be pointed out subsequently that

---

· *John Knight in his article, "John Fletcher's Influence on the Development of the Wesleyan Theology in America," *The Wesleyan Theological Journal*, XIII (Spring, 1978) wrongly reports that Telford's comments concerning Wesley's warning to Benson about Fletcher's "late discovery" referred to the equation of being "filled with the Spirit" and Christian perfection. Rather, Telford says it was Fletcher's equation of "receiving the Spirit" and Christian perfection (p. 27). Cf. *The Letters of John Wesley*, ed. John Telford (London: Epworth Press, 1931), v. 228. It is also most surprising for Knight to think that Wesley did not "connect Christian perfection . . . with Pentecost" (p. 27). In this regard, see Harald Lindström, *Wesley and Sanctification* (p. 135) and Lycurgus Starkey, *The Work of the Holy Spirit* (pp. 21, 33).

Wesley himself equated Christian perfection with a *special* reception of the Spirit in the book of Acts, even though he preferred not to speak of "receiving the Spirit" as a *general* description of perfection.

That Wesley used "filled with the Spirit" as descriptive of perfect love immediately after he had warned Benson against equating "receiving the Spirit" with Christian perfection suggests that he himself apparently distinguished between the general phrase "receiving the Spirit" and being "filled with the Spirit." In this respect, Wesley allowed for Fletcher's general equation of other uses of Pentecostal language (e.g., outpouring of the Spirit, filled with the Spirit) since he himself used it as such, even though infrequently.*

What is even more convincing about Wesley's apparent willingness to allow for the equation of Pentecostal language and Christian perfection is his comments about the Samaritans' and the Ephesians' *special* reception of the Spirit (Acts 8;19) in his *Explanatory Notes on the New Testament*. In both instances, Wesley allows for the possibility that their *unique* reception of the Spirit constituted their sanctification. In regard to the Samaritans' reception of the Spirit (Acts 8:15), Wesley asks if this could mean "His miraculous gifts, or His sanctifying graces?" He replies: "Probably in both." Of the Ephesians unique reception of the Spirit, Wesley raises the same possibility. He *asks* whether their reception of the Spirit refers to "the extraordinary gifts of the Spirit, as well as His sanctifying graces?" (See Wesley's *Notes* on Acts 19:2).

That Wesley had in mind entire sanctification in both of these instances is arguable on the following grounds.

1. Wesley most often meant *entire* sanctification when-

---

*In *A Plain Account of Christian Perfection*, Wesley equates "full of His Spirit" with being "perfected in love" (pp. 54-55). In one of his letters, he says that it was through the "outpouring of the Spirit" that one had experienced Christian perfection (*The Letters of John Wesley*, V, p. 81). In another instance, Wesley speaks of perfect love as "receiving a high degree of the Spirit of holiness" (*A Plain Account of Christian Perfection*, p. 60).

ever he used the word sanctification. Though he said that one ought to specify whether sanctification or entire sanctification is meant — since initial sanctification begins at the moment of justification — he rarely followed his own advice at this point, as Harald Lindström also shows.[203]

2. Wesley assumed that both the Samaritans and the Ephesians had experienced saving faith prior to their special reception of the Spirit. Of the Samaritans, Wesley interpreted their baptism in Acts 8:12 to mean that "they then saw and felt the real power of God, and submitted thereto." He further shows in his comment on Acts 8:14 that they experienced the word of God "by faith" through the preaching of Philip. Hence for Wesley, the Samaritans had saving faith prior to their reception of the Spirit.

Likewise in Acts 19:1ff, Wesley shows that the Ephesians had been "imperfectly instructed in Christianity," and hence their re-baptism was their formal initiation into the New Dispensation, which superseded the Old Dispensation. However, Wesley did not suggest that the Ephesians lacked saving faith prior to the preaching of Paul. That Wesley translated Acts 19:2 in accord with the King James Version — "Have you received the Holy Ghost *since* ye believed," — also suggests that he acknowledged them to be incomplete Christian believers. If Wesley thought that Paul intended to say that every believer *ipso facto* had experienced the unique reception of the Pentecostal Spirit at the time of his conversion, he probably would have translated Acts 19:2 — "Did you receive the Holy Spirit when you believed?" — since the Greek syntax also allows for this translation. In this respect, Wesley would not have hesitated to have changed the English text if he thought that it was incorrect, since he often did this, as he promised in his "Preface" to the *Explanatory Notes on the New Testament*: "I shall take the liberty, as occasion may require, to make here and there a small alteration" in the English translation.[204]

3. That Wesley let the translation of the KJV (which was obviously influenced by the theology of the Anglican Church) stand without alteration in Acts 19:2, and that he interpreted

the Samaritans' and Ephesians' unique experience of the Spirit as probably referring to their sanctification, seems to indicate a discernible influence of Anglican theology upon Wesley's thinking. As we will point out in Chapter seven, Acts 8:15-18 and Acts 19:2 are the two passages which Anglicanism had used for the theology of Confirmation in which the reception of the Spirit was given through the laying on of hands subsequent to the justifying faith received in baptism. In Anglican theology, this confirming grace was interpreted as the sanctifying and strengthening experience of the Christian life. Although Wesley ignored the rite of Confirmation for all practical purposes (probably because it denoted a formal and largely objectivistic experience of imputed righteousness instead of a subjective, evangelical experience of actual righteousness), his interpretation of the Samaritans' and Ephesians' unique experience of the Holy Spirit as a probable reference to their sanctification could very well reflect the influence of his Church's doctrine of Confirmation. In fact, it could be thought that Wesley's *Explanatory Notes* on both of these passages provided the basis for a reinterpretation of the liturgical rite of Confirmation along the lines of an evangelical experience of sanctifying grace. This "Wesleyan" reinterpretation of the Anglican doctrine of Confirmation is most evident in John Fletcher, who so freely alluded to Pentecostal language as descriptive of perfect love and who appealed to the Anglican rite of Confirmation as indirect support for the doctrine of perfect love. Here in Wesley's commentary notes on Acts 8:15 and Acts 19:2 may well be the discernible roots for the equation of Pentecostal language and Christian perfection!

4. A final consideration which shows that Wesley had in mind "entire sanctification" in reference to the Ephesians' special reception of the Spirit is indicated in *The Poetical Works of John and Charles Wesley*. In it the following verse is written as an interpretation of Acts 19:6, "The Holy Ghost came on them . . . .":

> Still the Holy Ghost descends
> The indwelling Comforter,

All the griefs and troubles ends
   Of those that Christ revere;
Works His miracles within,
Renews their hearts, and tongues, and eyes;
Makes an utter end of sin,
And wholly sanctifies."[205]

Wesley's interpretation of Cornelius' *special* reception of the Spirit (Acts 10:11) is also highly suggestive in this regard. He shows that Cornelius did not have "faith in Christ" (note on Acts 10:4), but he "believed in God the Father" (note on 10:48). He further shows that Cornelius, though not a Christian believer, was accepted by God "through Christ, though he knows Him not" (note on 10:35). Wesley further says of Cornelius' acceptance by God: "The assertion is express, and admits of no exception. He is in the favor [ = saving faith, for Wesley] of God, whether enjoying His written word and ordinances or not. Nevertheless, the addition of these is an unspeakable blessing to those who were before, in some measure, accepted." Wesley then shows that Cornelius' *special* reception of the Spirit meant that he and his household were "consecrated to God, as the first-fruits of the Gentiles" and that they were given "a clear and satisfactory evidence" of their equal acceptance with God (note on 10:44). Finally, Wesley interprets Cornelius' special reception of the Spirit to mean that he and his household had experienced "full Christian salvation, in this world and the world to come" (note on 11:14). It can thus be concluded that Wesley meant that Cornelius was entirely sanctified at the moment of his special reception of the Spirit, since he elsewhere equated "full salvation" with Christian perfection.[206] Further, Wesley's distinction between Cornelius' having "faith in God the Father" and having "faith in Christ" corresponds closely to his and Fletcher's doctrine of dispensations. It also parallels Fletcher's interpretation of Cornelius' reception of the Spirit as illustrative of one who experienced "the perfecting of holiness," even though he was "already in a state of salvation."[207]

Finally, it can be said that Wesley's equation of entire

sanctification and circumcision of the heart would necessarily commit him to this further equation of Pentecostal language and Christian perfection; for Deut. 30:6 (along with Jer. 31:31-32 and Ezek. 36:26f.) had its fulfillment on the Day of Pentecost. Fletcher in a succinct manner has shown the logic of this equation of Pentecostal language and Christian perfection through his exposition of these Old Testament passages:

> When the right foot of your faith stands on these evangelical precepts and proclamations, lest she should stagger for want of a promise every way adequate to such weighty commandments, let her place her left foot upon the following promises, which are extracted from the Old Testament: "The Lord thy God will circumcise thine heart, and the heart of thy seed, to love the Lord thy God with all thine heart, Deut. xxx, 6. I will give them a heart to know me, that I am the Lord, and they shall be my people, and I will be their God, [in a new and peculiar manner], for they shall return unto me with their whole heart. This shall be the covenant that I will make with the house of Israel. After those days, saith the Lord, I will put my law in their inward parts, and write it in their hearts, and will be their God, and they shall be my people, Jer. xxiv, 7; xxxi, 33. Then will I sprinkle clean water upon you, and ye shall be clean: from all your filthiness and from all your idols will I cleanse you: a new heart also will I give you, and a new spirit will I put within you: and I will take away the heart of stone out of your flesh, and I will give you a heart of flesh. And I will put my Spirit within you, and cause you to walk in my statutes, and ye shall keep my judgments and do them," Ezek. xxvi, 25-27.

> And let nobody suppose that the promises of *the circumcision* of the heart, *the cleansing, the clean water,* and *the Spirit*, which are mentioned in these scriptures, and by which the hearts of believers are to be made new, and God's law is to be so written therein, that they shall "keep his judgments and do them;" let none, I

say, suppose that these glorious promises belong only to the Jews; for their full accomplishment peculiarly refers to the Christian dispensation. Beside, if *sprinklings of the Spirit* were sufficient, under the Jewish dispensation, to raise the plant of Jewish perfection in Jewish believers, how much more will the revelation of "the horn of our salvation," and the *outpourings of the Spirit*, raise the plant of Christian perfection in faithful, Christian believers![208]

In this same context Fletcher further provides an exposition of Pentecostal passages in the New Testament (John 4:19, 14; 7:37ff.; 14:15, 23; Matt. 3:11; Mark 1:8; Luke 3:16; 24:49; Acts 1:4-5; 2:17, 33, 38) which he equates with perfect love.[209]

It can thus be seen that the equation of entire sanctification and Pentecostal language is strongly implied in Wesley's equation of circumcision of heart and perfect love as Fletcher plainly shows.

_____

[1]John Knight, "John Fletcher's influence on the Development of Wesleyan Theology in America," *Wesleyan Theological Journal*, XIII (Spring, 1978), pp. 16, 22f.

[2]Luke Tyerman, *Wesley's Designated Successor: The Life, Letters, and Literary Labours of the Rev. John William Fletcher* (London: Hodder and Stoughton, 1882, p. 7.

[3]*Ibid.*, pp. 14f.

[4]*Ibid.*, p. 23.

[5]*The Works of John Wesley*, XI, 306.

[6]*Ibid.*, XI, 42.

[7]Tyerman, p. 28.

[8]*The Letters of The Rev. John Wesley*, ed. John Telford, (London: The Epworth Press, 1921), IV, 300, cited in Knight, *Wesleyan Theological Journal*, XIII (Spring, 1978), 14.

[9]Tyerman, p. 346; cited in Knight, *The Wesleyan Theological Journal*, XIII, 14.

[10]*The Wesleyan Theological Journal*, p. 14.

[11]*Ibid.*, p. 13.

[12]Fletcher *Works*, I, 536.

[13]*The Letters of The Reverend John Wesley*, VI, 11.

[14]Fletcher, *Works*, I, 160.

[15]*Ibid.*, I, 575.

[16]*Ibid.*, I, 588.

[17]*Ibid.*, I, 589.

[18]*Ibid.*, I, 585, 591n., 593.

[19]*Ibid.*, I, 593.

[20]*Ibid.*, I, 590.

[21]*The Letters of The Reverend John Wesley*, V, 228, 215.

[22]*The Letters of The Reverend John Wesley*, IV, 272.

[23]Fletcher, *Checks*, I, 590-591.

[24]*The Standard Sermons of John Wesley*, II, 156.

[25]*Ibid.*, II, 157; cf. Fletcher, *Checks*, I, 589.

[26]*Sermons on Several Occasions* (New York: T. Mason & G. Lane, 1839), II, 383.

[27]*Ibid.*

[28]*Ibid.*, II, 385-388.

[29]*A Plain Account of Christian Perfection*, p. 55.

[30]*Ibid.*, p. 61.

[31]*Ibid.*, p. 60.

[32]Cf. Harald Lindström, *Wesley and Sanctification*, pp. 131, 155.

[33]*A Plain Account of Christian Perfection*, pp. 78-79.

[34]*Ibid.*, p. 80.

[35]*Ibid.*, pp. 79-80.

[36]*Ibid.*, pp. 23, 81-82; *The Letters of The Reverend John Wesley*, V, 280.

[37]*The Letters of The Reverend John Wesley*, V, 81.

[38]*The Works of John Wesley*, III, 116.

[39]*Ives Y. Congar*, p. 27.

[40]*Ibid.*, pp. 28-29.

[41]*Ibid.*

[42]*Ibid.*, pp. 11, 27, 92-93.

[43]*Ibid.*, pp. 31-32.

[44]Fletcher, *Works*, III, 177-178.

[45]Fletcher, II, 356.

[46]*Ibid.*, II, 356-357.

[47]*Ibid.*, I, 574.

[48]*Ibid.*, IV, 351.

[49]*Ibid.*, I, 585, 587; II, 622.

[50]*Ibid.*, II, 526.

[51]*Ibid.*

[52]*Ibid.*, 562.

[53]*Ibid.*, I, 590.

[54]*Ibid.*, II, 526.

[55]*Ibid.*, I. 592.

[56]*Ibid.*, I, 592-593.

[57]*Ibid.*, I, 593.

[58]*Ibid.*, I, 587.

[59]*Ibid.*

[60]*Ibid.*, I, 586.

[61]*Ibid.*, II, 538-539.

[62]*Ibid.*, II, 539.

[63]*Ibid.*, I, 574.

[64]*Ibid.*, I, 574.

[65]*Ibid.*, IV, 118-119.

[66]*Ibid.*, I, 586n., I, 585ff.

[67]Cited by Tyerman, p. 411.

[68]*Ibid.*, 412.

[69]Fletcher, *Works*, II, 538.

[70]*Ibid.*, I, 160-161.

[71]*Ibid.*, IV, 109.

[72]*Ibid.*, IV, 113-114.

[73]*Ibid.*, IV, 115; cf. *Ibid.*, IV, 287, where Fletcher says that being "baptized with the Holy Ghost ... can alone make a man a Christian."

[74]*Ibid.*, IV, 133.

[75]*Ibid.*, II, 356-357.

[76]*Ibid.*, IV, 134.

[77]*Ibid.*, IV, 119.

[78]*Ibid.*, IV, 118-119.

[79]*Ibid.*, III, 170.

[80]*Ibid.*, III, 171.

[81]*Ibid.*

[82]*Ibid.*, III, 170.

[83]*Ibid.*, III, 173.

[84]*Ibid.*, II, 558.

[85]*Ibid.*, II, 630.

[86]*The Standard Sermons of John Wesley*, II, 239.

[87]*Ibid.*, II, 240.

[88]*Ibid.*

[89]Fletcher, *Works*, I, 590n.; cf. I, 562.

[90]*Ibid.*, I, 575; cf. I, 562.

[91]*Christianity and Comparative Religion* (Downers Grove, Illinois: The Intervarsity Press, 1971), p. 97ff. Wesley's sermon, "On Faith" (*Sermons on Several Occasions*, II, 383ff.) shows that he believed that "heathen," Muslims, etc., in some cases had saving faith though they lacked the witness of the Spirit.

[92]Fletcher, *Works*, I, 590; II, 356.

[93]*Ibid.*, I, 574.

[94]Oscar Cullmann, *The Early Church* trans. and ed., A. J. B. Higgins (London: SCM Press, Ltd., 1956), pp. 116-125.

[95]Dunn, *Baptism with the Holy Spirit* (SCM Press Ltd., 1970), p. 77.

[96]*Works of John Wesley* (London: Wesleyan Conference Office, 1872), IX, 93.

[97]J. A. Bengel, *Gnomon of the New Testament*, I, 808-809.

[98]*Commentary on the Acts of the Apostles* (Grand Rapids: Wm. B. Eerdmans, 1949), I, 372.

[99]*The Interpreter's Bible*, ed. George Buttrick (New York: Abingdon Press, 1954), IX, 118, 123.

[100]Other references which date Saul's conversion on the road to Damascus include: A. Robertson and A. Plummer, *A Critical and Exegetical Commentary on I Corinthians*, Vol. XXXII; *The International Critical Commentary on the Holy Scriptures of the Old and New Testament*, ed. Samuel R. Driver, Alfred Plummer, and C. A. Briggs (Edinburgh: T. and T. Clark, 1959-1968), p. 178; G. T. Stokes, *The Acts of the Apostles*, Vol. II; *The Expositor's Bible*, ed. W. Robertson Nicoll (35 vols.; New York: A. C. Armstrong and Son, 1892), p. 48; Allan Menzies and William Edie, "Paul," *Encyclopedia of Religion and Ethics*, ed. Hastings, IX (1917), 682; J. Rawson Lumby, *The Acts of the Apostles, The Cambridge Bible for Schools* (Cambridge University Press, 1937), p. 192. William Neil, *The Acts of the Apostles, New Century Bible* (London: Oliphants, 1973), pp. 126-127; W. F. Albright and C. S. Mann, *The Acts of the Apostles, Anchor Bible*, intro. and trans. Johannes Munck (Garden City: Doubleday, 1967), p. 81; G. H. C. Macgregor and Theodore P. Ferris, *The Acts of the Apostles, The Interpreter's Bible* (Nashville: Abingdon Press, 1954), IX, 117ff.; A. C. Purdy, "Paul the Apostle," *The Interpreter's Dictionary of the Bible*, ed. George Buttrick and others (New York: Abingdon Press, 1962), K - Q, 684; Willi Marxsen, "The Resurrection of Jesus as a Historical and Theological Problem," *The Significance of the Message of the Resurrection for Faith in Jesus Christ*, ed. C. F. D. Moule (London: SCM Press, Ltd., 1968), p. 24.

[101]*The Standard Sermons of John Wesley*, II, 162-163.

[102]*Ibid.*, II, 162-163; I, 41-42.

[103]Harald Lindström, *Wesley and Sanctification*, p. 106.

[104]*The Standard Sermons of John Wesley*, I, 41-42.

[105]Fletcher, *Works*, I, 160, 574-575.

[106]Fletcher, I, 539, II, 356-357.

[107]*Ibid.*, I, 160, 536, 570, 591-594.

*234*

[108]*Ibid.*, I, 585n., 591n., 588-589.

[109]*The Letters of John Wesley*, VI, 137; cf. Tyerman, p. 310.

[110]*Works.*, I, 576, 588.

[111]*Ibid.*, I, 577f.

[112]*Ibid.*, II, 565.

[113]*Ibid.*, I, 167-168.

[114]*Ibid.*, II, 523.

[115]*Ibid.*, II, 648.

[116]*Ibid.*

[117]*Ibid.*, II, 636.

[118]*Ibid.*

[119]*Ibid.*

[120]*Ibid.*

[121]*Ibid.*, II, 632-633.

[122]*Ibid.*, II, 631.

[123]*Ibid.*, II, 632.

[124]*Ibid.*, II, 631.

[125]*Ibid.*, II, 648.

[126]*Ibid.*, II, 633.

[127]*Ibid.*, II, 634.

[128]Cited by Tyerman, pp. 468-469.

[129]Fletcher, *Works*, I, 580.

[130]*Ibid.*, I, 160.

[131]*Ibid.*, I, 270-271.

[132]*The Letters of John Wesley*, VI, 272.

[133]Cited by Tyerman, p. 182.

[134]Fletcher, Madeley, 24 November, 1771, to Charles Wesley, Ms. "Fletcher Volume," Methodist Archives and Research Center, John Rylands Library, the University of Manchester, p. 38. I am indebted to Timothy Smith for this information obtained from his research in the Rylands Library.

[135]Fletcher, *Works*, I, 588ff.

[136]*Ibid.*, I, 589.

[137]*Ibid.*, I, 590n., 593.

[138]*Ibid.*, I, 589.

[139]*Ibid.* cf. *Ibid.*, I, 580.

[140]Cited by Tyerman, p. 179.

[141]*Documents of Vatican II*, ed. Austin P. Hannery (Grand Rapids: Wm. B. Eerdmans, 1975), pp. 361f.; Fletcher, *Checks*, II, 657.

[142]*The Standard Sermons of John Wesley*, II, 157.

[143]*Ibid.*, II, 169.

[144]*Ibid.*, II, 171.

[145]*Ibid.*, cf. *The Letters of The Reverend John Wesley*, V, 43.

[146]*The Letters of The Reverend John Wesley*, V. 230.

[147]*The Standard Sermons of John Wesley*, I, 62.

[148]*Ibid.*, II, 113-114.

[149]Fletcher, *Works*, I, 592.

[150]*Ibid.*, I, 593.

[151]*Ibid.*, I, 594.

[152]*Ibid.*, I, 590n.

[153]*Ibid.*, I, 519n.

[154]*The Standard Sermons of John Wesley*, I, 93-94; cf. Fletcher, *Checks*, I, 593.

[155]That John Wesley was responsible for its publication is indicated at the end of the "Preface" after which Wesley attached the following note: "N.B. I have considerably shortened the following tracts; and marked the most useful parts of them with a *. J.W." cf. *The First Part of an Equal Check to Pharisaism and Antinomianism*; the third edition (London: Printed by G. Paramore, 1795). I am indebted to Timothy Smith for pointing this out to me.

[156]*The Standard Sermons of John Wesley*, I, 106-107.

[157]*The Works of John Wesley*, VII, 514.

[158]*Sermons on Several Occasions* (New York: Carlton and Phillips, 1853), II, 515.

[159]*Ibid.*, II, 518.

[160]Tyerman, p. 182.

[161]Fletcher, *Works* I, 160, 167, 168.

[162]*The Works of John Wesley,* XI, 306.

[163]"Theological Roots of the Wesleyan Understanding of the Holy Spirit," *Wesleyan Theological Journal*, XIV, No. 1 (Spring, 1979), p. 78.

[164]Fletcher, *Works*, II, 646; cf. *The Standard Sermons of John Wesley*, II, 457.

[165]Fletcher, II, 647.

[166]*The Letters of John Wesley*, VI, 146.

[167]*Ibid.*

[168]John Fletcher, Madeley, 21 May, 1775, to Charles Wesley, Ms. "Fletcher Volume, "p. 51. I am indebted to Timothy Smith for the contents of this letter obtained from his research in the Rylands Library.

[169]Wesley, *Works*, VI. 174-175.

[170]*Ibid*.

[171]Tyerman, p. 320; See above, footnote 155.

[172]Fletcher, I, 593.

[173]*Ibid*.

[174]*Ibid*., I, 594.

[175]*Ibid*., II, 525-526.

[176]*Ibid*., II, 630.

[177]*Ibid*., II, 525-526.

[178]*Ibid*., II, 526.

[179]*Ibid*.

[180]*Ibid*., II, 648.

[181]*Ibid*., II, 631, 648; I, 593.

[182]*Ibid*., II, 526, 631, 633, 647, 565.

[183]*Ibid*., I, 536; II, 629, 632.

[184]*Ibid*., II, 633, 645, 657; I, 590n., 592.

[185]*Ibid*., I, 593, 580, 590n; II, 636, 656.

[186]*Ibid*., I, 580, 590n., 593; II, 630.

[187]*Ibid*., I, 539, 574, 590n.; II, 633, 637, 652, 630.

[188]Cited by Tyerman, p. 465.

[189]Fletcher, II, 632.

[190]*Ibid*., I, 539.

[191]*Ibid*., I, 587; cf. I, 585f.

[192]*Ibid.*, I, 574.

[193]*Ibid.*

[194]*Ibid.*, I, 41.

[195]*Ibid.*, I, 579, 564; II, 356-357.

[196]*Ibid.*, II, 542.

[197]*Ibid.*, I, 585-587.

[198]*The Letters of John Wesley*, VI, 146.

[199]Cited by Tyerman, p. 411.

[200]*The Letters of John Wesley*, V, 228.

[201]*Ibid.*, V, 215.

[202]*Ibid.*, V, 229.

[203]Lindström, p. 127.

[204]*Explanatory Notes upon the New Testament*, p. 6.

[205]*The Poetical Works of John and Charles Wesley* (London: Wesleyan Methodist Conference Office, 1871), XII, 358.

[206]*The Standard Sermons of John Wesley*, II, 448; *A Plain Account of Christian Perfection*, p. 27; Lindström, p. 127.

[207]Fletcher, *Works*, I, 580; cf. *Ibid.*, I, 160.

[208]Fletcher, *Works*, II, 628; cf. *A Plain Account of Christian Perfection*, p. 35.

[209]*Ibid.*, II, 628ff.

# CHAPTER VII.

## THE WESLEYAN DOCTRINE OF CHRISTIAN PERFECTION AS A RE-INTERPRETATION OF THE ROMAN CATHOLIC AND ANGLICAN RITE OF CONFIRMATION

There is a most remarkable similarity between the Roman Catholic doctrine of confirmation and the Wesleyan doctrine of entire sanctification. In Roman Catholic theology, *baptism* has to do with inauguration into the Church; whereas *confirmation* has to do with the Pentecostal outpouring of the Holy Spirit, who empowers the individual believer to live the Christian life. Hence there are two sacraments of initiation, not just one. Without experiencing both baptism and confirmation one has not been duly initiated into the Christian life, for they "belong together in the single Christian initiation" and although they are "extended in time" they are "ultimately one."[1]

Roman Catholic scholars cite as exegetical support for the subsequent rite of confirmation the very same passages in the Book of Acts that Wesleyan exegetes cite for their distinction between the birth of the Spirit and the fulness of the Spirit. (Incidentally, if the Wesleyan tradition had a stronger emphasis upon the idea of the sacraments and the visibility of the Church as the body of Christ, such exegetical claims for the rite of confirmation by Roman Catholic scholars might not seem so unrealistic).*

---

*If I might express a personal conviction at this point, a strong emphasis upon the rite of confirmation could be a source for the revitalization of the corporate life of the Church as the body of Christ, as well as a source of enrichment for the spiritual life of young converts.

This similarity between the Roman Catholic doctrines of baptism and confirmation and the Wesleyan doctrines of conversion and entire sanctification has largely gone unnoticed. Yet it can be enlightening to those in the Wesleyan tradition to examine the common elements in their otherwise rather divergent traditions, especially since such a study could enhance one's understanding of the meaning of the baptism with the Spirit in the light of a more comprehensive doctrine of the Church as an organism — something which has been sorely lacking in the Wesleyan tradition.

The extensive but highly significant quotation which follows and which is taken from William J. O'Shea of the Catholic University of America shows the close similarity between the Catholic doctrine of confirmation and the Wesleyan doctrine of entire sanctification.

> The key to the whole problem seems to be in remembering that, according to Christian tradition going back to the third century, confirmation [the sacrament in which the baptized believer receives a Spirit-filled character] completes and perfects baptism. There is no need, therefore, of trying to discover something altogether different in confirmation from what is given in baptism. Some theologians, such as the late Gregory Dix, thought that the remission of sins was all that was given in baptism whereas the Spirit was given only in confirmation. But there is absolutely no warrant for thus deforming the sacrament of baptism. As we have seen, baptism is the sacrament of new birth. New birth is so often connected with the bath of water that one cannot hold otherwise. But new birth is impossible without the action of the Spirit — that Spirit who raised Jesus from the dead, who also quickens our mortal bodies to life.

O'Shea thus points out that baptism and confirmation are not in opposition to each other. Rather, confirmation "completes, brings to full development, what is already there" in baptism. In this respect, "there are Scripture texts which refer verbally to baptism, but the fulness of what is connoted there is attained only through confirmation." An example of this is "the Pentecost-event itself, because Pentecost was at once the baptism and the confirmation of the infant church." Consequently, there is no competition between the importance of baptism and confirmation.

> Rather there is continuity between them, and *the development of the same process of sanctification* [italics mine]. Baptism is a sacrament in its own right; it remits sin and gives grace. It could not do these things unless it gave the Holy Spirit. Precisely because baptism engenders in us life *in* the Spirit and the life *of* the Spirit, it awaits that completion and fullness which is necessary to make the baptized believer a perfect Christian. . . . By this sacrament the believer's being as a Christian is completed. He is clothed with the fullness of the Spirit after the likeness of Christ. In fact, the clue to the relationship of the two sacraments lies here. They both have for their aim to conform the believer to Christ, to reproduce Christ in him.[2]

It is clear that, like the Catholic doctrine of confirmation, the Wesleyan doctrine of entire sanctification means the perfection of sanctifying grace begun in conversion whereby "the believer's being as a Christian is completed" since "he is clothed with the fullness of the Spirit after the likeness of Christ."

It is also clear that for the Catholic doctrine of confirmation (like the Wesleyan doctrine of entire sanctification) there is "prescribed" a time lapse between "these two separate, yet related, anointings."[3] The definitive nature of this subsequent work of grace is such that it cannot be repeated for any baptized believer because it has to do with the perfection of character and if one's character is perfected in confirmation, there could be no need for further confirmation.[4] Hence confirmation, like entire sanctification, is a second definitive work of grace in the life of the Christian believer though the Wesleyan doctrine of entire sanctification does not absolutize the concepts of crisis and subsequency.

That there is a clear distinction between the beginning of the Christian life and a second definitive work of grace in Catholic theology can also be seen in the distinction that is made between Easter and Pentecost as a pattern of Christian experience.

> However theologians view the effects of the sacrament, all are agreed that confirmation is the sacrament that bestows the Holy Spirit in a special way. Just as we can say that baptism is the sacrament of the resurrection, so we can say that confirmation is the sacrament of the sending of the Spirit. As we associate baptism with Easter, so we associate confirmation with Pentecost.[5]

Like Reformed theologians today who reject Wesley's doctrine of a second work of grace, even so John Calvin engaged in a scathing attack upon the Roman Catholic theology of confirmation, with its emphasis upon a second experience which completes the work of grace begun in the new birth. Calvin specifically rejects the Catholic exegesis of Acts 19:1-2. For him the subsequent experience of the Spirit which the Ephesian believers had was a visible sign and manifestation of the Spirit which served a purpose peculiar to the evangelistic needs of the apostolic period. But the Catholic notion that the baptism with the Spirit was a perfection of the Christian life was to utter "horrible blasphemies."

> But the Papists are worthy of no pardon, who being not content with the ancient rite, durst thrust in rotten and filthy anointing, that it might be not only a confirmation of baptism, but also a more worthy sacrament, whereby they imagine that the faithful are made perfect who were before only half perfect, — whereby those are armed against the battle, who before had their sin only forgiven them. For they have not been afraid to spew out these horrible blasphemies.[6]

As has already been pointed out, for Wesleyan theology it is one thing to be "in Christ," yet another thing for Christ to be formed in us. Likewise, confirmation for Catholic theology means the believer is to be conformed to Christ. O'Shea writes:

> It was his own Spirit that Jesus poured forth abundantly on Pentecost, with the mission of continuing among men on the mystery of the incarnation. This is the Spirit poured out on us in confirmation. Its mission in us is the same: to bring us to the full measure of the age of Christ.
>
> Just as Jesus needed the presence and the action of the Spirit to realize to the full God the Father's design in him, we need the same Spirit to realize the divine plan in us. The divine plan is that we should be conformed to Christ, be made in his likeness.[7]

O'Shea further points out that "the difference between baptism and confirmation is the difference between giving life and enabling that life to reach its full potential. Confirmation gives us the power to be what we already are by baptism."[8]

Another highly significant comparison between Roman Catholic theology of confirmation and the Wesleyan doctrine of entire sanctification is that it is the Pentecostal gift of the Spirit who effects "Christlikeness" in the life of the baptized believer.

> These two separate, yet related, anointings must be reproduced in the life of the Christian. The first anointing of the Spirit takes place at baptism, making him the adopted son of God. The second takes place at confirmation when the Spirit descends upon him again to make him a prophet, to equip him with the gifts he needs to enable him to live fully the life of an adopted son, and to fulfill his mission in the Church. In confirmation he is empowered to function properly as a member of the priestly people, that is, to offer God spiritual and true worship in the true temple which is the body of Christ, the Church.[9]

What this means, then, is that every baptized believer is to have his own unique individual Pentecost. "The Spirit we receive in confirmation is the Spirit of Pentecost. That confirmation is the individual Christian's Pentecost is shown by the prayer at the end of the rite of confirmation."[10] O'Shea goes on to show that for "the Fathers and Doctors of the Church . . . what happened on Pentecost happens now to the individual Christian."[11]

In *The Sixteen Documents of Vatican II* there is a direct association of the "gift of the Holy Spirit" to the "perfection" of the believer's character. The chapter entitled, "The Universal Call to Holiness in the Church," cannot be surpassed as a concise statement on what holiness means, if its understanding of the Roman Catholic Church as the only true Church were eliminated. The call to holiness is the call for "individuals who, in their walk of life, tend toward the perfection of charity."[12]

Of special significance in these documents is the relating of the Pentecostal gift of the Spirit with perfect love.

> The Lord Jesus, the divine Teacher and Model of all perfection, preached holiness of life to each and everyone of His disciples of every condition. He Himself stands as the author and consumator of this holiness of life: 'Be you therefore perfect, even as your heavenly Father is perfect' . . . . Indeed He sent the Holy Spirit upon all men that He might move them inwardly to love God with their whole heart and their whole soul, with all their mind and all their strength and that they might love each other as Christ loves them.[13]

It is further urged: "Thus it is evident to everyone, that all the faithful of Christ of whatever rank or status, are called to the fullness of the Christian life and to the perfection of charity."[14]

What is significant is that Roman Catholic theology appeals to the same biblical passages as does Wesleyan theology to support its doctrine of holiness, as well as to support its distinction between baptized believers and perfect Christians who have been filled with the Holy Spirit in the rite of confirmation.[15]

Even in Wesley's day it was said often enough that his doctrine of entire sanctification was highly influenced by Roman Catholic theology.[16] What should also be evident is that John Fletcher's relating the gift of the Holy Spirit to Christian perfection has its historical roots in Roman Catholic theology as well.[17] In this respect, John Wesley's Anglican heritage was too easily forgotten by his followers in the succeeding generations. Though Wesley may have departed from some of the liturgical and traditional aspects of his Anglican background, it should be kept in mind that at heart he was a loyal churchman, steeped in the Anglican tradition. He always insisted that his teachings were thoroughly Anglican.[18]

Unfortunately, Wesley's followers forgot about his heritage and largely dropped his Anglicanism. What has happened as a result is that the Wesleyan emphasis on holiness has appeared all too often as an aberration. Instead of understanding and appreciating the Anglican heritage which serves as the basis of the Wesleyan doctrine of holiness, the Wesleyan-Arminian tradition cut itself off from dialogue with the Anglican tradition. Hence, Wesley's doctrine of entire sanctification has been made to appear as an innovation within church history, as well as a mere inference, if not an imposition on Scripture. As a result, other theological traditions do not often take seriously the Wesleyan doctrine of Christian perfection.

At this point it should be remembered that Wesley firmly locates the source of his doctrine of entire sanctification within the Anglican tradition, especially in such thinkers as Jeremy Taylor.[19] For Taylor it was the ordinance of confirmation which effected perfection of character. It is through "the overflowings of the Spirit" that one comes to "receive perfective graces" and becomes "a perfect Christian."[20] He felt so strongly about this rite that he wrote "A Discourse of Confirmation," in which he sought to defend it against those who neglected its importance. For him, it is the Pentecostal reception of the Spirit in confirmation which makes the life of holiness possible. Confirmation, if it is met with inward faith, makes the baptized believer a "perfect Christian."[21] He further says: "Until we receive the spirit of . . . confirmation, we are but babes in Christ, in the meanest sense, infants that can do nothing, that cannot speak, that cannot resist any violence, exposed to every rudeness, and perishing by every temptation."[22] Likewise, Wesley distinguishes between "*a babe in Christ*" and "those who *are strong* in the Lord." The former refers to believers, the latter to the entirely sanctified believer.[23]

Jeremy Taylor defends the rite of confirmation on the basis of Acts 8. He says that though the Samaritans became believers as a result of Philip's ministry, they needed "a τελείωσις, 'something to make them perfect.' "[24] He also argues in the same way with regard to the Ephesian believers in Acts 19. Following both Roman Catholic and Anglican tradition,[25] Taylor makes a clear distinction between the work of the Spirit in regeneration (baptism) in which our sins are forgiven and a subsequent experience of the Pentecostal Spirit (confirmation) who "enkindles charity and the love of God."[26] In further describing the subsequent working of the Spirit in the life of the baptized believer, he writes:

> "The Holy Ghost is promised to all men" . . . . Confirmation, or prayer- and imposition of the bishop's hand is the solemnity and rite used in Scriptures for the conveying of that promise, and the effect is felt in all the sanctifications and changes of the soul. . . . Hear what the Scriptures yet further say in this mystery: "Now he which confirmeth or stablisheth us with you in Christ, and hath anointed us, is God: who hath also sealed us, and given the earnest of the Spirit in our hearts." Here is a description of the whole mysterious part of this rite.[27]

That Anglican (following Roman Catholic) theology interprets the reception of the Spirit by the Samaritans and the Ephesians in Acts 8 and 19 as confirming and sanctifying grace subsequent to their becoming baptized believers is most probably why Wesley himself in his *Explanatory Notes on the New Testament* gives these same passages a similar interpretation (see Chapter VI). In this respect, Wesley surely must have known that the Pentecostal reception of the Spirit by the Samaritans and Ephesians had served as the basis for the rite of confirmation from the earliest times of Christian tradition.[28]

Hence Wesley could hardly have been unaware of the liturgical rites of baptism and confirmation and what they signified, even though there are few references to confirmation in Wesley's writings.* In the Anglican ritual of confirmation, which was revised in 1662 and used in Wesley's day, the following is found in one of the prayers: "Confirm and settle the godly Resolutions They have now made. Sanctify Them throughout that They may become the Temples of the Holy Ghost."[29] The sanctifying work of the Holy Spirit is mentioned elsewhere in the ritual as well. It seems to admit of supposition that Wesley must have been aware of the similarity of his doctrines of conversion and entire sanctification with the Anglican rites of baptism and confirmation.

It is also apparent that John Fletcher was not unaware of his Anglican theology, which specifically linked Pentecostal language to the subsequent work of "perfecting" grace in confirmation. This can be seen in Fletcher's remarks addressed particularly to Anglican clergymen, who rejected Wesley's doctrine of Christian perfection. He reminds them at their baptism that they "were ranked among Christ's soldiers, and received a Christian name, in token that ... [they] would 'keep God's holy will and commandments all the days of ... [their] life." He further reminds them that at their subsequent confirmation they vowed to '"keep God's holy will and commandments' so as utterly 'to abolish the whole body

---

*Ole E. Borgen points out in his book, *John Wesley on the Sacraments* (Nashville: Abingdon Press, 1972), that Wesley did not include the ordinance of confirmation in the *Sunday Service*. He also points out that Wesley called the Roman Catholic doctrine of confirmation "an abuse." Wesley does quote the Office of Confirmation from the *Prayer Book* to defend his doctrine of the inner assurance of the Holy Spirit (Borgen, p. 170). In general, however, Wesley showed no interest in the rite of confirmation (Borgen, p. 276).

of sin.' " Hence for them to reject Christian perfection is "to pull down what he [the bishop] confirmed, and to demolish the perfection which he made you vow to attain, and to 'walk in all the days of your life.' "[30]

Fletcher also appeals directly to the Anglican rite of confirmation to illustrate his doctrine of dispensations, in which a distinction is made between the faith of "imperfect Christians who, like the apostles before the day of Pentecost, are yet strangers to the great outpouring of the Spirit" and the faith of "Christians complete in Christ" because they have "faith 'in the Holy Ghost.' "[31] After his having given several sources to substantiate his doctrine of dispensations, he shows that the ordinance of confirmation was "originally intended to lead young believers to the fulness of the Christian dispensation."[32] Hence it seems apparent that Fletcher was following the lead of the Anglican doctrine of confirmation when he described the Samaritan's reception of the sanctifying Spirit as subsequent to their becoming Christian believers, especially since this particular passage in Acts 8:14ff. is given as the exegetical basis for the rite of confirmation.[33]

It can thus be said that the genius of John Wesley and John Fletcher was not that they created a doctrine of entire sanctification, but that they gave it a more evangelical interpretation by ridding it of its largely objectivistic and sacramentarian weight.

James Dunn, *Baptism in the Holy Spirit*, is thus methodologically correct to address himself at the same time both to the Wesleyan doctrine of a subsequent experience of the Holy Spirit in the life of a believer, on the one hand, and to the Roman Catholic theology of the sacraments on the other hand.[34] For their basic difference is that the sacrament of confirmation is largely formalistic.

Perhaps it should also be acknowledged that Wesley's and Fletcher's reinterpretation of confirmation along the lines of an evangelical experience too easily dropped the significance of the liturgical rite of confirmation. There are at least three advantages which could have been gained if Wesley had brought the ordinance of confirmation into direct association with his concept of Christian perfection. First, it could have saved the doctrine from some of its more extravagant subjectivism to which it has often been prone. Second, it could have made the doctrine more closely connected with the body-life of the Church. Third, it would have served as a perpetual and public witness and reminder to the Church of God's sanctifying grace, even as baptism has so functioned as a constant public reminder of God's justifying love and regenerating grace. To be sure, this is not to suggest that confirmation ought to become a "third sacrament" for Protestants, but it could become a significant ordinance in the life of the Church. After all, even for Protestants, the Christian life is mediated through the "organism" of the Church, the body of Christ.

It can thus be seen that while the Reformed tradition allows for only one beginning event of the Christian life, the Wesleyan, Anglican, and Catholic traditions allow for a second definitive work of grace for the maintenance of the Christian life.* To be sure, for Roman Catholic theology, freedom from sin and the actual restoration of character occurs subjectively for most baptized believers in purgatory — except for saints who are perfected in love in this life.[35] Yet objectively, and to some extent experientially, this perfection is realized in confirmation. Likewise in Anglican theology, the grace received objectively in confirmation is presumably appropriated progressively throughout one's life, until its full realization in glorification.

---

*The Episcopal Church in the U.S.A. has altered its understanding of confirmation in *The Proposed Book of Common Prayer*. The reception of the Spirit is now acknowledged to be given at baptism as well as at confirmation. There has been a desire for some in the Episcopal Church even to do away with the rite of confirmation, since it allegedly takes away from the significance of baptism, as well as it allegedly is exegetically indefensible. In this respect, it is being argued that since every believer has the Spirit, there is no basis for a second ordinance of the Christian life. (Cf. Leonel L. Mitchell, "The Theology of Christian Imitation and *The Proposed Book of Common Prayer*," *Anglican Theological Review*, LX [October, 1978], 399-419.

That confirmation, however, is not viewed exclusively in an objectivistic fashion in Roman Catholic theology is made clear by Austin Milner:

> The effect of the sacrament may be completely blocked by his lack of faith or sinful disposition, yet he remains one over whom the Church has prayed and proclaimed the outpouring of the Holy Spirit. As soon as the blocks to this grace from his side are removed, the action of Christ in the sacrament will take effect.[36]

Karl Rahner, *A New Baptism in the Spirit: Confirmation Today* seems to move toward a more evangelical understanding of the baptism with the Spirit within Roman Catholicism. Though he still links the baptism with the Spirit to confirmation, he appreciates the charismatic renewal within the Church, with its strong emphasis upon the need for a personal "baptism with the Spirit" which comes after confirmation. His mediating position between the liturgical rite of confirmation and an evangelical experience of the "baptism with the Spirit" is expressed in this way: "Why, then, may we not look forward to a new, revitalized understanding of Confirmation, the sacrament of the Spirit, on the basis of these experiences bursting forth everywhere in the Church today?"[37]

A similar question could be put to Wesleyans at this point: "May we not look forward to a new, revitalized understanding of Christian perfection, the fulness of the Spirit, on the basis of a new appreciation of the sacraments and of the Church as an organism – the entire body of Christ – when we no longer overly stress individual experience in isolation from the corporate church?"

It seems to me that the Wesleyan doctrine of entire sanctification could profit greatly through an intensive study of the Roman Catholic theology of the Holy Spirit in the life of the Church, while at the same time avoiding formalistic and extreme sacramentarian notions of grace.

Finally, to insist upon one grand beginning moment of conversion without any definitive, subsequent, sanctifying grace as does the Reformed tradition is to ignore the many

biblical passages which summon the believer to holiness and
perfection of heart. Both the Wesleyan and Roman Catholic
traditions stress this point.[38]

In this respect one of the key verses which Wesleyans have
used to show the relation between Pentecostal language and
entire sanctification is Acts 15:8-9, where Peter declares
that the disciples, along with the house of Cornelius, had
their "hearts cleansed by faith" through the baptism with the
Spirit. John Calvin also points out that this passage involves

> a double manner of purging, because Christ doth offer
> and present us clean and just in the sight of his Father,
> by putting away our sins daily, which he hath once
> purged by his blood; secondly, because, by mortifying
> the lusts of the flesh by his Spirit, he reformeth us
> unto holiness of life. I do willingly comprehend both
> kinds of purging under these words; because Luke doth
> not touch one kind of purging only, but he teacheth
> that the whole perfection therefore consisteth without
> the ceremonies of the law.[39]

Calvin further acknowledges that "we are bidden to 'love
God with all our heart, with all our soul, and with all our
faculties' [Deut. 6:5; Matt. 22:37]."[40] Yet he argues against
the possibility of achieving this state of grace because

> if we search the remotest past, I say that none of the
> saints, clad in the body of death [cf. Rom. 7:24], has
> attained to that goal of love so as to love God "with all
> his heart, all his mind, all his soul, and all his might".
> . . . I further say that there will be no one hereafter
> who will teach the goal of true perfection without
> sloughing off the weight of the body.[41]

For Calvin, and the Reformed tradition in general, at
conversion God

> clothes us with the innocence of Christ and accepts it
> as ours that by the benefits of it he may hold us as

> holy, pure, and innocent. . . . Covered with this purity
> [of Christ], the sordidness and uncleanness of our
> imperfections are not ascribed to us but are hidden
> as if buried.[42]

Hence, purity of heart is imputed to the believer in Christ, though in practice he strives to actualize it. The Wesleyan tradition, on the other hand, stresses that the righteousness of Christ can be truly actualized in the life of the justified believer through the sanctifying Spirit.

While James Dunn[43] and Karl Barth,[44] along with John Calvin in his exegesis of Acts 15:8-9, show that the baptism with the Spirit specifically denotes the sanctifying fulness of the Christian life, it is surprising that some in the Wesleyan tradition (e.g., J. B. Atkinson)[45] separate "the baptism with the Spirit" from the doctrine of Christian perfection. To do so could create the impression that the experience of perfect love is artificially tacked on as an addendum to Pentecostal reality, thereby calling into question its significance and validity.

It also seems hermeneutically inappropriate for those in the Wesleyan tradition to attempt an exegesis of the doctrine of entire sanctification while ignoring the experience of that tradition. Just as no one today can ignore 2,000 years of Church tradition in his interpretation of the New Testament,[46] even so we cannot ignore Charles Wesley, John Fletcher, and the subsequent holiness tradition in interpreting John Wesley's doctrine of entire sanctification. To be sure, the Bible is our primary source of theology; but traditon, experience, and reason are also essential sources of theology as well. Wesley made this point clear. That is why he insisted that something must be wrong with our exegesis if experience and tradition contradict it.[47]

Since the association of entire sanctification with the baptism with the Holy Spirit has been a main part of our Wesleyan tradition since the time of John Wesley, it should occasion a serious pause in our thinking if that association is altogether wrong. Nevertheless, it must be frankly said that tradition can be wrong. And, to be sure, there have been extremes and abuses in the Wesleyan tradition in this regard, but let's not "throw out the baby with the bath water."

Further, before one disassociates entire sanctification from Pentecostal language too hastily, one ought to consider the long exegetical tradition in Roman Catholic theology of a similar association. If there is not taught in Scripture any definitive experience of the baptism with the Spirit in a sanctifying work subsequent to regeneration, then the exegetical scholarship of the Roman Catholic tradition has also been negated.[48] While the Catholic theological structure of baptism and confirmation imposed on these exegetical foundations may be in need of readjustment, their exegetical bases for distinguishing between the beginning of the Christian life symbolized in water baptism and the subsequent establishing (or confirming) grace of God through the Spirit's fulness seems to be an impressive (though indirect) support for, if not a substantiation of, the Wesleyan position.

---

[1] Karl Rahner, *Foundations of Christian Faith*, p. 416.

[2] William J. O'Shea, *Sacraments of Initiation* (Englewood Cliffs: Prentice-Hall, 1965), p. 62.

[3] *Ibid.*, p. 63.

[4] Cf. Karl Rahner, *A New Baptism in the Spirit: Confirmation Today* (Denville, N.J.: Dimension Books, 1965), pp. 19-20; *Foundations of Christian Faith*, pp. 416-417.

[5] O'Shea, pp. 48-49.

[6] John Calvin, *Commentary on the Book of Acts* (Grand Rapids: Eerdmans, 1949), II, 211.

[7] O'Shea, p. 65.

[8] *Ibid.*, p. 66.

[9] *Ibid.*, p. 63.

[10] *Ibid.*

[11] *Ibid.*

[12] *The Sixteen Documents of Vatican II* and *The Instruction on the Liturgy*, N.C.W.C. translation (St. Paul Editions; Boston: Daughters of St. Paul, N.D.), p. 151.

[13] *Ibid.*, pp. 151-152.

[14] *Ibid.*

[15] Cf. O'Shea, pp. 54-55.

[16] John Fletcher, *Checks*, I, 270.

[17] Cf. Fletcher, *Checks*, I, 592-593; II, 632, 636.

[18] "A serious clergyman desired to know, in what points we differed from the Church of England. I answered, 'To the best of my knowledge, in none. The doctrines we preach are the doctrines of the Church of England; indeed, the fundamental doctrines of the Church, clearly laid down, both in his Prayers, Articles, and Homilies.' He asked, 'In what points then, do you differ from the other clergy of the Church of England?' I answered, 'In none from that part of the clergy who adhere to the doctrines of the Church; but from that part of the clergy who dissent from the Church, (though they own it not), I differ in the following: — First, they speak of justification, either as the same thing with sanctification, or as something consequent upon it. I believe justification to be wholly distinct from sanctification and necessarily antecedent to it.'" *The Journal of the Rev. John Wesley*, ed. Nehemiah Curnack (London: Charles H. Kelley, n.d), II, 274-275. For an extensive comparison between Wesley's doctrine of Christian perfection and the Anglican Church, see John Fletcher's *Check*, II, 506-516.

[19] Wesley, *A Plain Account of Christian Perfection*, p. 5.

[20] *The whole Works of the Right Reverend Jeremy Taylor* (London: Henry G. Bohn, 1867, III, 14.

[21] *Ibid.*

[22] *Ibid.*, p. 6.

[23] *Standard Sermons*, II, 169.

[24]*The Whole Works of the Right Reverend Jeremy Taylor*, III, 13.

[25]*Ibid.*, pp. 17ff.

[26]*Ibid.*, I, 763.

[27]*Ibid.*, III, 27.

[28]Cf. Jeremy Taylor, III, 17ff.

[29]Peter J. Jagger, *Christian Initiation 1582-1969, Rites of Baptism and Confirmation Since the Reformation Period* (London: SPCK, 1970), p. 32.

[30]Fletcher, *Checks*, II, 617.

[31]*Ibid.*, I, pp. 590-591.

[32]*Ibid.*, I, p. 594.

[33]*Ibid.*, II, p. 648.

[34]James D. G. Dunn, *The Baptism in the Holy Spirit* (SCM Press Ltd., 1970), pp. 1-3.

[35]Rahner, *Theological Investigations,* III, p. 153f.

[36]Austin Milner, *The Theology of Confirmation* (Notre Dame, Ind.: Fides Publishers, Inc., 1971), p. 102.

[37]Rahner, *A New Baptism in the Spirit* . . . , p. 7.

[38]O'Shea, p. 55; *Sixteen Documents of Vatican II*, pp. 151ff.

[39]*Commentary on the Book of Acts*, edited from the original English Translation of Christopher Fetherstone by Henry Heveridge (Grand Rapids: Wm. B. Eerdmans, 1949), II, 51.

[40]*Institutes of the Christian Religion*, I, 604.

[41]*Ibid.*, I, 353.

[42]*Ibid.*, I, 779.

[43]Dunn, p. 156.

[44]Karl Barth in his *Church Dogmatics*, IV, Part IV shows that circumcision of heart by the Spirit means to be "completely renewed" (p. 8) and that "the baptism with the Holy Spirit . . . cleanses, renews, and changes man truly and totally" (p. 34). He further shows that "the baptism of the Spirit . . . is the totality of salvation, the full justification, sanctification, and vocation of man brought about in Jesus Christ" (*ibid.*, p. 35). He further says that the baptism with the Spirit denotes "whole grace and wholly adequate grace" (p. 35). To be sure, Barth's theology of "whole grace" and "full . . . sanctification" is defined in terms of the Reformed view of imputation (pp. 41-42, 38, 40).

[45]J. B. Atkinson, *The Beauty of Holiness* (London: The Epworth Press, 1953), p. 151.

[46]Paul Tillich, Systematic Theology, I, 36.

[47]*A Plain Account of Christian Perfection*, p. 58.

[48]Austin Milner, pp. 11-41.

# CHAPTER VIII.

## PENTECOSTAL LANGUAGE AND SANCTIFYING GRACE

In my discussions with some in the Wesleyan tradition it appears that the association of entire sanctification with the baptism with the Holy Spirit has become problematic, if not explicitly denied. One easily suspects that the charismatic adoption of the baptism language may be a major factor for this growing uneasiness, yet there is no reason why a ruthless probing of the exegetical foundations should not be had. The primary issue before us in this chapter is, then, not the theology of entire sanctification. On that point evangelicals in the Wesleyan tradition are generally agreed. However, it should be said that the relationship of entire sanctification to circumcision of heart has a significant bearing on the relationship of Pentecostal language to entire sanctification, and in my discussions with some Wesleyan scholars it seems apparent that they equate circumcision of heart with conversion-initiation. Thus the doctrine of entire sanctification is also a part of the concern of this chapter but the primary issue is: is entire sanctification effected through the infilling of the Holy Spirit?

James D. G. Dunn, *Baptism in the Holy Spirit*[1] has received considerable attention among those in the Wesleyan tradition; at least so it seems to me in my conversations with my colleagues, students, and others. Dunn's scholarly exegetical-theological treatise is pivotal. One can hardly discuss this doctrine without reference to the issues raised by Dunn, an ordained minister of the Church of Scotland and lecturer in New Testament at the University of Nottingham.

What I propose to do in part is to capitalize on his exegetical-theological conclusions, either as support for what I perceive to be the truth in this matter or as an opportunity to take an opposing point of view. This dialogical approach will serve two functions. It will make it unnecessary for me to spend time reproducing those findings in his work with which I so thoroughly agree. It will also help to get the areas of disagreement and conflict out into the open, where they belong if theological formulation is to be better stated and exegetically based.

## 1. Some Areas of General Agreement with Dunn's Theology of the Holy Spirit

Let us first focus attention upon those areas of exegetical-theological agreement with Dunn.

(1) Pentecost was a unique and unrepeatable event in *salvation history*, for the Holy Spirit in an unprecedented way became operative in the world through the Church.[2]

(2) Pentecost marked the new era of divine grace. To be sure, this does not mean that the regenerating grace of God was inoperative before the day of Pentecost, but in regard to the history of salvation, only on the day of Pentecost, when the gift of the Spirit was given, did the grace of God become operative in a unique way.[3]

(3) The Pentecostal gift of the Holy Spirit is the fulfilment of the Old Testament prophecy of the last days in which "God's holy spirit" would be "purgative and refining for those who had repented."[4] For Wesley, entire sanctification is the purifying of the believer's heart from sin whereby he is enabled to love God with all his heart.[5] For Dunn, it would *appear* from his exegetical work that such an experience is what the New Testament expects to be normative. Presumably Dunn does not really think this ideal can be actualized, but rather interprets this biblical demand for perfect

love in accord with Calvin's imputation theory. Nevertheless, Dunn shows exegetically that it is the Pentecostal gift of the Spirit who purifies the heart.

(4) The Pentecostal gift is the fulfilment of the Old Testament promise of the new law written on the heart whereby one loves God with all his heart, soul, and mind. Dunn writes:

> Among the specific promises of the Father for the messianic time and the new covenant the parallel between Ezek. 36.27 and Jer. 31.33 is particularly noticeable: both promise ability to keep the law, the law written in the heart (the enabling factor in Jeremiah) being precisely equivalent to the gift of the Spirit (the enabling factor in Ezekiel). In any new covenant theology, therefore, the Spirit is to be seen as the agent of the new covenant and its supreme blessing — the one who will write the law in their hearts, the one we may say is the law written in their hearts.[6]

(5) The Pentecostal gift is the agent of spiritual circumcision of the heart which "is a total stripping away of the body of flesh ( = the body of sin [Rom. 6.6] = the body of death [Rom. 7.24])."[7] Dunn further writes:

> Spiritual circumcision also is the work of the Spirit and the gift of the Spirit. The circumcision which matters is the circumcision of the heart effected by the Spirit (Rom. 2.28f.). We are the circumcision, because we have been circumcised by the Spirit, and having thus received the Spirit, we worship by the Spirit of God (Phil. 3.3). . . . The gift of the Spirit is therefore to be equated with the circumcision of the heart (cf. Deut. 30.6 with Jer. 31.33 and Ezek. 36.26f.)[8]

I also endorse his equation of the "circumcision of the heart" with the "baptism in the Spirit."[9] It was pointed out in the previous chapter that Wesley equated "circumcision of the heart" with entire sanctification. It is also significant that Wesley appeals to these same Pentecostal passages (Deut.

30.6; Jer. 31.33; Ezek. 36.26f.) as texts to support his doctrine of Christian perfection.[10]

(6) The Pentecostal gift is the agent of sanctification, for it is the Holy Spirit who sanctifies.[11] In particular, Dunn shows that the cleansing of the hearts of the 120 believers on the day of Pentecost was effected by the baptism with the Holy Spirit.[12] It should be noted that Dunn, as a Reformed scholar, would most likely interpret this cleansing in relative terms, in so far as the believer's *actual* cleansing is concerned; although he would allow that *cleansing* would be *entire* in so far as the believer's *ideal* standing in Christ is concerned.

However, for Wesley cleansing from all sin can be effected in the heart of the believer in this life. He quotes I John 1:9 as a text to differentiate between the two works of grace: forgiveness of sins relates to justification, whereas "a perfect Christian" is one who is "cleansed from all unrighteousness" and thus "freed from evil thoughts and evil tempers."[13]

Wesley particularly shows that there is a "wide difference between the Jewish and the Christian dispensation" and that this difference is seen primarily in the fact that "the Holy Ghost was not yet given in His sanctifying graces, as He was after Jesus was glorified."[14] Hence, through the Pentecostal gift of the Spirit the experience of actual righteousness has become a universal possibility.

The significance of the sanctifying grace of the Spirit is well expressed poetically by Charles Wesley's Pentecost hymn, "Love Divine":[15]

> Love divine, all loves excelling,
> Joy of heaven, to earth come down;
> Fix in us Thy humble dwelling,
> All Thy faithful mercies crown!
> Jesus, Thou art all compassion,
> Pure, unbounded love Thou art,
> Visit us with Thy Salvation,
> Enter every trembling heart.
>
> Breathe, O breathe Thy loving Spirit
> Into every troubled breast!

Let us all in Thee inherit,
Let us find that second rest.
Take away our bent to sinning,
Alpha and Omega be;
End of faith, as its beginning,
Set our hearts at liberty.

Come, Almighty to deliver,
Let us all Thy grace receive;
Suddenly return and never,
Never more Thy Temples leave,
Thee we would be always blessing,
Serve Thee as Thy hosts above,
Pray, and praise thee without ceasing,
Glory in Thy perfect love.

Finish, then, Thy new creation;
Pure and spotless let us be;
Let us see Thy great salvation
Perfectly restored in Thee:
Changed from glory into glory,
Till in heav'n we take our place,
Till we cast our crowns before Thee,
Lost in wonder, love and praise.

(7) The gift of the Spirit is not the same as the manifestations and gifts of the Spirit.[16] Wesley specifically equates the gift of the Spirit and the fruit of the Spirit in his sermon, "Scriptural Christianity." He shows that "the *extraordinary gifts* of the Holy Ghost" were given with "a sparing hand." He suggests that "perhaps not one in a thousand" and "probably none but the teachers in the Church, and only some of them (I Cor. xii.28-30)" possessed the *gifts* of the Spirit. Yet the gift of the Spirit himself is to be received by all believers in all ages, whereas the *gifts* of the Spirit are not universally given to all believers. The "more excellent purpose" for which the gift of the Spirit is given is to fill believers with the fruit of the Spirit — "to give them . . . the mind which was in Christ, those holy fruits of the Spirit . . . to fill them with 'love, joy, peace, long-suffering, gentleness' (Gal. v. 22-24)."[17]

(8) The baptism with the Spirit (Matt. 3:11; Mark 1:8; Luke 3:16; John 1:33; Acts 1:5; Acts 11:15-16), the reception (λαμβάνειν) of the Spirit (John 7:39; 14:17; 20:22; Acts 1:8; 2:38; 8:15, 17, 19; 10:47; 19:2), the Spirit "falling upon" (ἐπιπίπτειν) (Acts 8:16; 10:44; 11:15), the Spirit "coming upon" (ἐπέλθοντος) (Acts 1:8; 19:6), "filled with the Spirit" (Acts 2:4; 9:17) are equivalent phrases *in these particular passages* to denote the sanctifying grace of Pentecost.[18] Other instances of being "filled with the Spirit" in the Book of Acts (e.g., Acts 4:8, 31) probably are to be interpreted as typical of the Old Testament prophetic type of fulness of the Spirit whereby the prophet is enabled to *speak* the Word of God, rather than indicating the ethical type of "fulness of the Spirit" which marked the arrival of Pentecostal grace under the New Covenant.

(9) Dunn points out that in the case of the disciples their regeneration preceded their baptism in the Spirit. He also points out that there were two distinct events in the life of Jesus which have soteriological significance. One event was his identification with sinful men, in which he was baptized with water, representing man's need for repentance.[19] The other distinct event was his baptism in the Spirit, in which he was the first to enter the New Covenant.[20] In both cases the significance of these two events for Dunn is that it marks the transition from the Old Covenant to the New Covenant. Hence, "what Jordan was to Jesus, Pentecost was to the disciples. As Jesus entered the new age and covenant by being baptized in the Spirit at Jordan, so the disciples followed him in like manner at Pentecost."[21]

Since the disciples' baptism with the Spirit is acknowledged to be subsequent to their regeneration, one wonders why Dunn does not try to argue that they were not really converted until Pentecost, in accord with his exegesis of the Samaritans and Ephesians (Acts 8 and 19). His concession in regard to the disciples' time-lapse between their regeneration and baptism with the Spirit seems to annul the requirements of his exegesis of other Pentecostal passages in the Book of Acts.

## 2. An Exegetical-Theological Analysis of Pentecostal Passages in the Book of Acts

Up to this point the areas of general agreement with Dunn have been noted, especially his equation of Pentecostal language with circumcision of heart and loving God with all the heart. The substantive difference which this writer has with Dunn's position is his disallowance of two definitive works of grace.

Dunn's emphasis that salvation is a "single complex event" is indisputable. On the other hand, his insistence that no longer is there a "chronological disjointedness" in which conversion and the baptism with the Spirit are separated in time, since we have now entered the Pentecostal era in which the two events form "a chronological unity" is not so certain as he assumes.[23] His reasoning is as follows. The apostles were regenerated before Pentecost, but this does not justify "taking the apostles' experience as *the* or *a possible* pattern for experience today."[24] Why? because "the disciples' experience was determined by the process of salvation-history." He further says: "With Pentecost the transition phase comes to an end; the old stage of salvation-history was wholly past and the new stage wholly in operation. Henceforth entry into the blessings of the new dispensation is immediate, whereas for the apostles it was 'staggered'."[25] To be sure, he admits that the gospel of "John certainly shows that it may not be possible to equate Spirit-baptism with regeneration, *but only in the case of the apostles.*"[26] Henceforth, "he who believes receives the Spirit in his cleansing, regenerating, baptismal power, bringing the forgiveness and life of the new dispensation."[27]

Though Dunn is certainly right to stress the single complex event of salvation in the life of the individual believer, there is no reason why he should insist upon its "chronological unity." It seems justifiable to say that there are two coordinate moments in the single complex event of salvation and that there may be a time lapse between these two distinct but coordinate moments of conversion and the Spirit's baptism. Nor is it necessary to think of these distinct but coordinate moments as a "chronological disjointedness"; for these moments are genuinely continuous though temporally distinct.

One of the things that I have liked so much about the theological concept of salvation history (a theological term widely used in contemporary theology) is its dynamic understanding of time. Salvation history is a continuous, albeit flexible and fluctuating, line running from creation to the eschaton (Cullmann). A number of unique events have occurred on this time line at the center of which is the Christ event. At no point, however, is any one event discontinuous with what is in the past or in the future. The present embraces the past and is moving forward by the pressure of the future. The past is never merely past and the present is never merely present, for the present which becmes past has its truth in God who is the power of the unbounded future (Pannenberg). Hence, the depth of one's spiritual life is determined by the orientation of his own personal history of salvation to the broader scope of salvation history. The idea of salvation history accords well with Fletcher's *flexible* dispensationalism,* and it is quite in keeping with covenantal language.

This concept of salvation history surely allows for a more dynamic understanding of time than a *rigid* dispensationalist idea of biblical history with its mechanical dissection of history into static periods of time. One of the implications of a theology of salvation history is that some may not be enjoying the full blessing of the New Covenant. Their own personal history of salvation may be stalled at some particular point on the time line of salvation history. Simply living in the Pentecostal, New Covenant age of salvation history does not *ipso facto* mean all people are universally and unilaterally Spirit-filled Christians. Nor does it mean that when one becomes a Christian he appropriates the full blessing of the New Covenant, even though the emphasis — especially in Paul's writ-

---

*Fletcher's dispensationalism, of course, has nothing to do with millenial views of the end time.

ing — is rightly that the norm of the Chiristian life is the holy life evidenced by the fruit of the Spirit. Yet many Christians have a personal history of salvation, which is in a very real but qualified sense pre-Pentecostal. Some have a personal history of salvation which is pre-Christian, or pre-Mosaic, or pre-Abrahamic! C. S. Lewis in his autobiography, *Surprised by Joy*, tells of the time when he gave in and "admitted God was God," yet his conversion to theism was not a conversion to Christ, which came later.

It seems to me that Dunn's soteriological monism freezes up the working of the Spirit. Does not the Spirit deal with each person according to his own personal salvation history? On some occasions the Spirit's baptism may come with one's incorporation into the body of Christ (Acts 2:37-38). On other occasions, the Spirit's baptism may follow his conversion to Christ. The cases of the Samaritans (Acts 8), Paul (Acts 9), and the Ephesians (Acts 19) seem to overrule Dunn's contention that the "staggered" experience of the disciples cannot be normative for today, if the obvious sense of these Pentecostal passages are allowed to speak for themselves.

(1) The Samaritans' experience in Acts 8 would seem to suggest a time lapse between conversion and the Spirit's baptism. Dunn's attempt to explain this away by suggesting that the Samaritans only gave intellectual assent ($\dot{\epsilon}\pi\dot{\iota}\sigma\tau\epsilon\upsilon\sigma\alpha\nu$ $\tau\tilde{\omega}$ $\Phi\iota\lambda\dot{\iota}\pi\pi\omega$) to Philip's preaching is not convincing. Acts 8:14 says the Samaritans had "received the Word of God," a parallel to Acts 2:41, where it is said of those converted by Peter's Pentecostal sermon that they "received his word." To receive the Word of God is to experience the reality of God, for God is his Word. When Peter and John later came to Samaria, they "received the Holy Spirit" subsequent to their having "received the word of God" through Philip. Hence Dunn's failure to observe the two parallel terms, "received the word of God" and "received the Holy Spirit," is a fatal oversight is his exegesis.[28] Further, that Simon Magus "believed" and was "baptized" even though Peter observed his lack of true repentance is hardly evidence that the

rest of the Samaritan "believers" were still "in the bond of iniquity."

(2) Dunn's exegesis of Acts 19:1, 2 seems unnatural. His argument that the word "disciples" does not mean true Christian disciples because of the indefinite pronoun, τινας μαθητάς, is a non sequitur.[29]   On another occasion Luke refers to Ananias as a "certain disciple" [cf. τις μαθητὴς ἐν Δαμασκῷ (Acts 9:10) with εἰς Ἔφεσον . . . τινας μαθητάς (Acts 19:1)]. Are we here to conclude that the use of the indefinite pronoun suggests that Ananias was less than truly Christian?

This case of the Ephesians is a parallel to that of Apollos, who only knew John's baptism though he had been "instructed in the way of the Lord" and had been "taught *accurately* the things concerning Jesus" (Acts 18:25). F. F. Bruce points out the connection between Apollos and the Ephesians in this way:

> When Luke uses the term "disciples" without qualification, as he does of these men, he elsewhere means disciples of Jesus; and Paul appears to have recognized them as Christian believers since he asks them if they received the Holy Spirit when they believed. Luke does not bring them into direct relation with Apollos, to whom he has devoted the preceding paragraph (probably he derived this incident and the Apollos episode from two different sources), but since Apollos also is said to have known "only the baptism of John," for all his accurate knowledge of the story of Jesus (18:25), it is natural to conclude that they had learned of the Christian way along a similar line of transmission, deviating from that acknowledged by both Luke and Paul. However, when Paul realized the defective character of these disciples' faith and practice, he gave them further instruction and they "were baptized into the name of the Lord Jesus" — the only instance of rebaptism in the New Testament. . . . It may be that the Ephesian disciples had received John's baptism more recently, when the age of the Spirit had already been inaugurated,

in which case John's baptism might have been thought to be no longer valid.[30]

Because these two passages stand in such close juxtaposition and because "they learned of the Christian way along a similar line of transmission" (Bruce), it seems to admit of supposition that Apollos was a "pre-Pentecostal" convert. Note the following progression of thought:

(a) Apollos "was an eloquent man, *well versed* (δυνατός) in the Scriptures" (vs. 24).

(b) "He had been *instructed* (κατηχημένος – catechism, instruction, not a piecemeal and rumored knowledge) in the way of the Lord" (vs. 25).

(c) "*taught accurately* (ἀκριβῶς) the things concerning Jesus" (this emphasis upon his accurate knowledge of Jesus could hardly have been stressed if he failed to understand the central confession of the gospel that "Jesus is Lord." If his "catechism" had been other than "Jesus is Lord" it would have been an "inaccurate" knowledge).

(d) Priscilla and Aquila "expounded to him the way of God *more accurately* (ἀκριβέστερον) (26). They did not change his understanding of who Jesus was; rather, they added to his incomplete knowledge. It seems only natural to suppose that Apollos (like the Ephesians) was a Christian disciple, but had not been baptized with the Holy Spirit.

(e) "He *powerfully* (not merely *well versed*, but now with added fervor and unction, vehemently εὐτόνως) confuted the Jews in public, showing by the scriptures that the Christ was Jesus" (vs. 28).

Though Dunn calls into question the authentic nature of the Ephesian (and by implication Apollos') contact with Christianity, he does admit that "we may not simply dub them 'disciples of John the Baptist' " since the "use of μαθηταί requires some connection with Christianity, and presumably Paul must have had some reason for addressing them as οἱ πιστεύσαντες."[31]

(3) Saul's encounter with the risen Lord on the way to Damascus seems to imply that he was really converted. To

suggest he was not converted until his arrival three days later in Damascus seems to be a case of special pleading.[32] Dunn fails to remember that Paul's encounter with the Lord was not without its preparation. He well knew the meaning of the gospel with its blasphemous claim that Jesus is Lord. Most forcefully was this message spoken by Stephen. To say, as Dunn does, that Saul, "a dazed and shocked man," could not have been brought into "full Christian commitment all in a matter of seconds"[33] ignores his previous contact with the gospel. Consenting to the death of Stephen, Saul heard his last words: *"Lord Jesus*, receive my spirit . . . *Lord*, do not hold this sin against them" (Acts 7:59). With Saul's exposure to Stephen's message and martyrdom, and with his vision of the naked presence of God in Jesus Christ on the road to Damascus, it is impossible to think of his confusing who God was in that moment and simply speaking to him as "Sir"; though, of course, κύριος in other contexts may be so translated (cf. John 12:21).

Saul's question, "Who are you, Lord?" was hardly a question in the sense of seeking factual information. It was more like a confession admitting Jesus was Lord. Only Jesus as Lord can reveal himself to be such. Despite his rabbinic learning and adherence to the Law, Saul had now come to admit that he could not work his way to God; he could not discover through his own human efforts and reasoning the knowledge of God. And now, on the road, he comes to see that the knowledge of God is revealed through Christ and Christ alone. "Who are you, Lord?" The question is the answer. The Lord is whom he reveals himself to be: "I am Jesus." When Paul came to Damascus, Ananias did not have to give him theological instruction; he only needed to administer the sacrament of baptism, symbolizing the washing away of his sins (Acts 22:16; cf. 26:12-21).

To be sure, Paul became blind. Was this physical blindness symbolic of spiritual blindness? Was his groping about illustrative of his spiritual imbalance? Or was it not rather the result of his having seen the glory of God which engulfs and overwhelms. God's presence is like a consuming fire (Heb.

12:29). To come up against the stark reality of God so suddenly is to be struck down in fear and trembling. When Isaiah saw the Lord, the shock was great: the foundations of the threshold shook, the house was filled with smoke, he could see nothing but the Lord high and lifted up, and he cried out, "woe is me." Smoke may have blinded his eyes to everything else in the Temple, but he nonetheless saw the Lord. This all-consuming experience of the divine is expressed by Abraham Heschel this way:

> God to the Biblical man is a Being whose manifestation is more than flesh and blood can bear. One cannot see Him, one cannot hear Him and remain alive (Exodus 33:20; Deuteronomy 4:33). "A dread, a great darkness" fell upon Abraham (Genesis 15:12). To perceive Him is to be crushed by His majesty. . . . When aflame with His presence, the world is consumed.[34]

Saul may not have been able to see anything with his physical eyes because of the all-consuming presence of the Lord, but his spiritual sight was clear: He saw the Lord. "Have I not seen ($\dot{\epsilon}\dot{\omega}\rho\alpha\kappa\alpha$) Jesus our Lord?" he tells the Corinthians. "Am I not an apostle?" (I Cor. 9:1). $\dot{o}\rho\dot{\alpha}\omega$ is the word Jesus often used in speaking of his pre-existent state with his Father. He bears witness to what he had seen ($\dot{o}\rho\dot{\alpha}\omega$) when he was with his Father in glory.[35] $'O\rho\dot{\alpha}\omega$ thus suggests an existential reality; it is personal knowledge which is the most intimate knowledge that one can ever have. By contrast, $\vartheta\epsilon\omega\rho\dot{\epsilon}\omega$ denotes *"deliberate* contemplation."[36] $\Theta\epsilon\omega\rho\dot{\epsilon}\omega$ is more theoretical, less personal. $B\lambda\dot{\epsilon}\pi\omega$ stresses "outward" and physical sight.[37] Saul was thus without sight ($B\lambda\dot{\epsilon}\pi\omega\nu$). The men with him heard a voice, but saw ($\vartheta\epsilon\omega\rho\dot{\epsilon}\omega$ spectator knowledge) no one. Saul saw ($\dot{o}\rho\dot{\alpha}\omega$, personal knowledge) the Lord Jesus (I Cor. 9:1). (Cf. Gal. 1:16 — $\dot{\alpha}\pi o\kappa\alpha\lambda\dot{\upsilon}\psi\alpha\iota$ $\tau\dot{o}\nu\, \Upsilon\dot{\iota}\dot{o}\nu\, \alpha\dot{\upsilon}\tau o\tilde{\upsilon}\, \dot{\epsilon}\nu\, \dot{\epsilon}\mu o\dot{\iota}$).

The aorist passive of $\dot{o}\rho\dot{\alpha}\omega$ is $\dot{\omega}\phi\vartheta\eta$ (appeared) which is used particularly in reference to the appearances of the risen Lord to the apostles and others; (cf. I Cor. 15:5, 6, and espec-

ially verse 8, where Paul says "he appeared also to me").
It is significant that Ananias says in Acts 9:17: "Brother Saul,
The Lord Jesus who *appeared* to you" (ὀφθείς, which stresses
a personal knowledge of the risen Lord). G.G. Findlay says:
"'Ιησοῦν. . . ἑώρακα . . . is a unique expression with P[aul]"
which denotes "that actual beholding of the human and glorified Redeemer which befell him on the way to Damascus;
from this dated both his faith and his mission. . . . The visible
and glorious man who then appeared, declared Himself as
'Jesus'; from that instant Saul knew that he had seen the crucified Jesus risen and reigning. . . . Personal knowledge of
the Lord and a 'word from His mouth' (Acts xxii.14) were
necessary to constitute an Apostle in the primary sense."[38]

Further, to suggest "Brother Saul" means Ananias greeted
Saul as a "fellow Jew" rather than a Christian brother[39]
seems to go against the obvious sense of the text; for Ananias
greeted Saul as one who had a personal knowledge (ὁράω)
of the Lord Jesus (Acts 9:17). Bengel shows that in *this*
context Ananias called Saul a brother "by the old Jewish
bond, and by the new tie of Christianity."[40] Likewise,
F. F. Bruce shows in his commentary note on Acts 9:17 in
*The New Bible Commentary* that in this context "brother"
means that Ananias greeted Saul as "a fellow-Christian."

### 3. Concluding Remarks

Dunn has rightly shown throughout his work, *Baptism in
the Holy Spirit*, that the emphasis in Paul's writing is always
upon the full blessing of the New Covenant. Likewise, writing
from the Roman Catholic viewpoint O'Shea, of the Catholic
University, in distinguishing between baptism (conversion-
initiation) and confirmation ("receiving the Spirit") writes:
"The New Testament writers spoke of the effects of the
redemption as a whole, without distinguishing too much (or
perhaps enough) the role of each of these rites in the scheme
of things."[41] Also, Karl Rahner points out that Paul is not
concerned with how the ascent to Christian perfection is

achieved, but rather Paul's emphasis is that we are to be perfect as Christ is.[42]

Paul's writings are thus largely hortatory and kerygmatic; he does not attempt logically to order the work of salvation. Paul talks of nothing less than the adequacy of God's grace to destroy all sin and to impart Christ's righteousness to the believer. Likewise, Rudolf Bultmann shows that Paul's concern is not primarily with the forgiveness of sins; rather, Paul's concern is freedom from sin.[43] Dunn's conclusion of what it means to be a Christian is: "That man is a Christian who has received the gift of the Holy Spirit by committing himself to the risen Jesus as Lord, and who lives accordingly."[44] Also, Wesley says that "every real Christian" is perfect in love and free from sin.[45]

One thing seems quite certain. If Dunn's exegetical-theological conclusions are defensible in regard to his soteriological monism, then most people whom we call new converts really are not even converted, for the Pauline ideal of the Christian life is seldom realized so quickly at the initial step of faith. Perhaps Dunn would theologically allow for a progressive realization of the full blessing of the New Covenant, though his *exegetical* consideration implies *full* salvation is experienced at *conversion-initiation*.

Further, if Dunn's analysis of the baptism with the Spirit is correct, then Wesley's doctrine of entire sanctification is wrong. Dunn insists that circumcision of heart, purity of heart, the fulness of the blessing of the New Covenant arc realized in the moment of conversion (i.e., for him, at the Spirit's baptism). But Wesley insists that circumcision of the heart, which he defines as "the being so 'renewed in the spirit of our mind,' as to be 'perfect as our Father in heaven is perfect,'"[46] is subsequent to conversion-initiation.

To be sure there is only one Christian life, not two, and its ideal is a life free from sin. This freedom is made possible by Pentecostal grace. Yet many Christians may not be enjoying the full blessing of the New Covenant. They have life, but not the abundant life of a heart purified by love. Ideal Christians are those of whom it can be said that "God's

love has been *poured* [ἐκκέχυται, Pentecostal language –
Acts 2:18; 10:45] into our hearts through the Holy Spirit
which has been *given* [δοθέντος, Pentecostal language –
Acts 5:32; 8:18; 11:17; 15:3] to us" (Rom. 5:5).

---

[1]*Baptism with the Holy Spirit* (SCM Press Ltd., 1970).

[2]*Ibid* pp. 53-54.

[3]*Ibid.*, pp. 52ff.

[4]*Ibid.*, p. 13.

[5]Cf. *Standard Sermons of John Wesley*, II, 173.

[6]Dunn, pp. 47-48.

[7]*Ibid.*, p. 153.

[8]*Ibid.*, p. 156.

[9]*Ibid.*, p 146, 156.

[10]*Standard Sermons of John Wesley*, II, 173-174; cf. *A Plain Account of Christian Perfection*, p. 35.

[11]Dunn, pp. 106, 120, 163, 164.

[12]*Ibid.*, pp. 81-82.

[13]*Standard Sermons of John Wesley*, II, 173.

[14]*Ibid.*, II, 162; cf. *A Plain Account of Christian Perfection*, p. 17.

[15]Cf. John Fletcher, *Checks*, II, 652-653.

[16]Cf. Dunn, pp. 56ff.

[17]*Standard Sermons of John Wesley*, I, 92-93; cf. Fletcher, *Checks*, I, 593.

[18]Dunn, pp. 56ff.

[19]*Ibid.*, p. 36.

[20]*Ibid.*, p. 32.

[21]*Ibid.*, p. 40.

[22]*Ibid.*, p. 37.

[23]*Ibid.*, p. 183.

[24]*Ibid.*, p. 181.

[25]*Ibid.*, p. 182.

[26]*Ibid.*

[27]*Ibid.*

[28]*Ibid.*, p. 65.

[29]*Ibid.*, p. 84.

[30]F. F. Bruce, "The Holy Spirit in the Acts of the Apostles," *Interpretation* 27:2 (April, 1973), 176.

[31]Dunn, p. 84.

[32]*Ibid.*, p. 76.

[33]*Ibid.,* p. 74.

[34]*God in Search of Man* (New York: Harper, 1955), p. 191.

[35]*A Greek-English Lexicon,* trans. Arndt and Gingrich, p. 581.

[36]Marvin R. Vincent, *Word Studies in the New Testament* (Grand Rapids: Wm. B. Eerdmans, 1946), II, 59.

[37]*Ibid.,* II, 59, 66.

[38]"St. Paul's First Epistle to the Corinthians," *The Expositor's Greek Testament,* ed., W. Robertson Nicoll (Grand Rapids: Wm. B. Eerdmans, 1961), II, 845.

[39]Dunn, p. 74.

[40]J. A. Bengel, *Gnomon of the New Testament,* trans. C. T. Lewis and Marvin Vincent (New York: Sheldon and Company, 1860), I, 811.

[41]O'Shea, *Sacraments of Initiation,* p. 62.

[42]Rahner, *Theological Investigations,* III, 5.

[43]Bultmann, *Theology of the New Testament,* I, 287.

[44]Dunn, p. 229.

[45]*The Standard Sermons of John Wesley,* II, 171.

[46]*Ibid.,* I, 268.

# INDEX OF NAMES